beautiful people

MITSUKAZU MIHARA

HAMBURG // LONDON // LOS ANGELES // TOKYO

Beautiful People
by Mitsukazu Mihara

Translation - Haruko Furukawa
English Adaptation - Nathan Johnson
Retouch and Lettering - Jennifer Carbajal
Production Artist - James Dashiell
Cover Design - Thea Willis

Editor - Rob Tokar
Digital Imaging Manager - Chris Buford
Production Managers - Jennifer Miller and Mutsumi Miyazaki
Managing Editor - Lindsey Johnston
VP of Production - Ron Klamert
Publisher and E.I.C. - Mike Kiley
President and C.O.O. - John Parker
C.E.O. - Stuart Levy

A  Manga

TOKYOPOP Inc.
5900 Wilshire Blvd. Suite 2000
Los Angeles, CA 90036

E-mail: info@TOKYOPOP.com
Come visit us online at www.TOKYOPOP.com

ISBN: 1-59816-243-8

First TOKYOPOP printing: February 2006

10 9 8 7 6 5 4 3 2 1

Printed in Canada

beautiful people

MITSUKAZU MIHARA

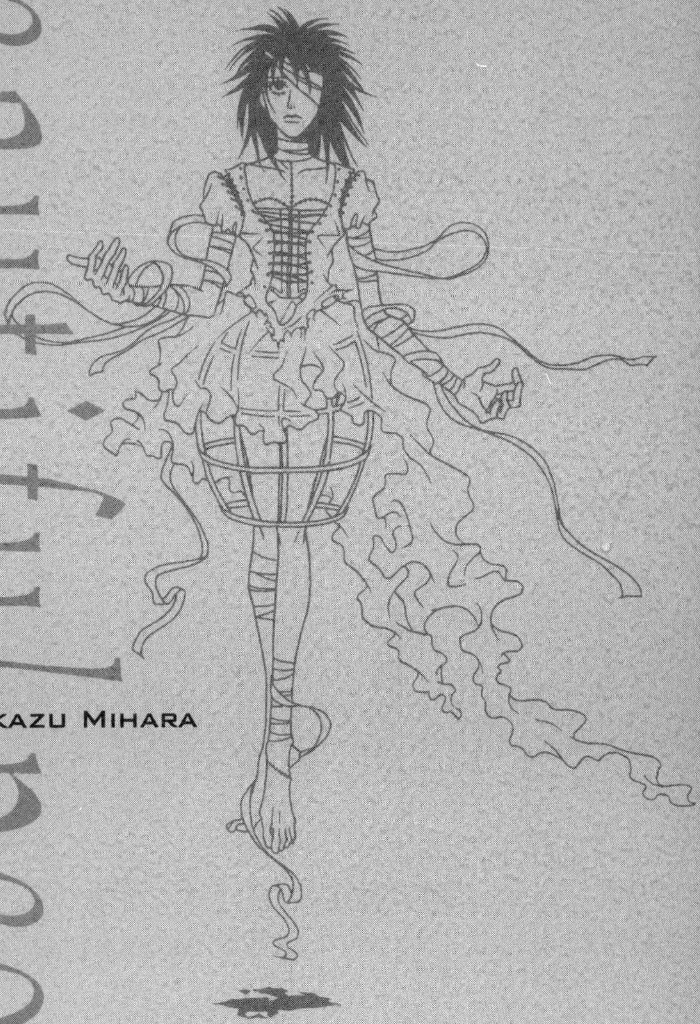

beautiful people
CONTENTS

Princess White Snow ——————————— 5
World's End ——————————————— 27
Electric Angel ———————————————— 51
The Lady Stalker ——————————————— 75
beautiful people ——————————————— 99
Blue Sky ——————————————————131

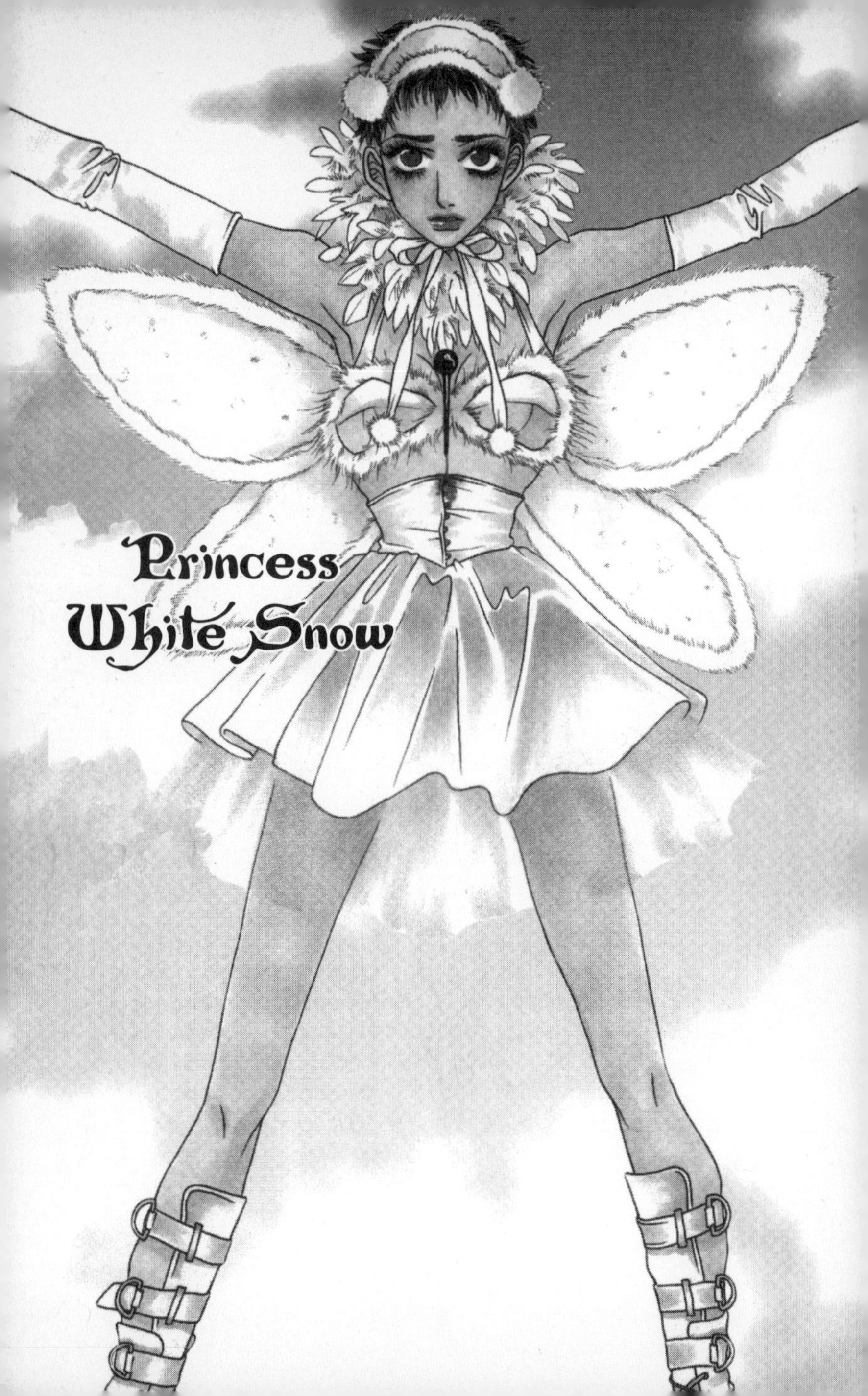
Princess
White Snow

beautiful
people™

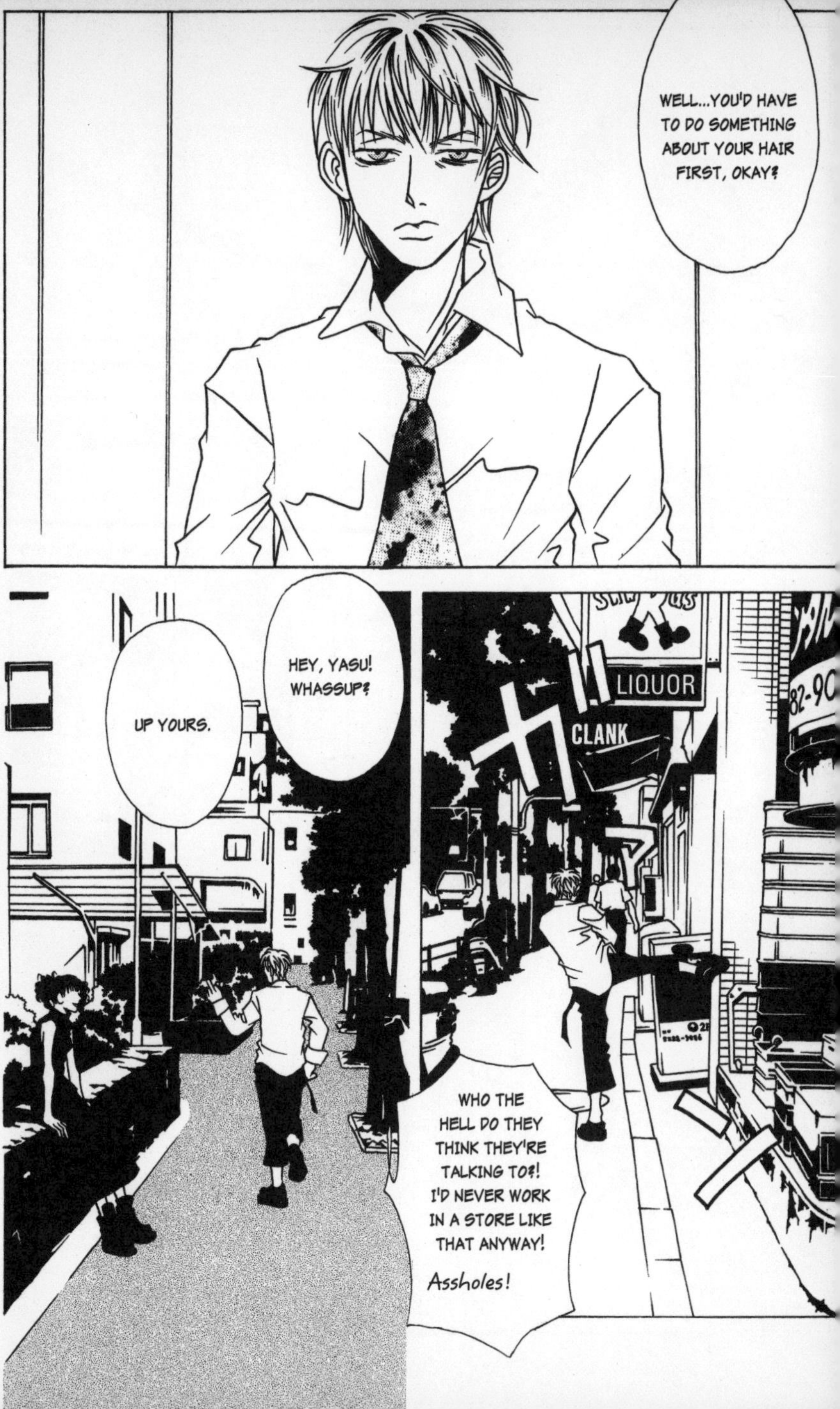
WELL...YOU'D HAVE TO DO SOMETHING ABOUT YOUR HAIR FIRST, OKAY?
LIQUOR
82-90
CLANK
WHO THE HELL DO THEY THINK THEY'RE TALKING TO?! I'D NEVER WORK IN A STORE LIKE THAT ANYWAY!
Assholes!
HEY, YASU! WHASSUP?
UP YOURS.

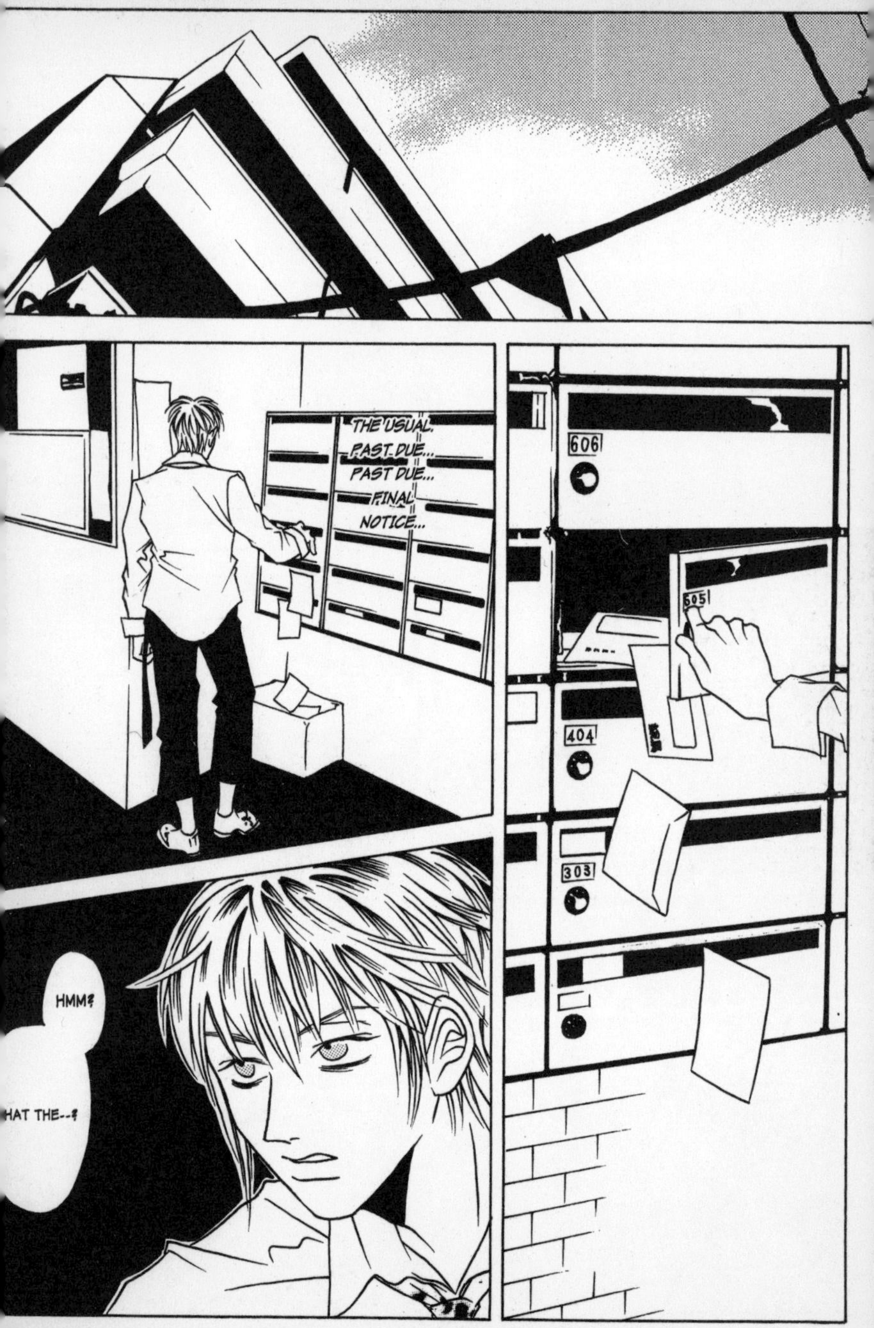
606
505
404
303
THE USUAL.
PAST DUE...
PAST DUE...
FINAL NOTICE...
HMM?
HAT THE--?

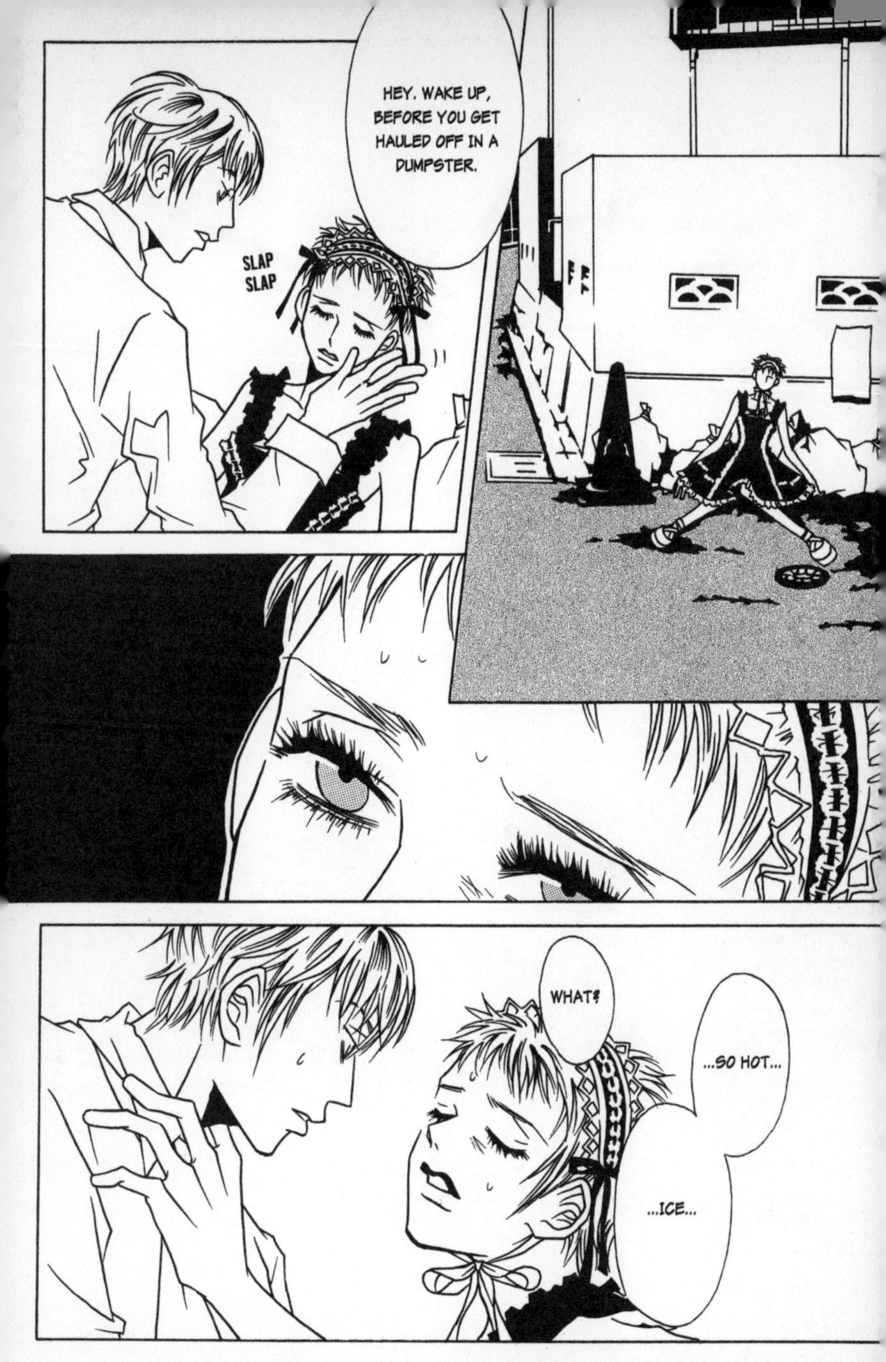
HEY. WAKE UP, BEFORE YOU GET HAULED OFF IN A DUMPSTER.
SLAP SLAP
...SO HOT...
...ICE...
WHAT?

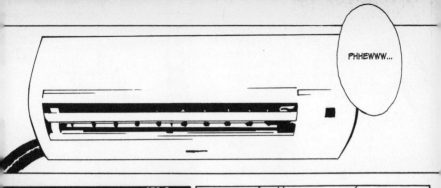

PHHEWWW...

THANK YOU VERY MUCH. I DON'T DO WELL WITH THE HEAT.

I HAD A PLACE, BUT I JUST GOT KICKED OUT.

YEAH, I KNOW HOW THAT GOES! THAT'S WHAT HAPPENS IF YOU DON'T PAY RENT FOR LONG ENOUGH!

THIS IS THE GREATEST!

IS SHE A GIFT FROM GOD?

♥

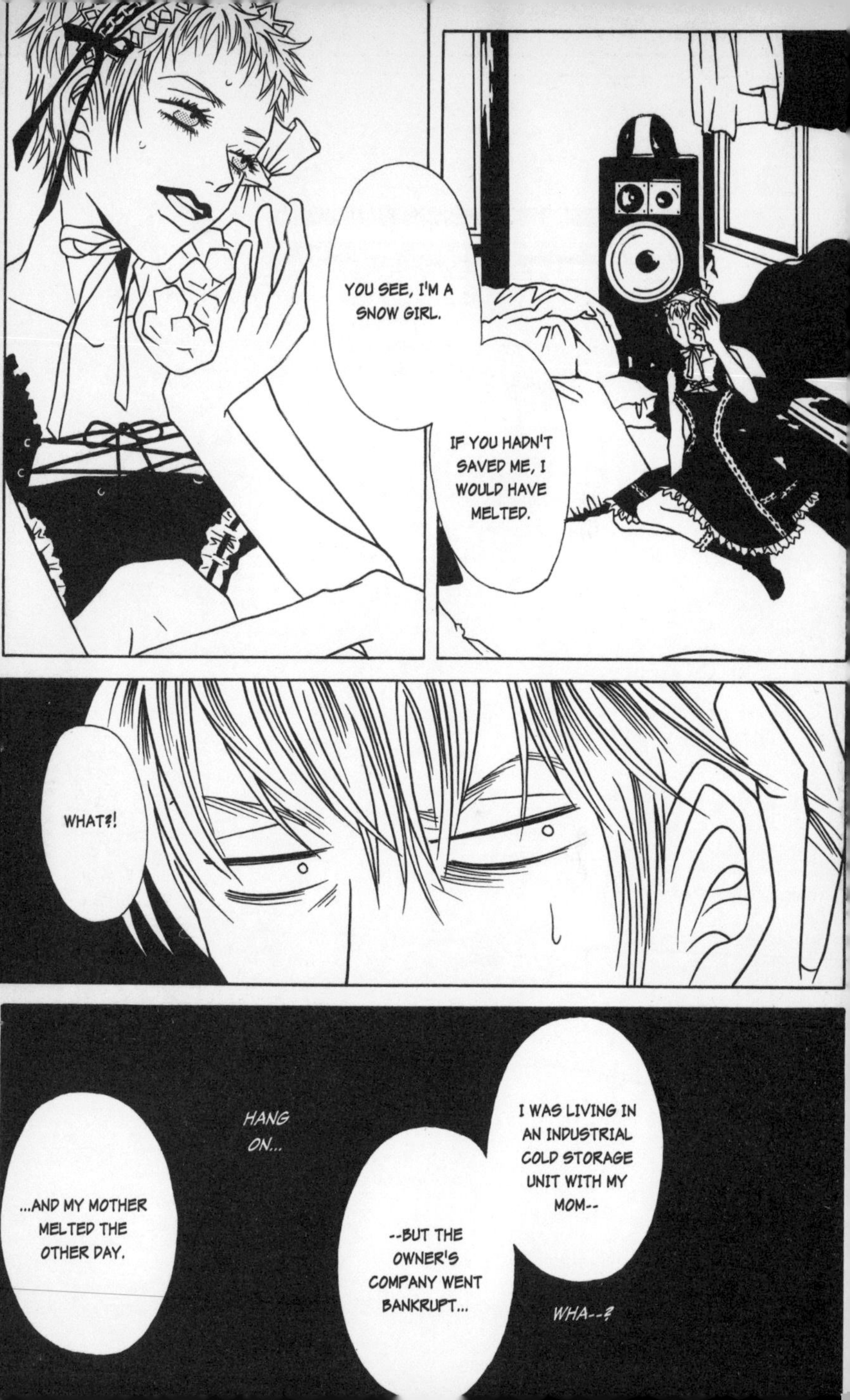
YOU SEE, I'M A SNOW GIRL.
IF YOU HADN'T SAVED ME, I WOULD HAVE MELTED.
WHAT?!
I WAS LIVING IN AN INDUSTRIAL COLD STORAGE UNIT WITH MY MOM--
--BUT THE OWNER'S COMPANY WENT BANKRUPT...
WHA--?
HANG ON...
...AND MY MOTHER MELTED THE OTHER DAY.

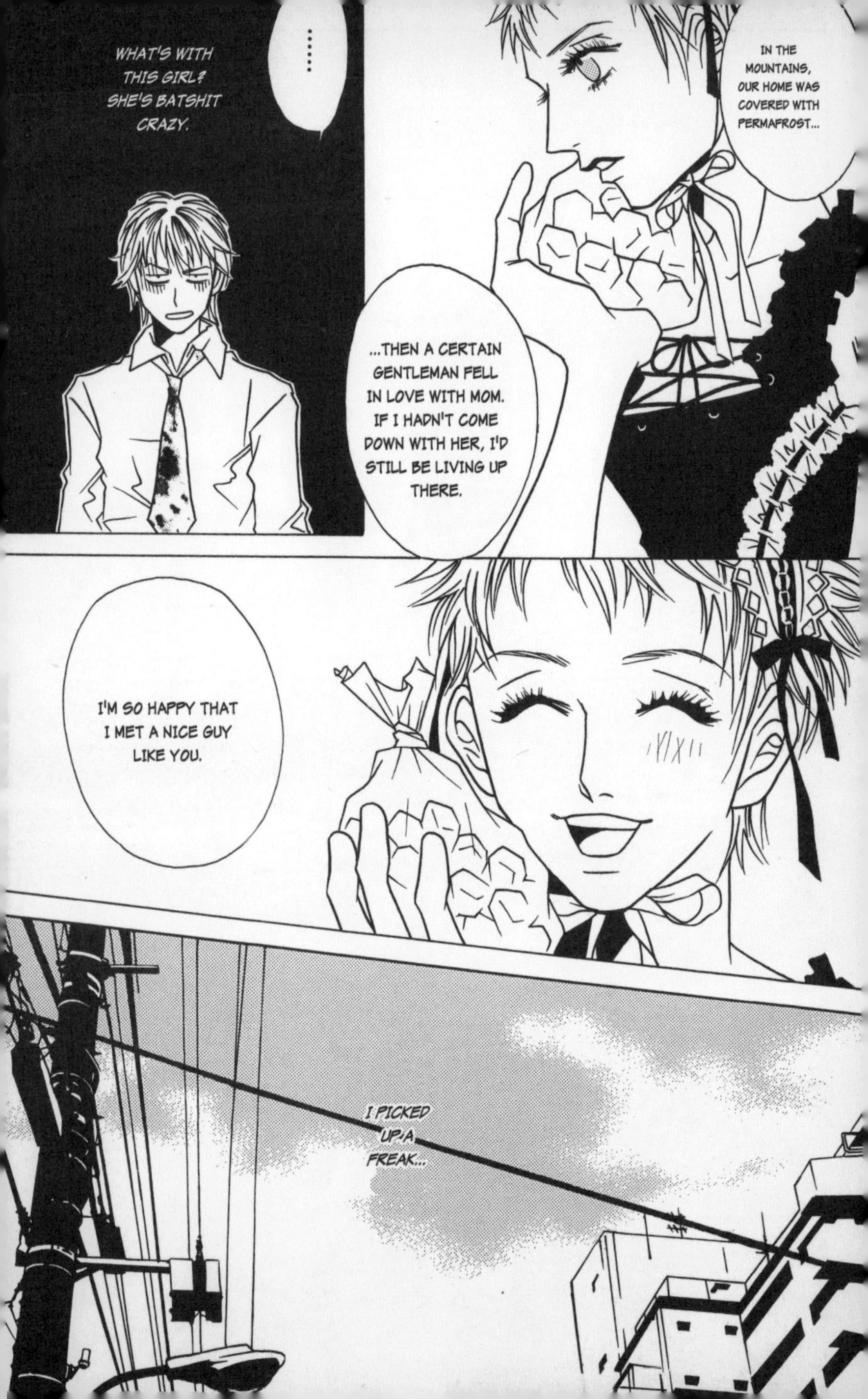
IN THE MOUNTAINS, OUR HOME WAS COVERED WITH PERMAFROST...
...THEN A CERTAIN GENTLEMAN FELL IN LOVE WITH MOM. IF I HADN'T COME DOWN WITH HER, I'D STILL BE LIVING UP THERE.
......
WHAT'S WITH THIS GIRL? SHE'S BATSHIT CRAZY.
I'M SO HAPPY THAT I MET A NICE GUY LIKE YOU.
I PICKED UP A FREAK...

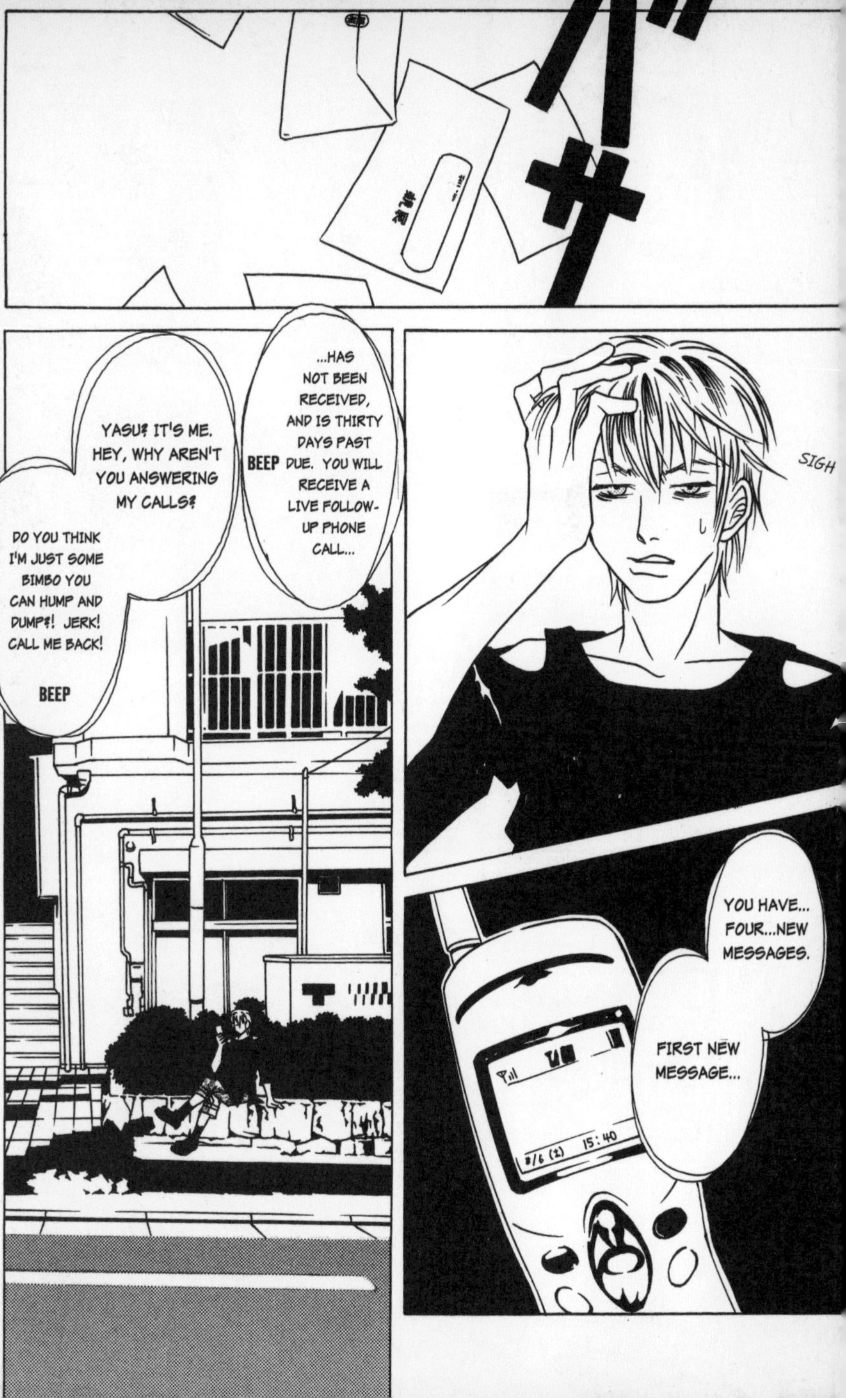

バサ
SIGH
YOU HAVE... FOUR...NEW MESSAGES.
FIRST NEW MESSAGE...
...HAS NOT BEEN RECEIVED, AND IS THIRTY DAYS PAST DUE. YOU WILL RECEIVE A LIVE FOLLOW-UP PHONE CALL...
BEEP
YASU? IT'S ME. HEY, WHY AREN'T YOU ANSWERING MY CALLS?
DO YOU THINK I'M JUST SOME BIMBO YOU CAN HUMP AND DUMP?! JERK! CALL ME BACK!
BEEP

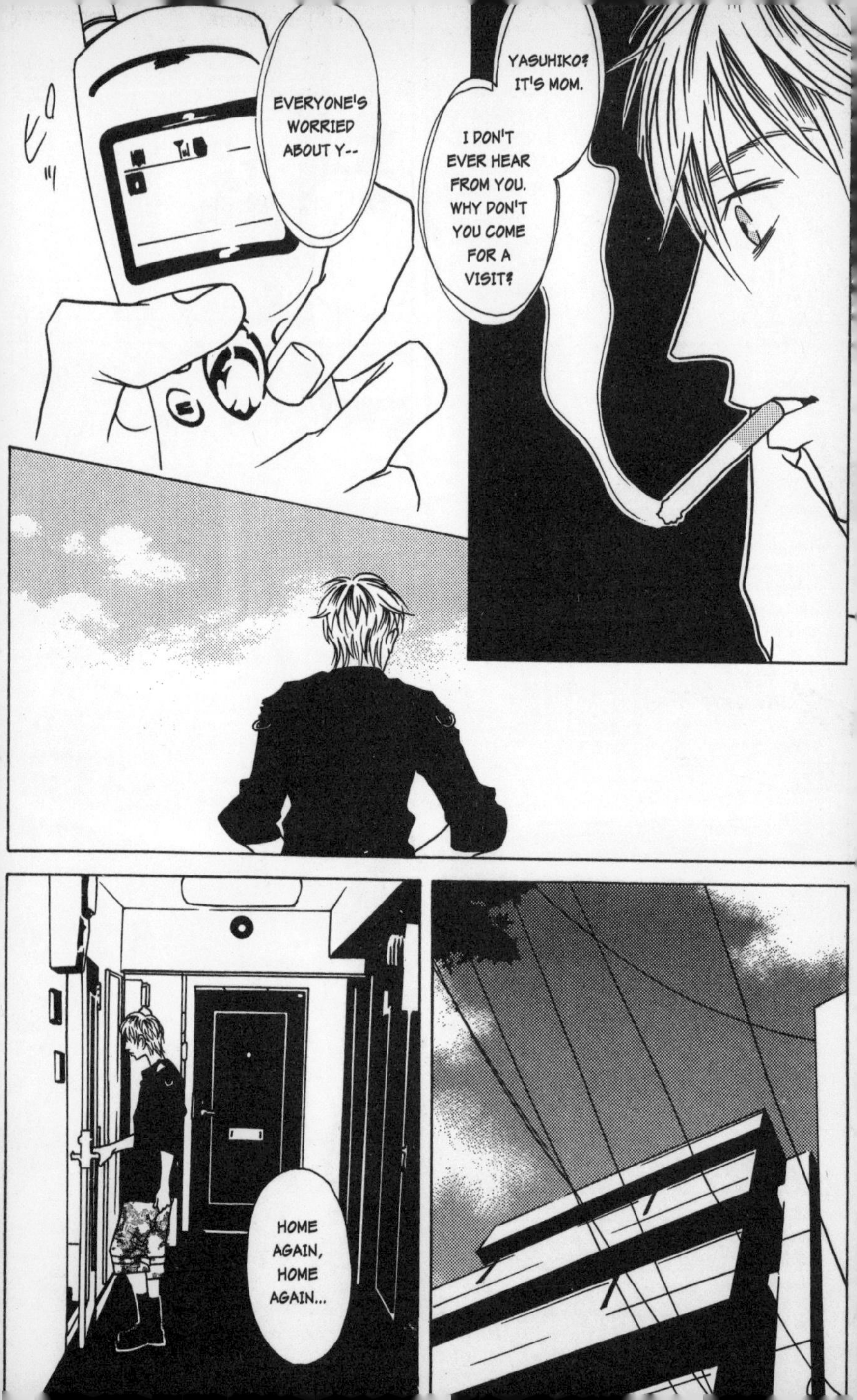
YASUHIKO? IT'S MOM.
I DON'T EVER HEAR FROM YOU. WHY DON'T YOU COME FOR A VISIT?
EVERYONE'S WORRIED ABOUT Y--
HOME AGAIN, HOME AGAIN...

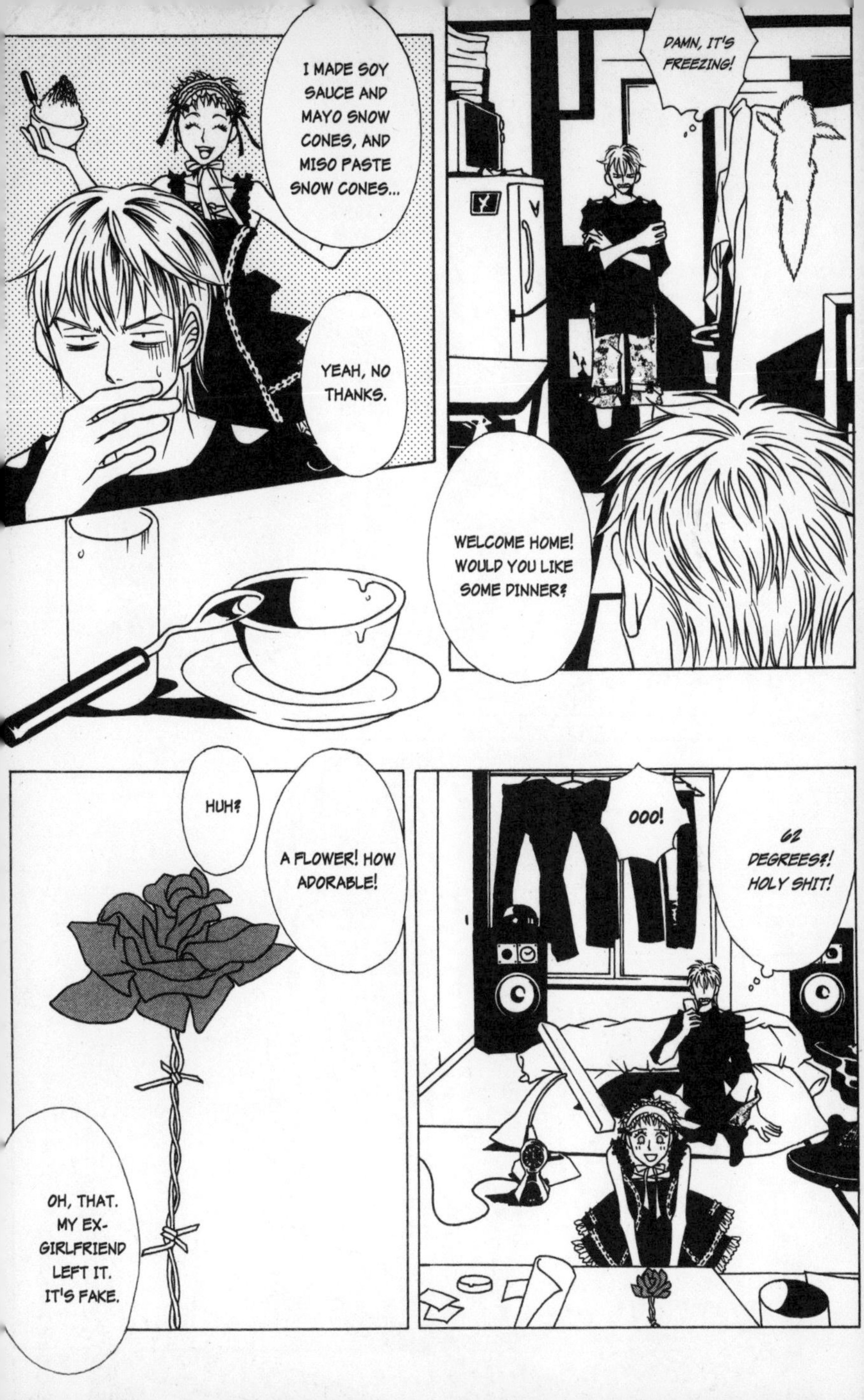
DAMN, IT'S FREEZING!
WELCOME HOME! WOULD YOU LIKE SOME DINNER?
I MADE SOY SAUCE AND MAYO SNOW CONES, AND MISO PASTE SNOW CONES...
YEAH, NO THANKS.
62 DEGREES?! HOLY SHIT!
OOO!
HUH?
A FLOWER! HOW ADORABLE!
OH, THAT. MY EX-GIRLFRIEND LEFT IT. IT'S FAKE.

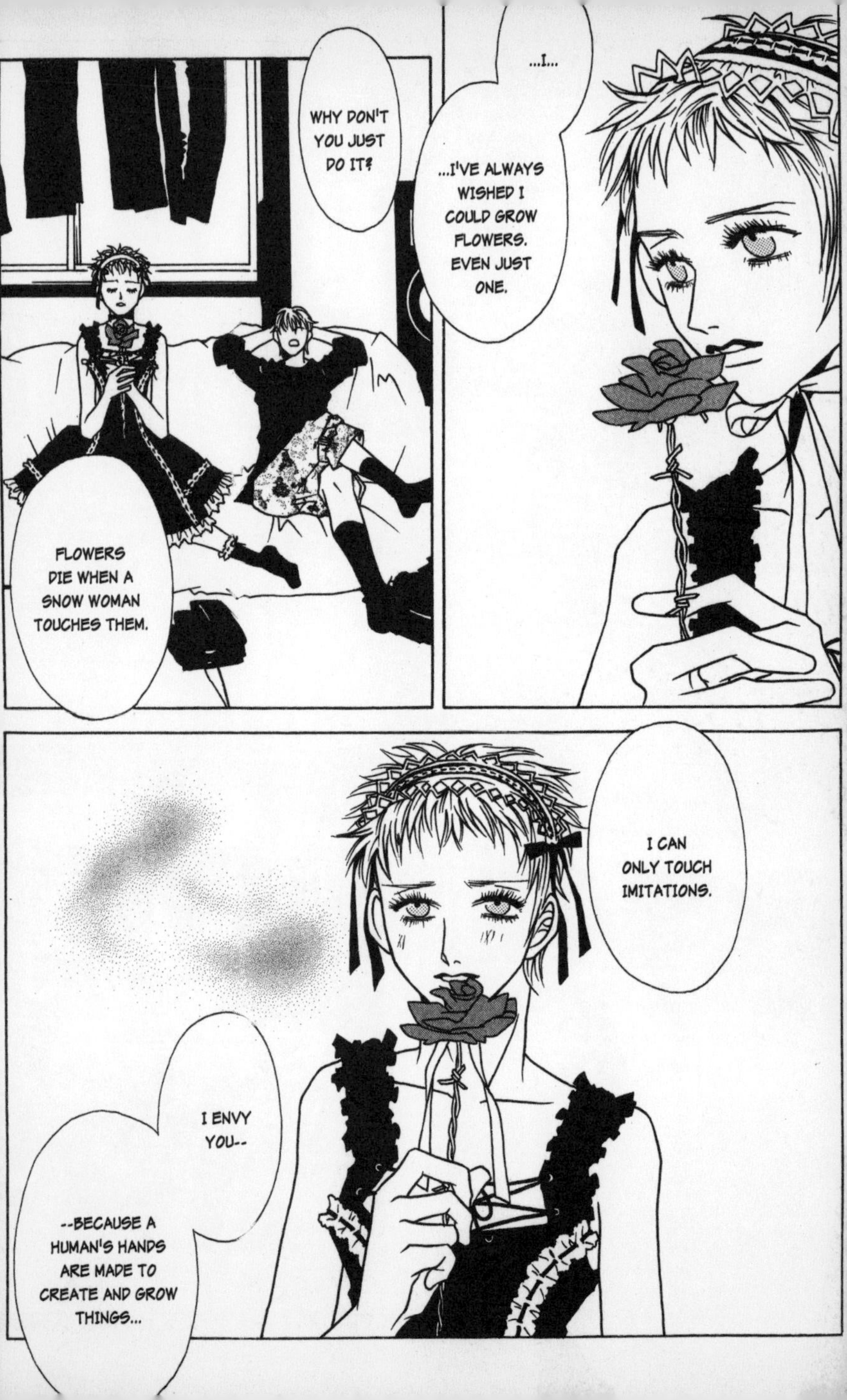
...I...
...I'VE ALWAYS WISHED I COULD GROW FLOWERS. EVEN JUST ONE.
WHY DON'T YOU JUST DO IT?
FLOWERS DIE WHEN A SNOW WOMAN TOUCHES THEM.
I CAN ONLY TOUCH IMITATIONS.
I ENVY YOU--
--BECAUSE A HUMAN'S HANDS ARE MADE TO CREATE AND GROW THINGS...

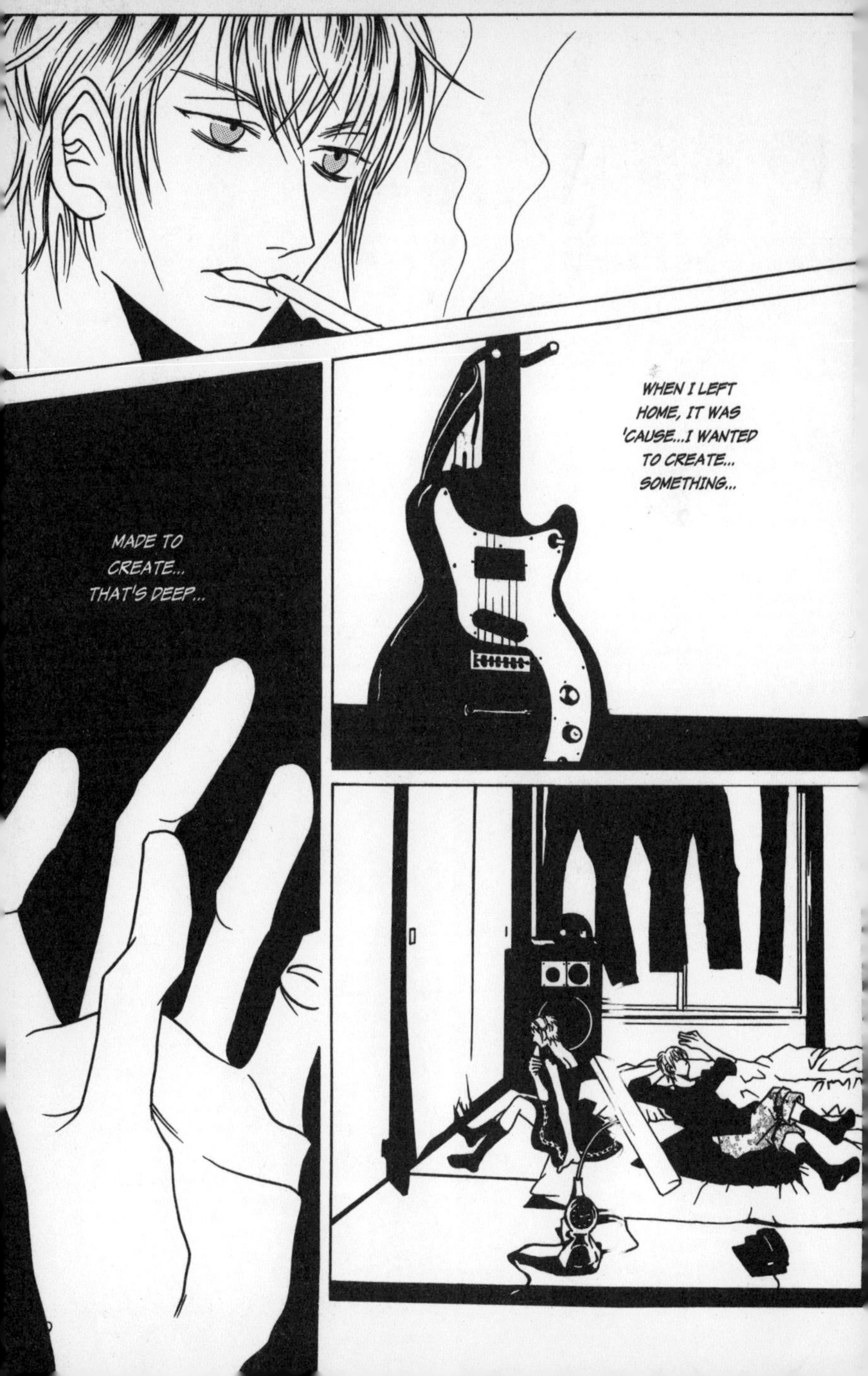
WHEN I LEFT HOME, IT WAS 'CAUSE...I WANTED TO CREATE... SOMETHING...
MADE TO CREATE... THAT'S DEEP...

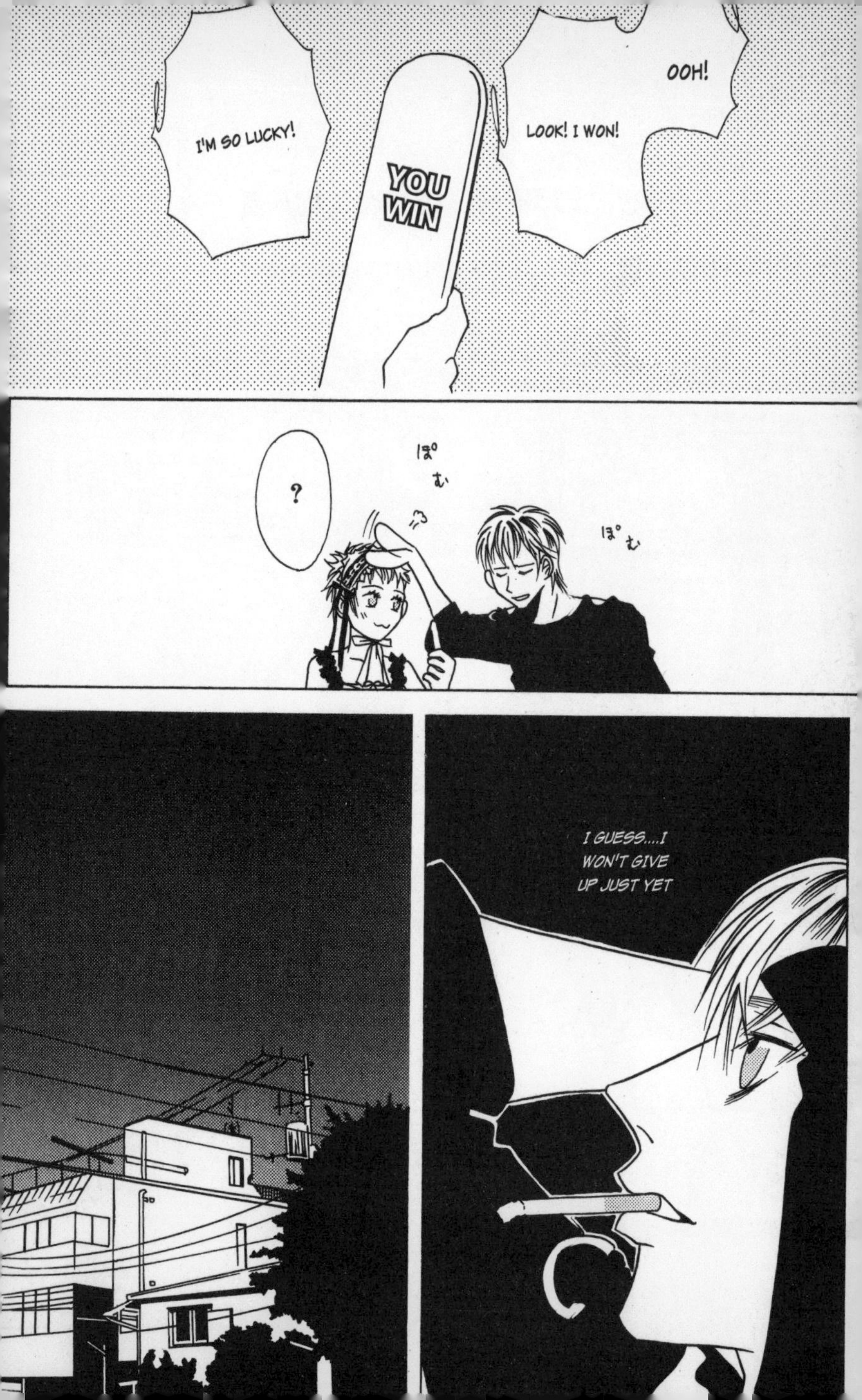
OOH!
LOOK! I WON!
YOU WIN
I'M SO LUCKY!
ぽむ
ぽむ
?
I GUESS....I WON'T GIVE UP JUST YET

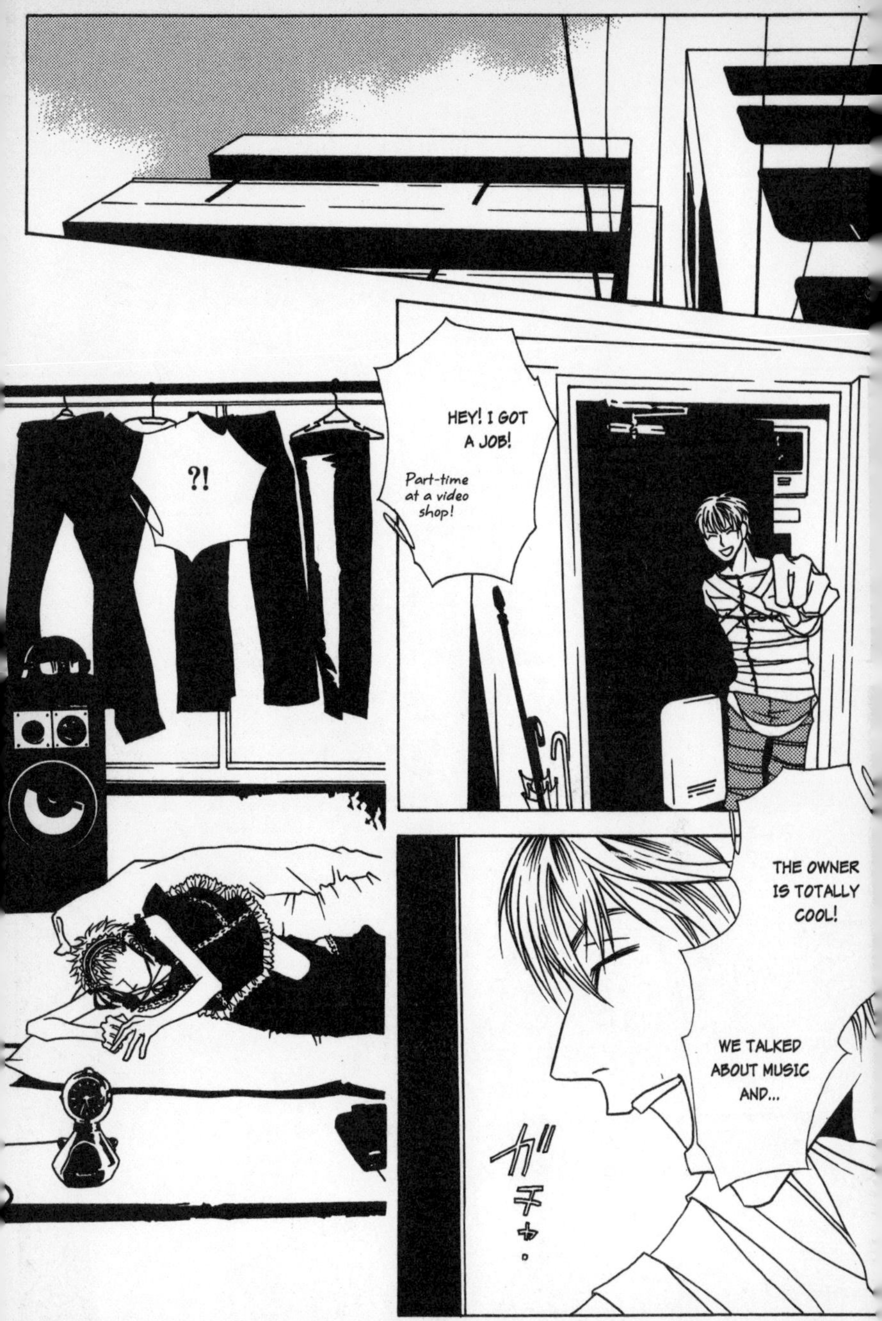
HEY! I GOT A JOB!
Part-time at a video shop!
THE OWNER IS TOTALLY COOL!
WE TALKED ABOUT MUSIC AND...
ガチャ。
?!

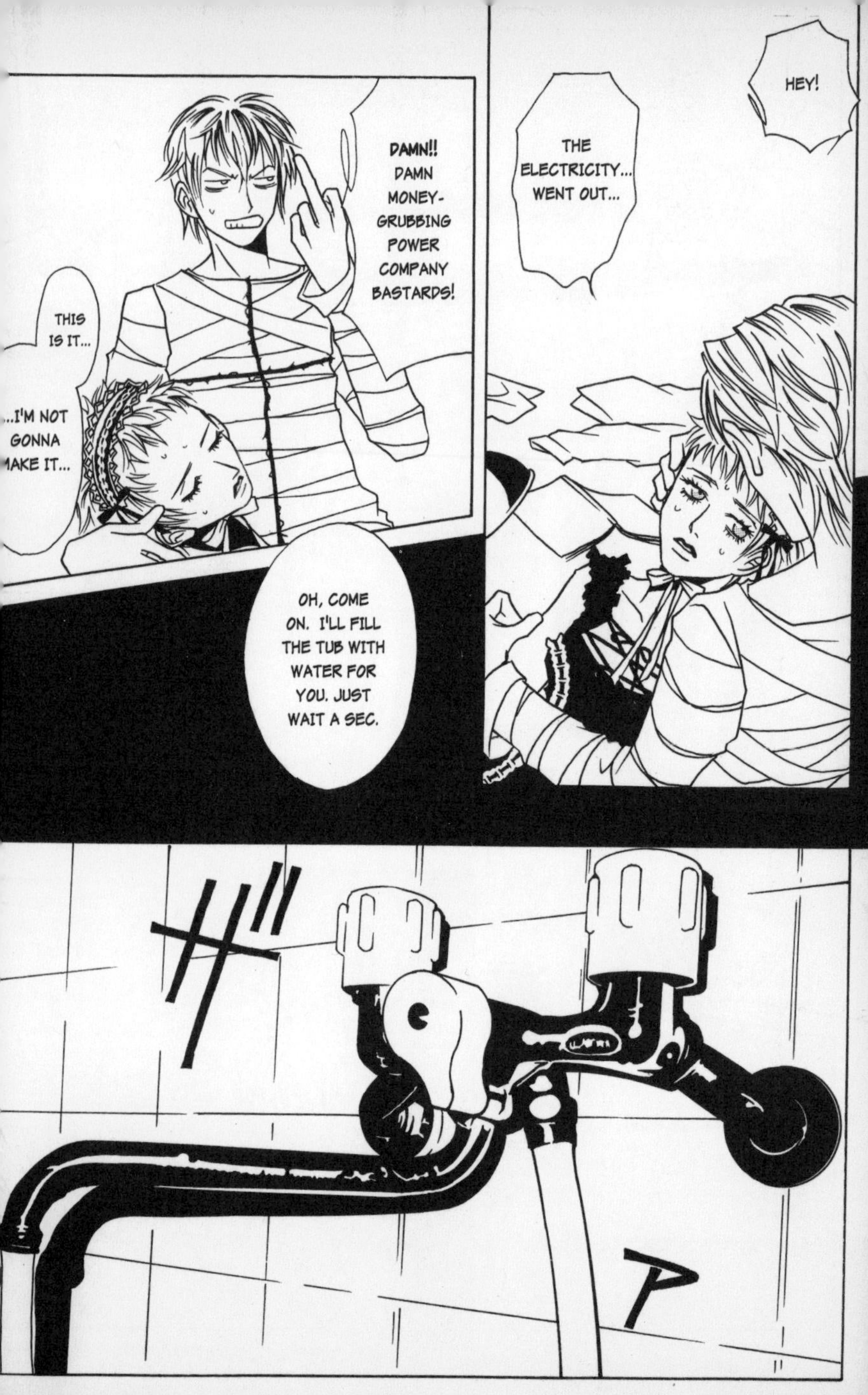
HEY!
THE ELECTRICITY... WENT OUT...
DAMN!! DAMN MONEY-GRUBBING POWER COMPANY BASTARDS!
THIS IS IT...
...I'M NOT GONNA MAKE IT...
OH, COME ON. I'LL FILL THE TUB WITH WATER FOR YOU. JUST WAIT A SEC.

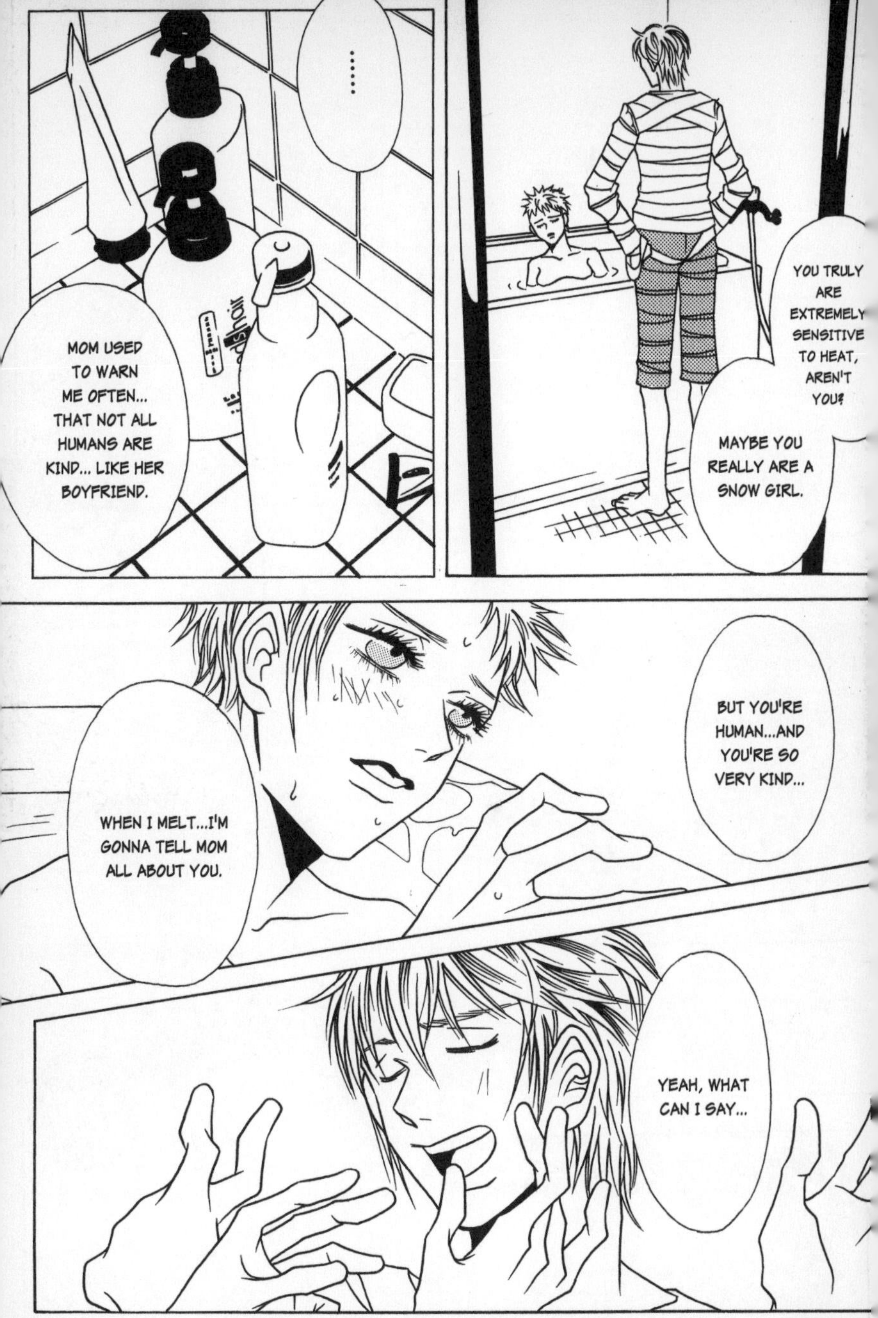
YOU TRULY ARE EXTREMELY SENSITIVE TO HEAT, AREN'T YOU?
MAYBE YOU REALLY ARE A SNOW GIRL.
......
MOM USED TO WARN ME OFTEN... THAT NOT ALL HUMANS ARE KIND... LIKE HER BOYFRIEND.
BUT YOU'RE HUMAN...AND YOU'RE SO VERY KIND...
WHEN I MELT...I'M GONNA TELL MOM ALL ABOUT YOU.
YEAH, WHAT CAN I SAY...

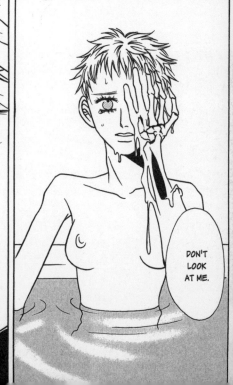

DON'T
LOOK
AT ME.

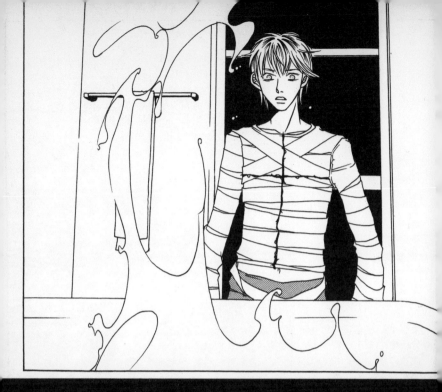

IT HAPPENED
ALL AT ONCE...

...AND SHE WAS
GONE.

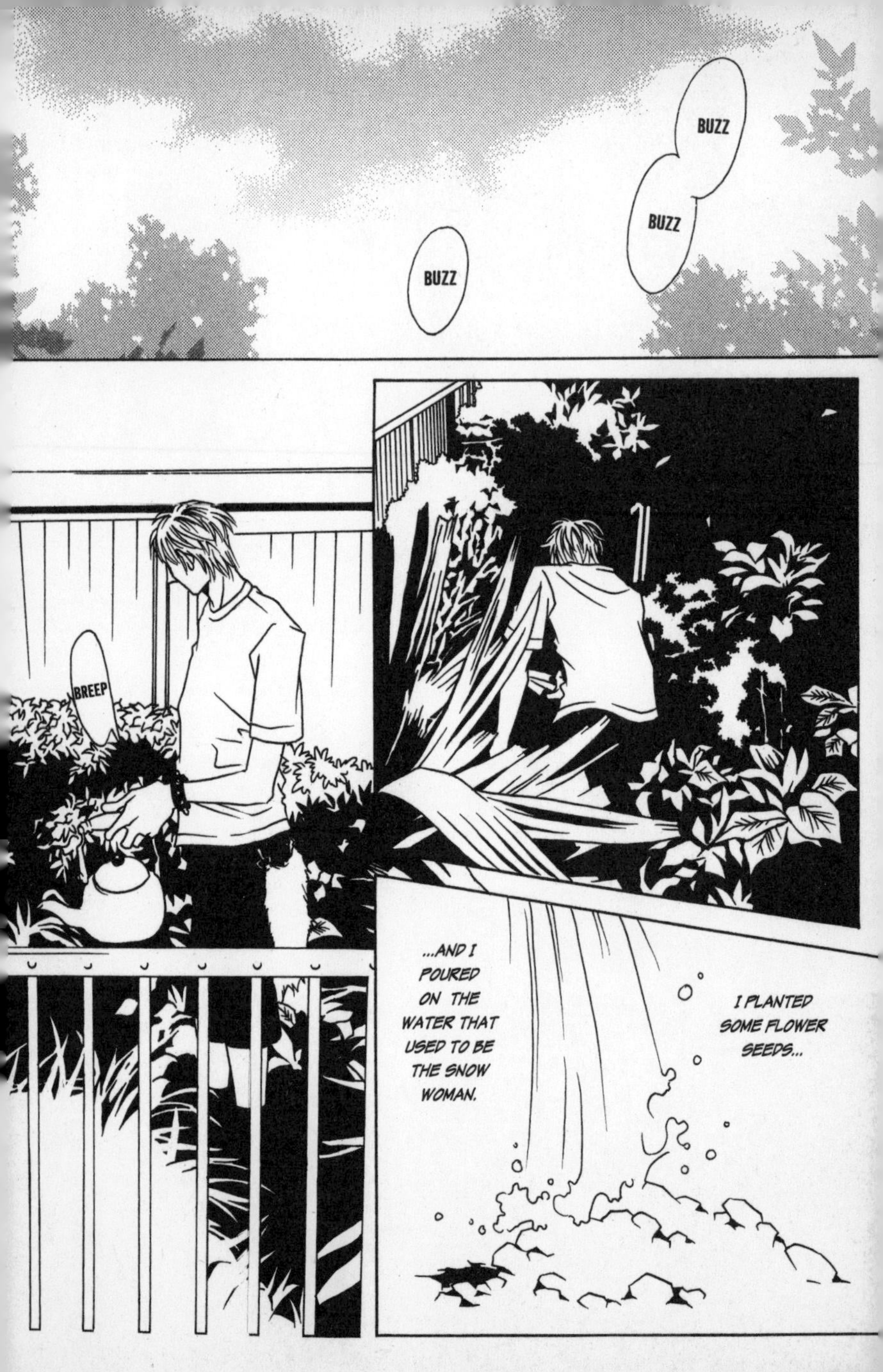
BUZZ
BUZZ
BUZZ
I PLANTED SOME FLOWER SEEDS...
...AND I POURED ON THE WATER THAT USED TO BE THE SNOW WOMAN.
BREEP

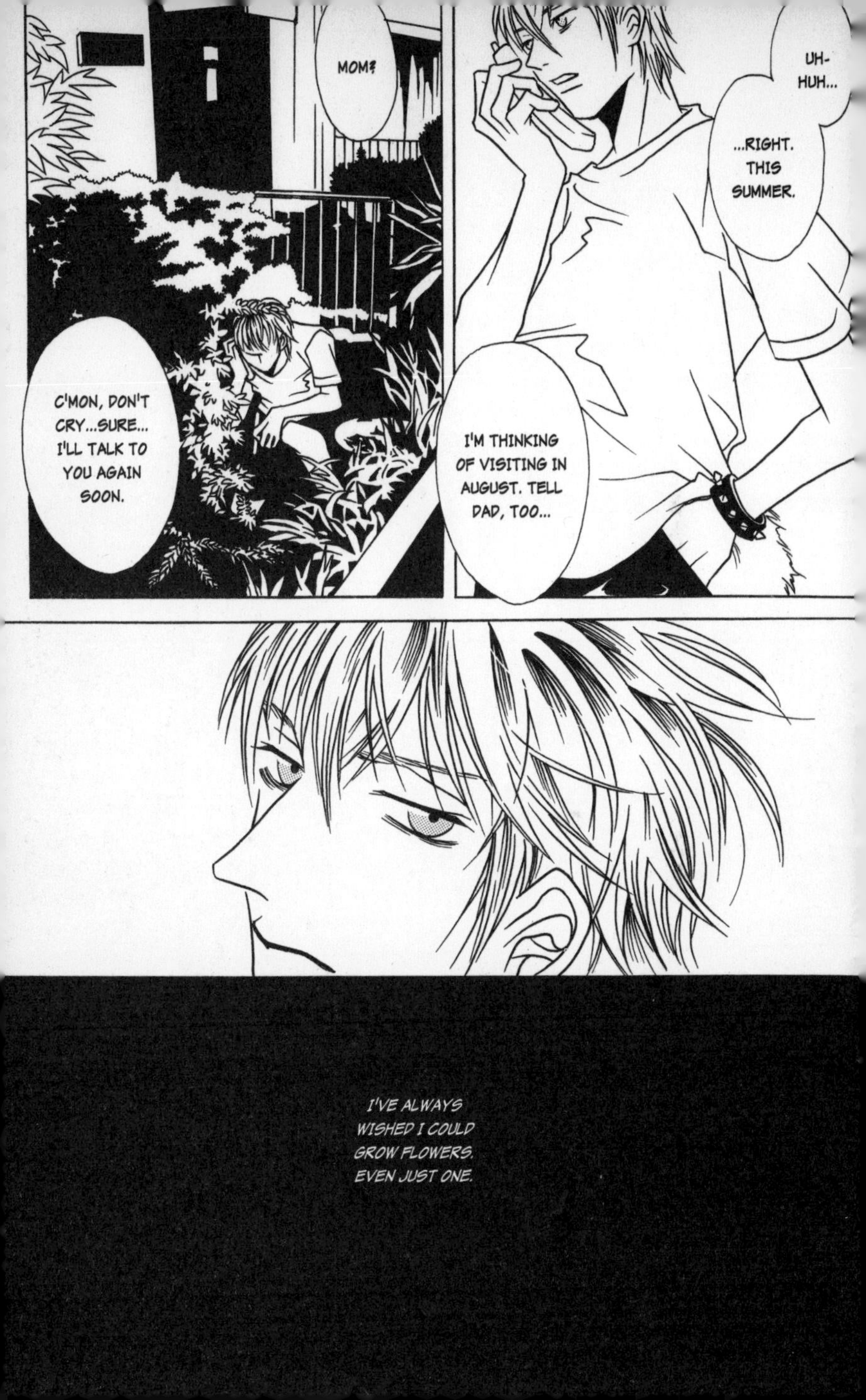
UH-HUH...
...RIGHT. THIS SUMMER.
I'M THINKING OF VISITING IN AUGUST. TELL DAD, TOO...
MOM?
C'MON, DON'T CRY...SURE... I'LL TALK TO YOU AGAIN SOON.
I'VE ALWAYS WISHED I COULD GROW FLOWERS. EVEN JUST ONE.

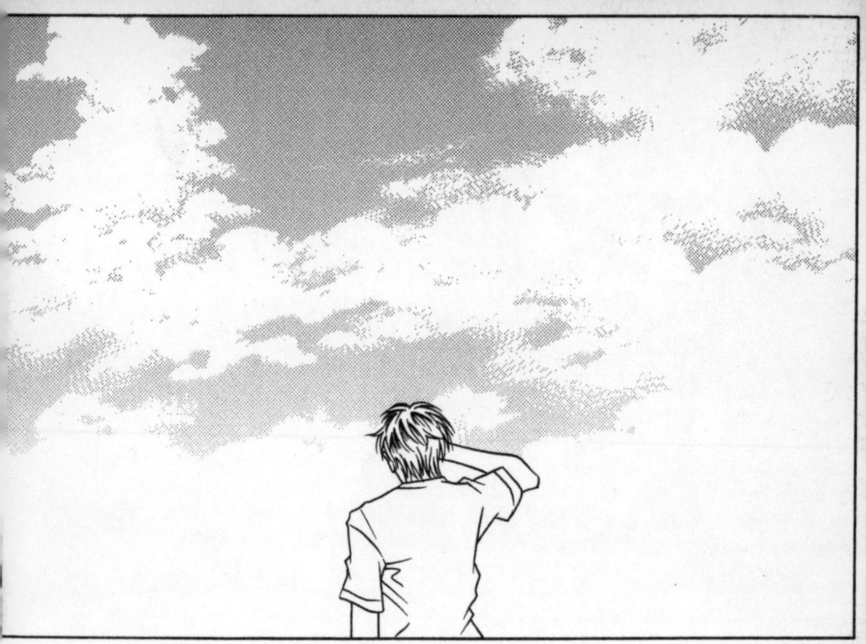

BY THIS TIME
NEXT YEAR, SHE'LL
GET HER WISH.

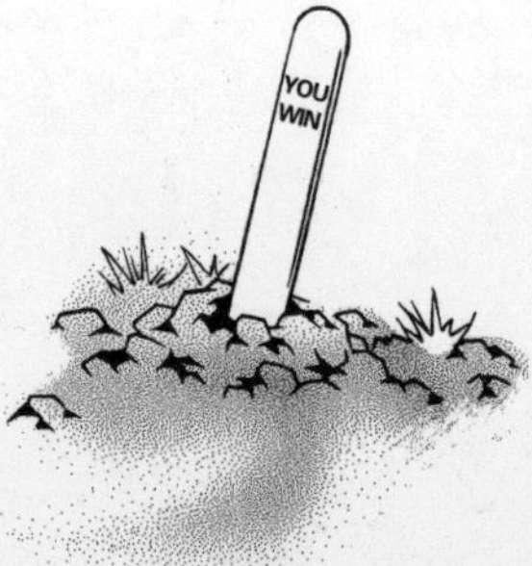
YOU WIN

END

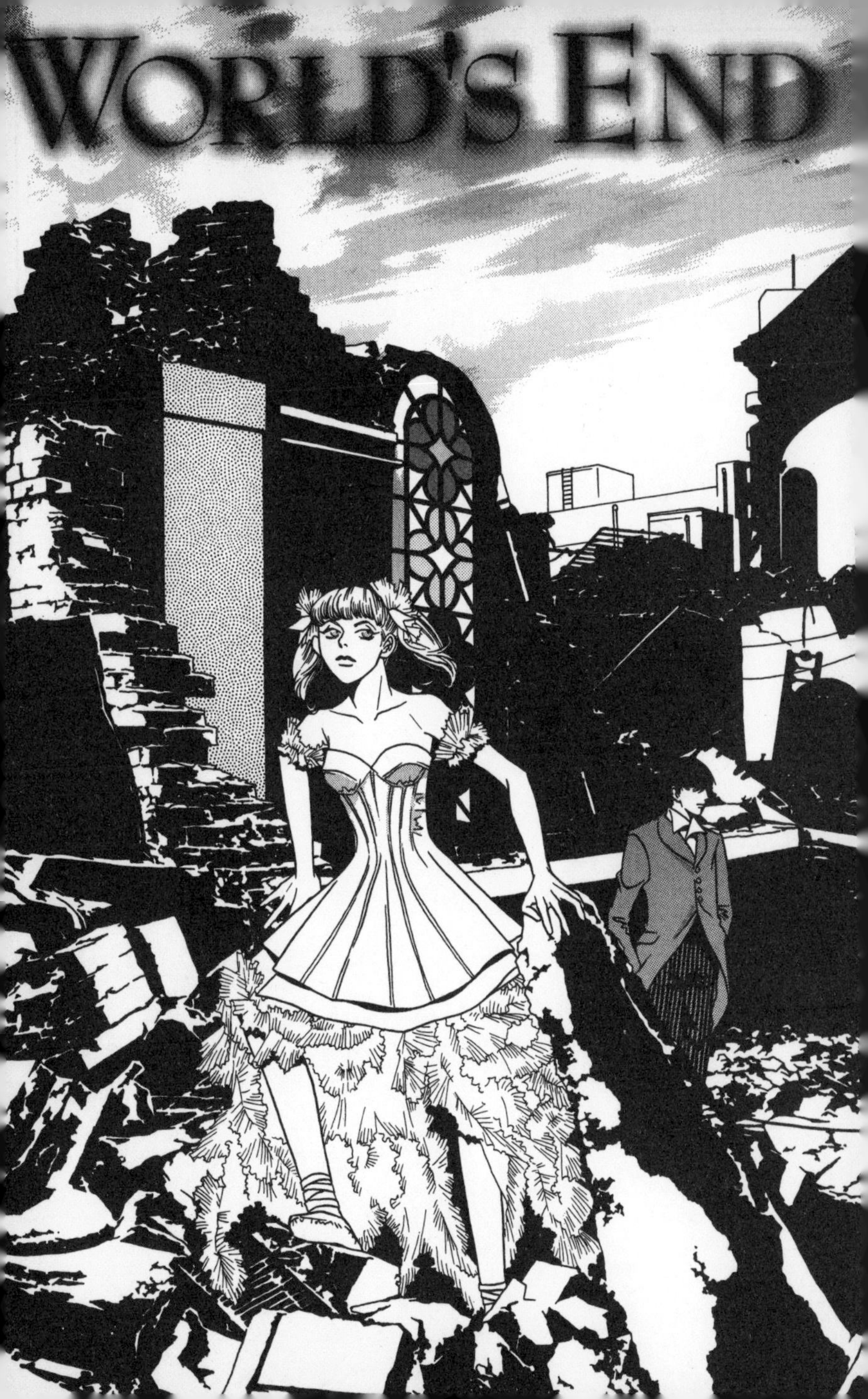
WORLD'S END

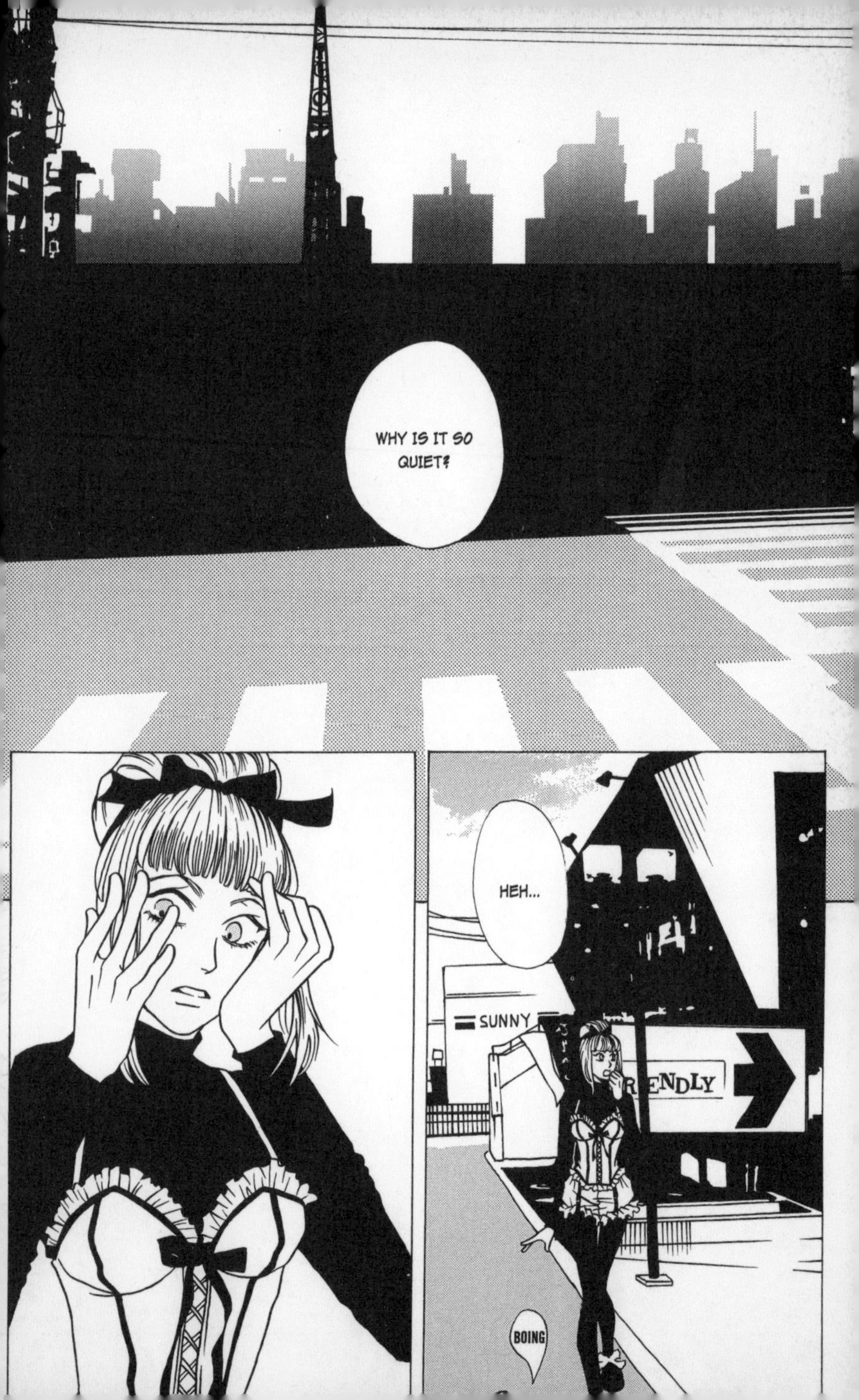
WHY IS IT SO QUIET?
HEH...
SUNNY
BOING

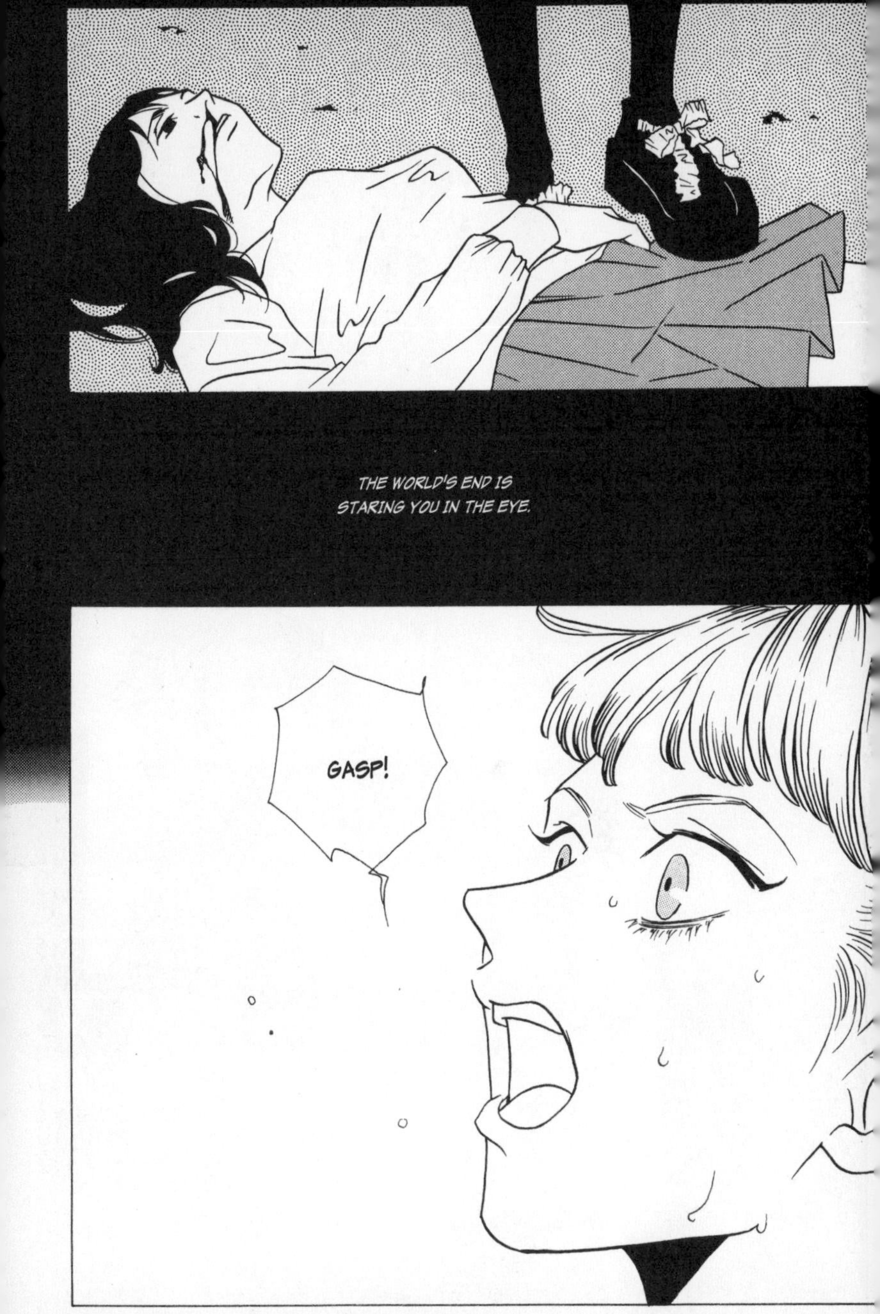
THE WORLD'S END IS
STARING YOU IN THE EYE.
GASP!

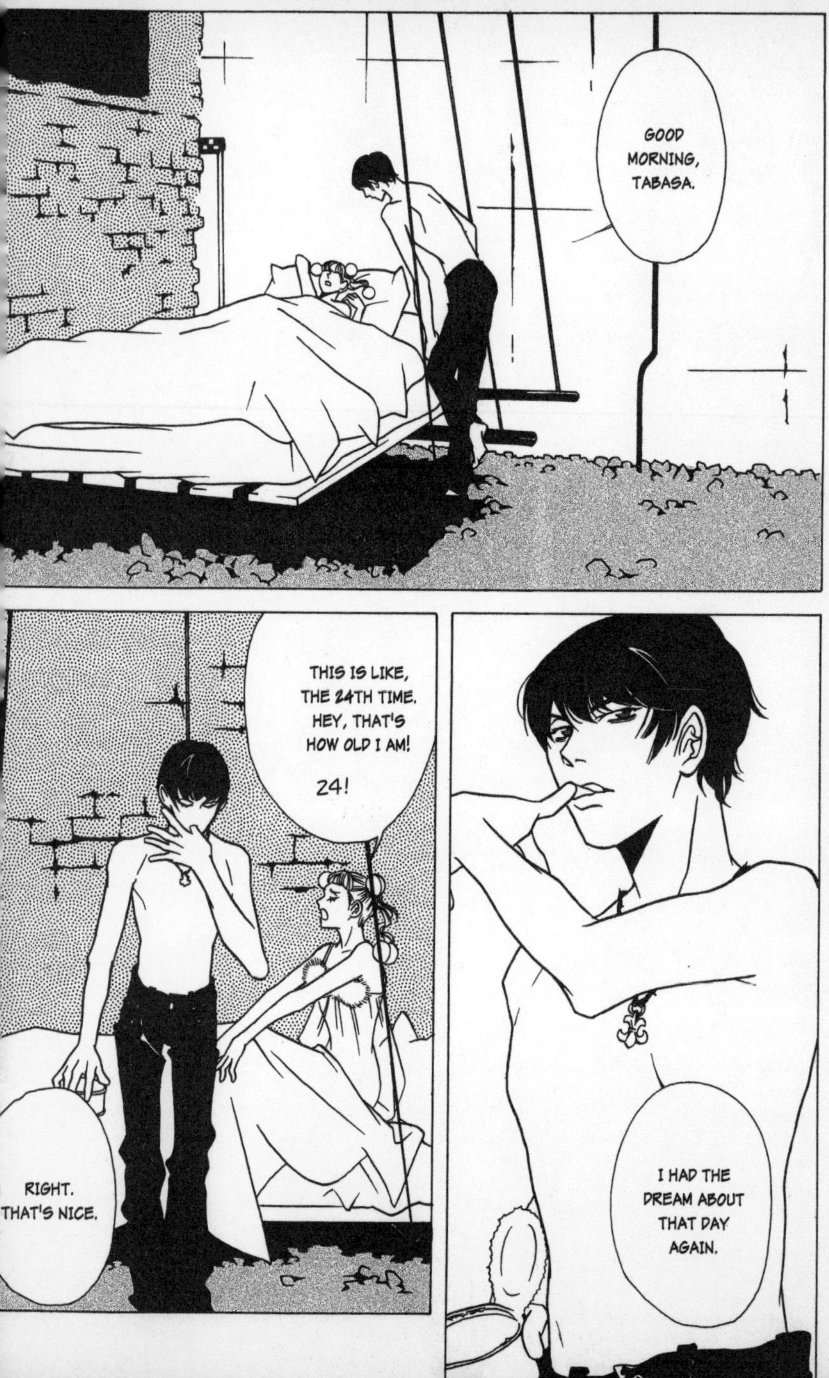
GOOD MORNING, TABASA.
I HAD THE DREAM ABOUT THAT DAY AGAIN.
THIS IS LIKE, THE 24TH TIME. HEY, THAT'S HOW OLD I AM!
24!
RIGHT. THAT'S NICE.

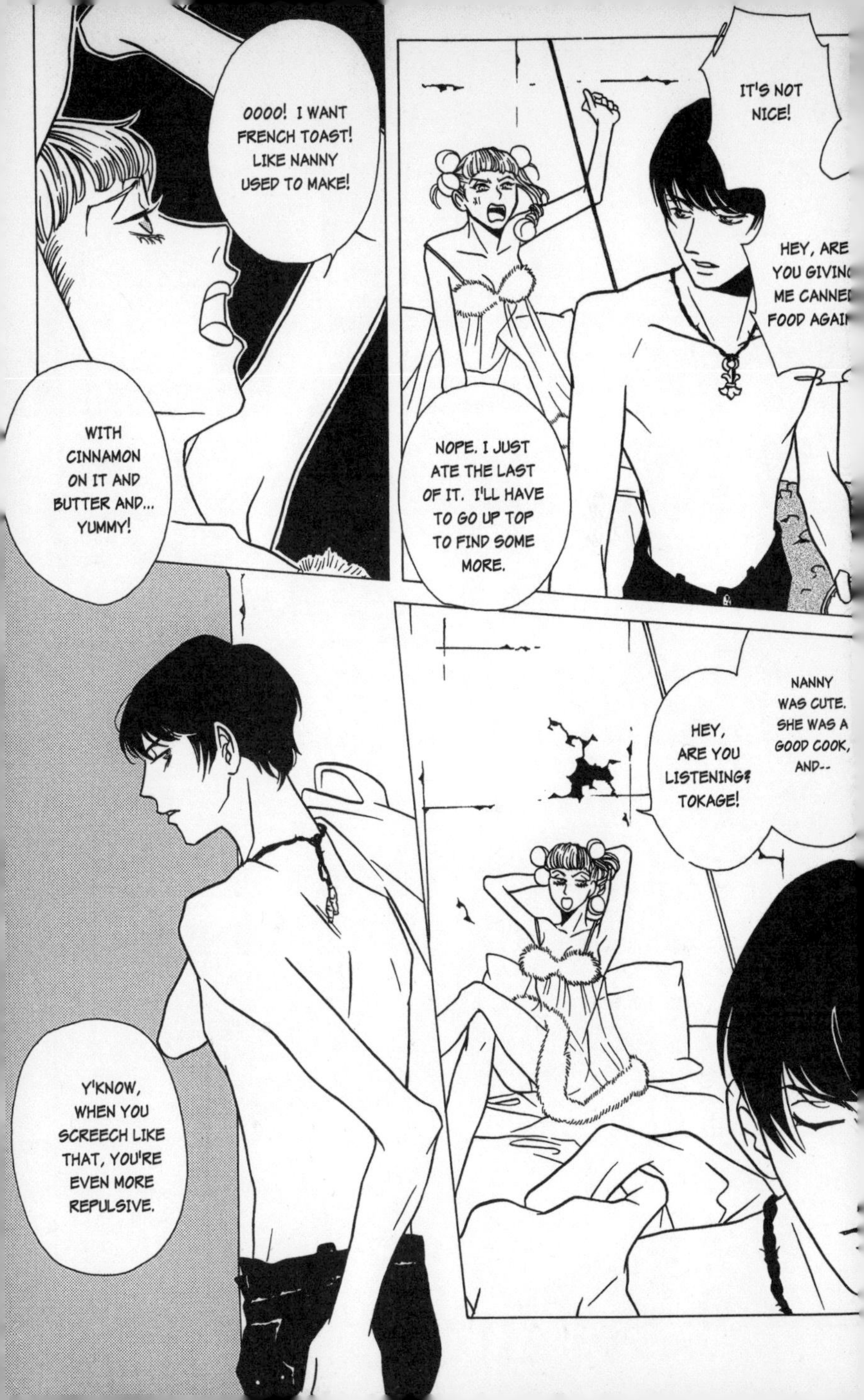
HEY, ARE YOU GIVIN ME CANNE FOOD AGAI
IT'S NOT NICE!
NOPE. I JUST ATE THE LAST OF IT. I'LL HAVE TO GO UP TOP TO FIND SOME MORE.
OOOO! I WANT FRENCH TOAST! LIKE NANNY USED TO MAKE!
WITH CINNAMON ON IT AND BUTTER AND... YUMMY!
NANNY WAS CUTE. SHE WAS A GOOD COOK, AND--
HEY, ARE YOU LISTENING? TOKAGE!
Y'KNOW, WHEN YOU SCREECH LIKE THAT, YOU'RE EVEN MORE REPULSIVE.

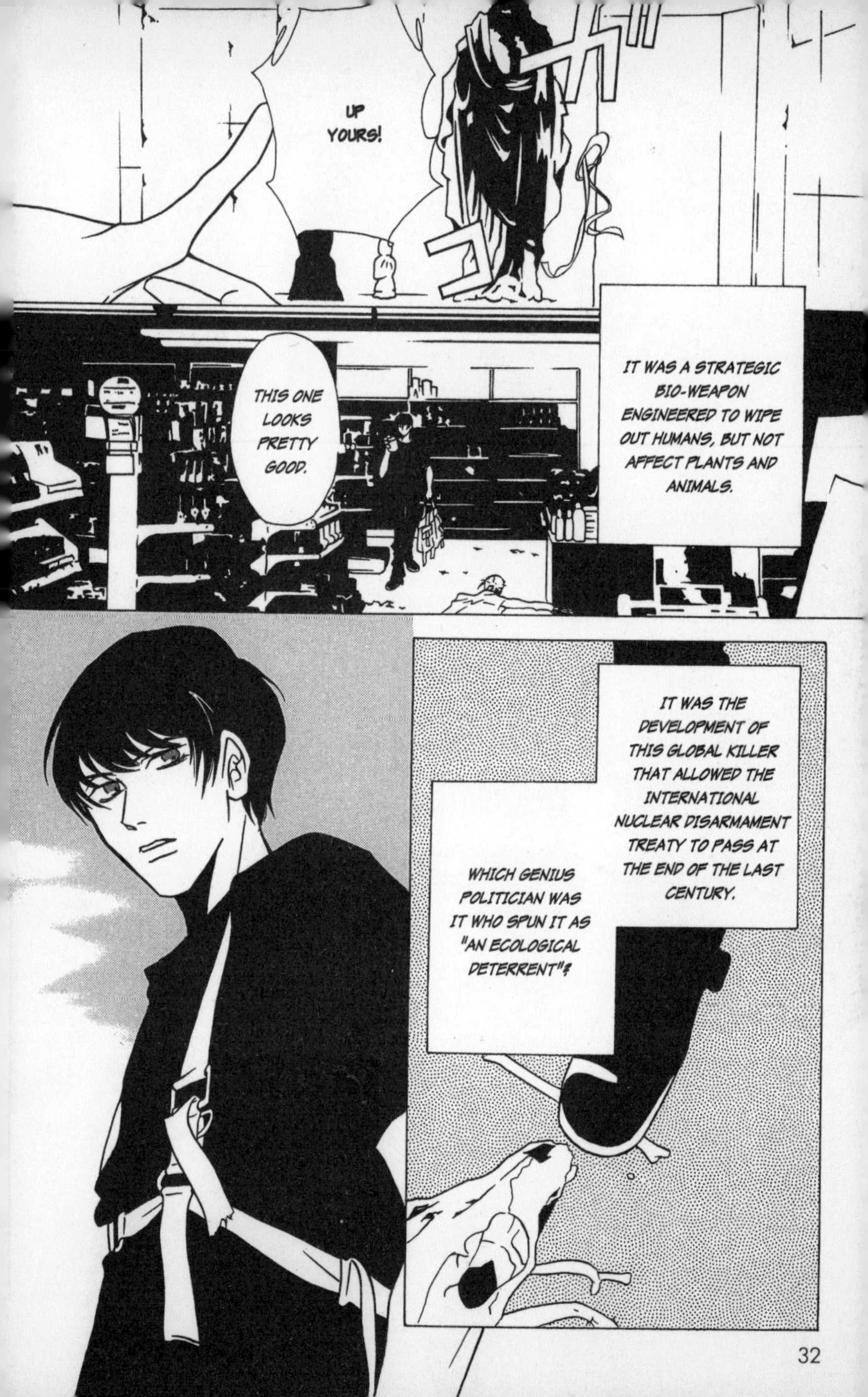
UP YOURS!
IT WAS A STRATEGIC BIO-WEAPON ENGINEERED TO WIPE OUT HUMANS, BUT NOT AFFECT PLANTS AND ANIMALS.
THIS ONE LOOKS PRETTY GOOD.
IT WAS THE DEVELOPMENT OF THIS GLOBAL KILLER THAT ALLOWED THE INTERNATIONAL NUCLEAR DISARMAMENT TREATY TO PASS AT THE END OF THE LAST CENTURY.
WHICH GENIUS POLITICIAN WAS IT WHO SPUN IT AS "AN ECOLOGICAL DETERRENT"?

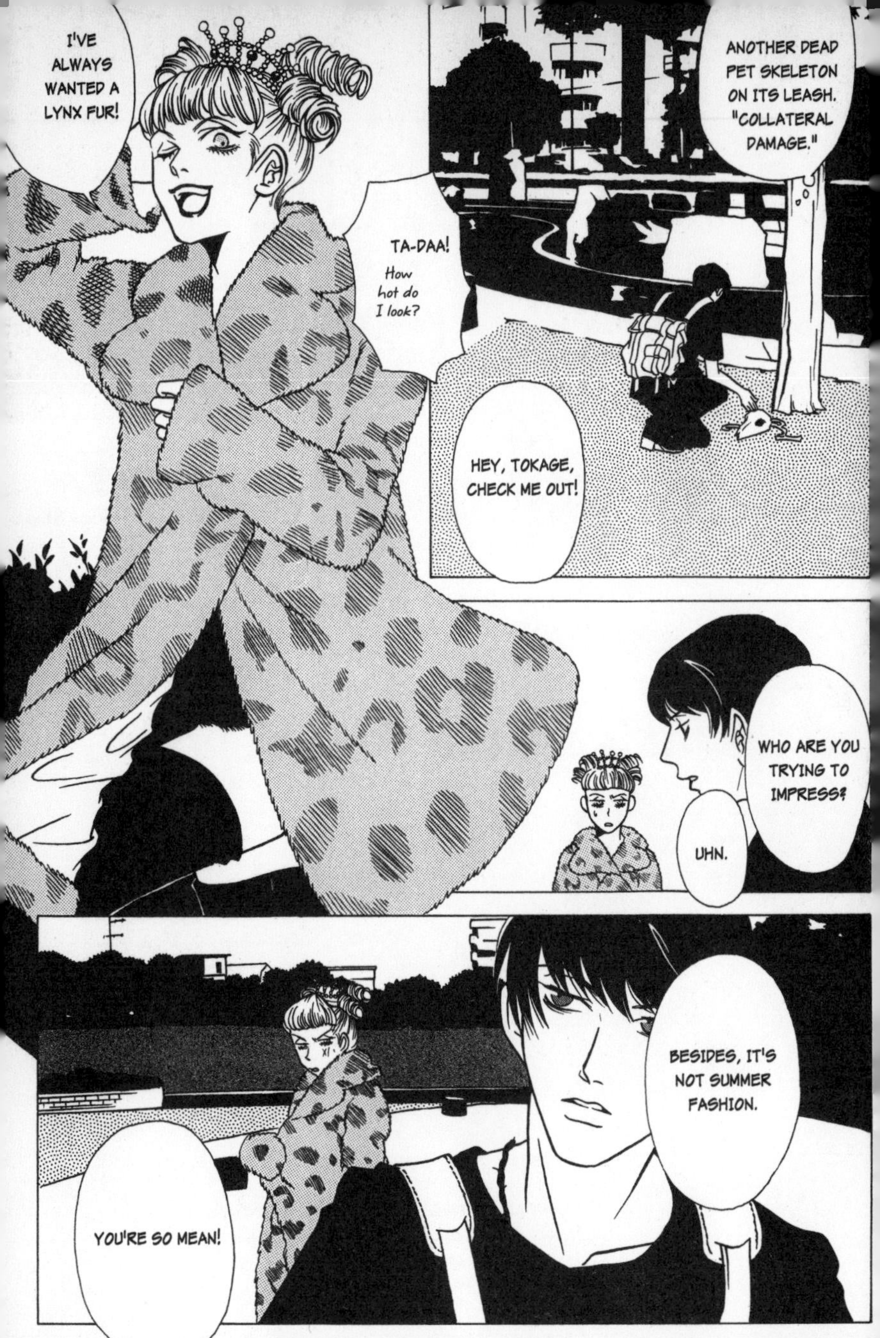
ANOTHER DEAD PET SKELETON ON ITS LEASH. "COLLATERAL DAMAGE."
HEY, TOKAGE, CHECK ME OUT!
WHO ARE YOU TRYING TO IMPRESS?
UHN.
TA-DAA!
How hot do I look?
I'VE ALWAYS WANTED A LYNX FUR!
BESIDES, IT'S NOT SUMMER FASHION.
YOU'RE SO MEAN!

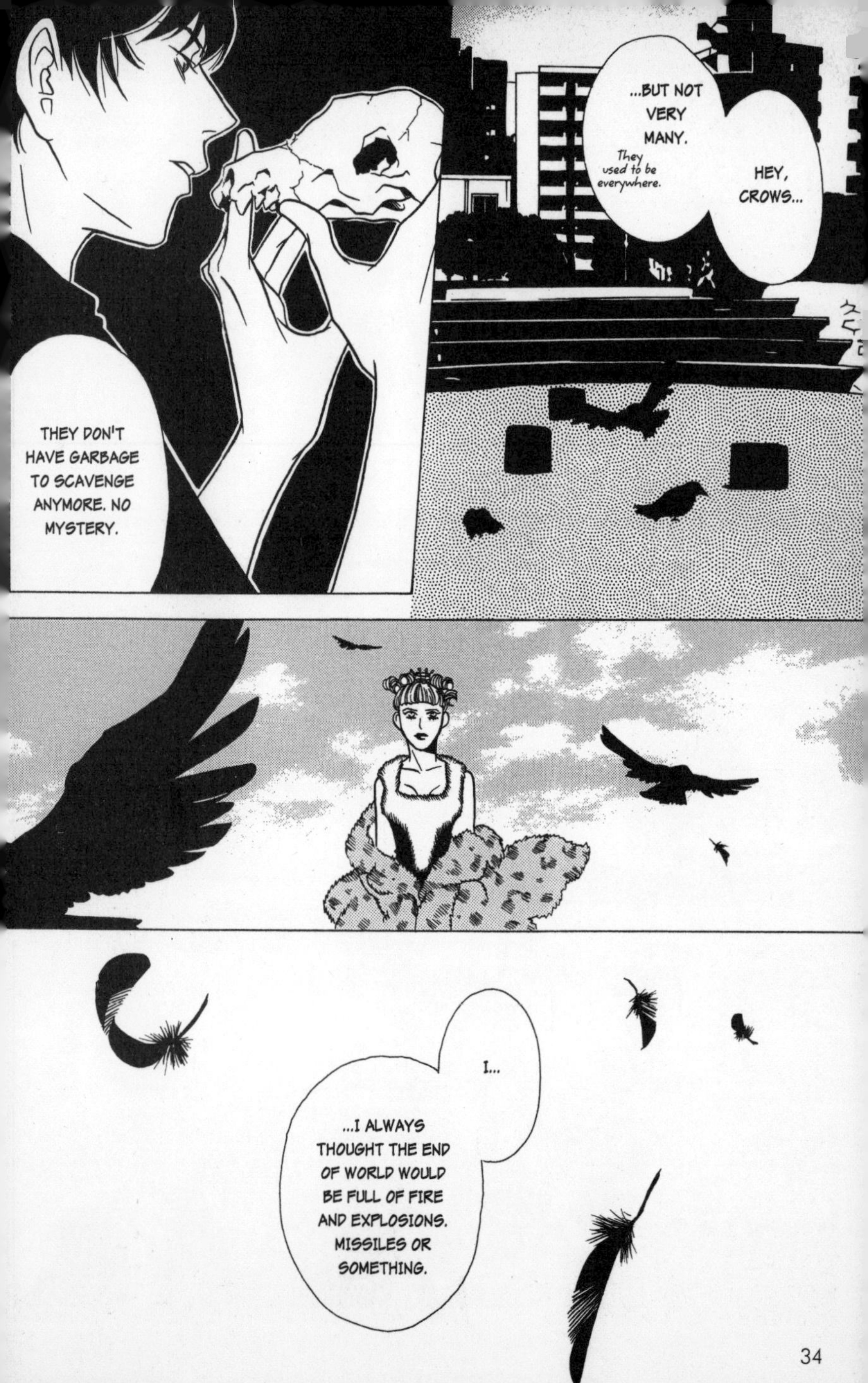
HEY, CROWS...
...BUT NOT VERY MANY.
They used to be everywhere.
THEY DON'T HAVE GARBAGE TO SCAVENGE ANYMORE. NO MYSTERY.
I...
...I ALWAYS THOUGHT THE END OF WORLD WOULD BE FULL OF FIRE AND EXPLOSIONS. MISSILES OR SOMETHING.

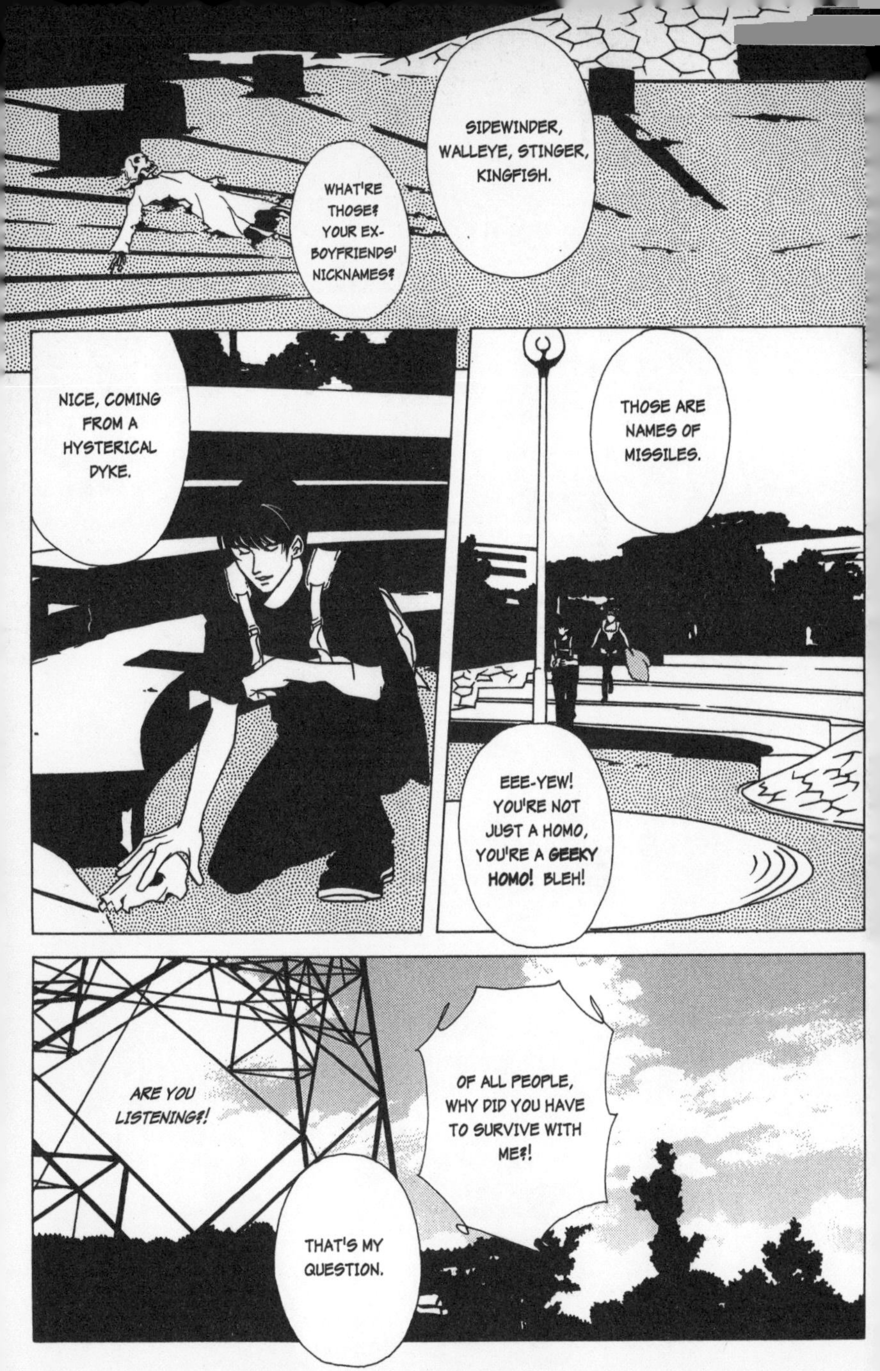
SIDEWINDER, WALLEYE, STINGER, KINGFISH.
WHAT'RE THOSE? YOUR EX-BOYFRIENDS' NICKNAMES?
THOSE ARE NAMES OF MISSILES.
EEE-YEW! YOU'RE NOT JUST A HOMO, YOU'RE A GEEKY HOMO! BLEH!
NICE, COMING FROM A HYSTERICAL DYKE.
OF ALL PEOPLE, WHY DID YOU HAVE TO SURVIVE WITH ME?!
ARE YOU LISTENING?!
THAT'S MY QUESTION.

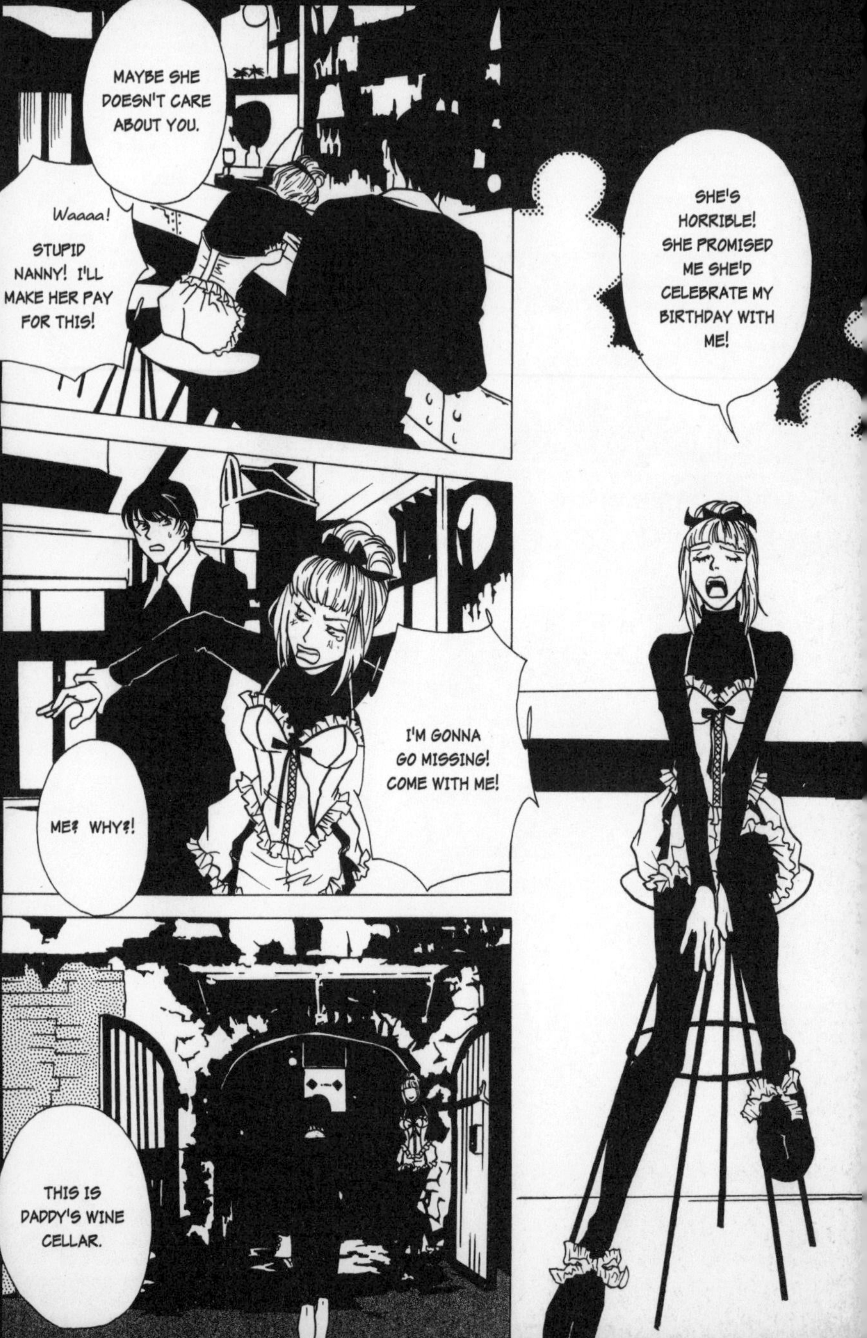
SHE'S HORRIBLE! SHE PROMISED ME SHE'D CELEBRATE MY BIRTHDAY WITH ME!
MAYBE SHE DOESN'T CARE ABOUT YOU.
Waaaa!
STUPID NANNY! I'LL MAKE HER PAY FOR THIS!
I'M GONNA GO MISSING! COME WITH ME!
ME? WHY?!
THIS IS DADDY'S WINE CELLAR.

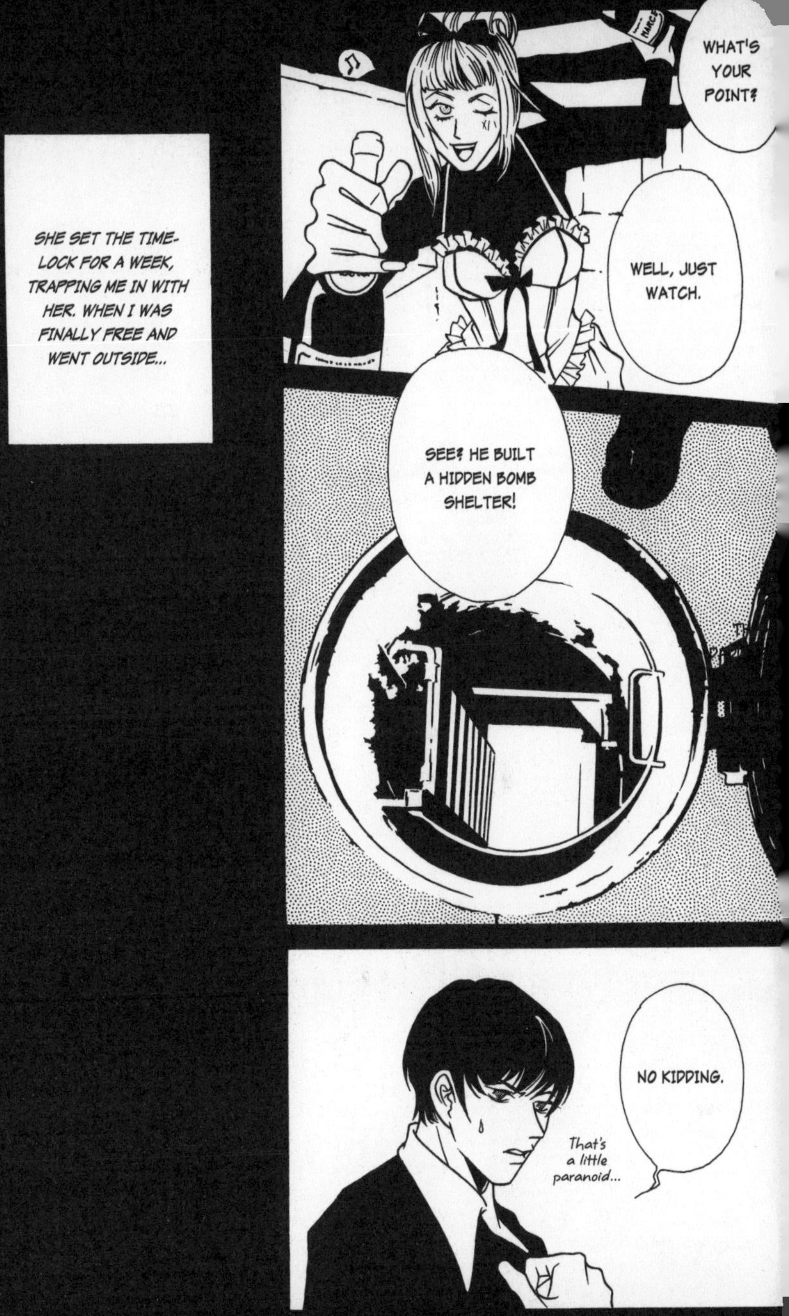
WHAT'S YOUR POINT?
WELL, JUST WATCH.
SEE? HE BUILT A HIDDEN BOMB SHELTER!
NO KIDDING.
That's a little paranoid...
SHE SET THE TIME-LOCK FOR A WEEK, TRAPPING ME IN WITH HER. WHEN I WAS FINALLY FREE AND WENT OUTSIDE...

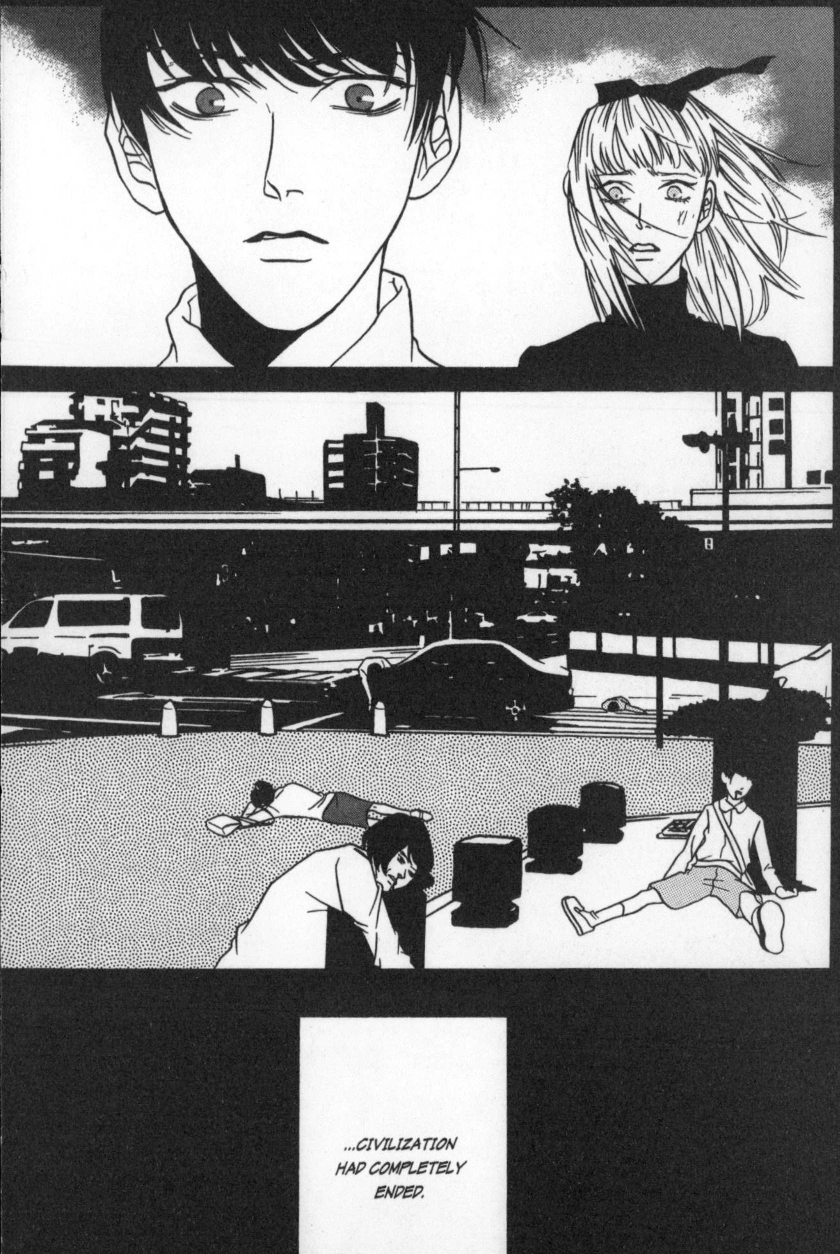
...CIVILIZATION HAD COMPLETELY ENDED.

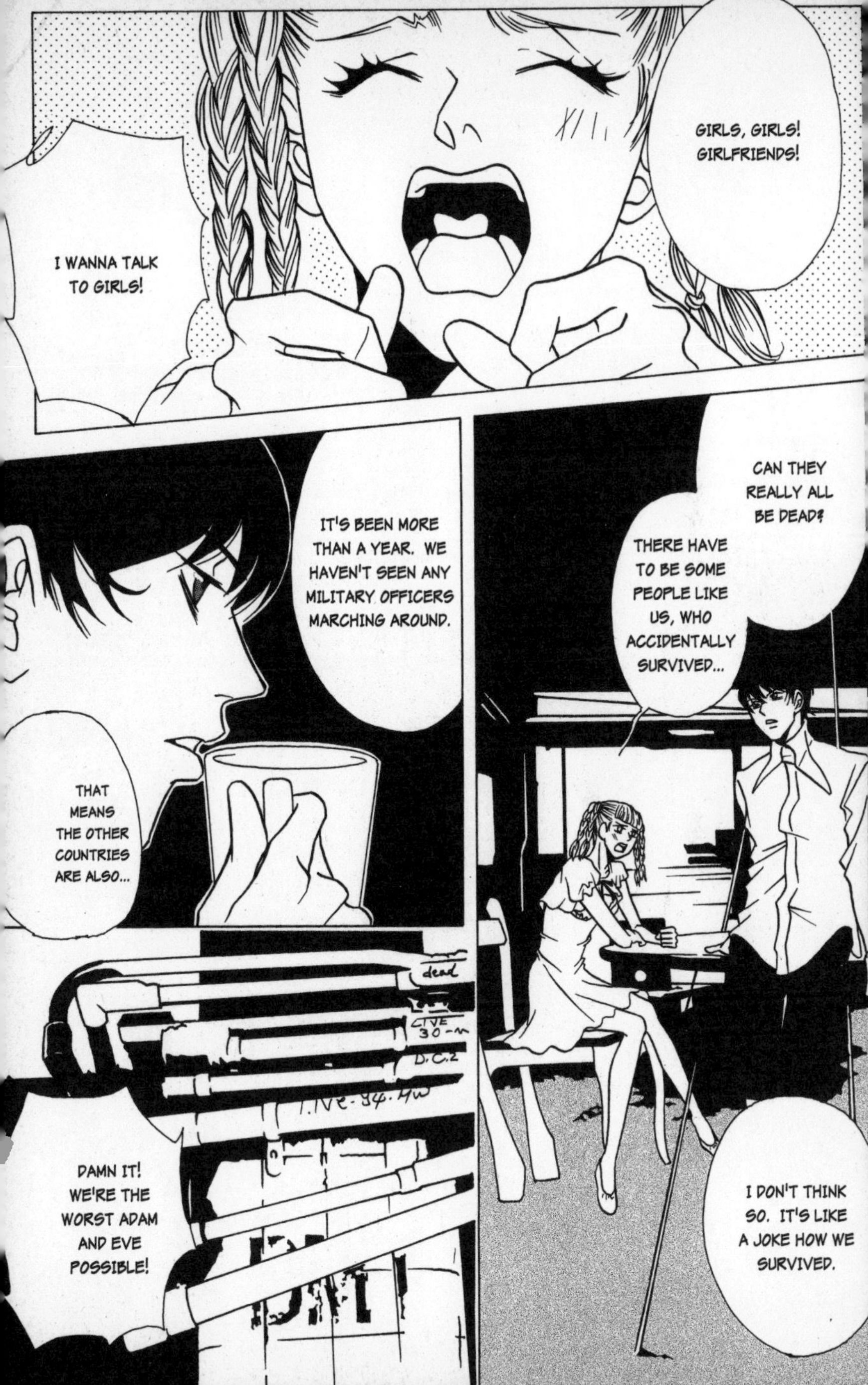
GIRLS, GIRLS! GIRLFRIENDS!
I WANNA TALK TO GIRLS!
CAN THEY REALLY ALL BE DEAD?
THERE HAVE TO BE SOME PEOPLE LIKE US, WHO ACCIDENTALLY SURVIVED...
I DON'T THINK SO. IT'S LIKE A JOKE HOW WE SURVIVED.
IT'S BEEN MORE THAN A YEAR. WE HAVEN'T SEEN ANY MILITARY OFFICERS MARCHING AROUND.
THAT MEANS THE OTHER COUNTRIES ARE ALSO...
DAMN IT! WE'RE THE WORST ADAM AND EVE POSSIBLE!

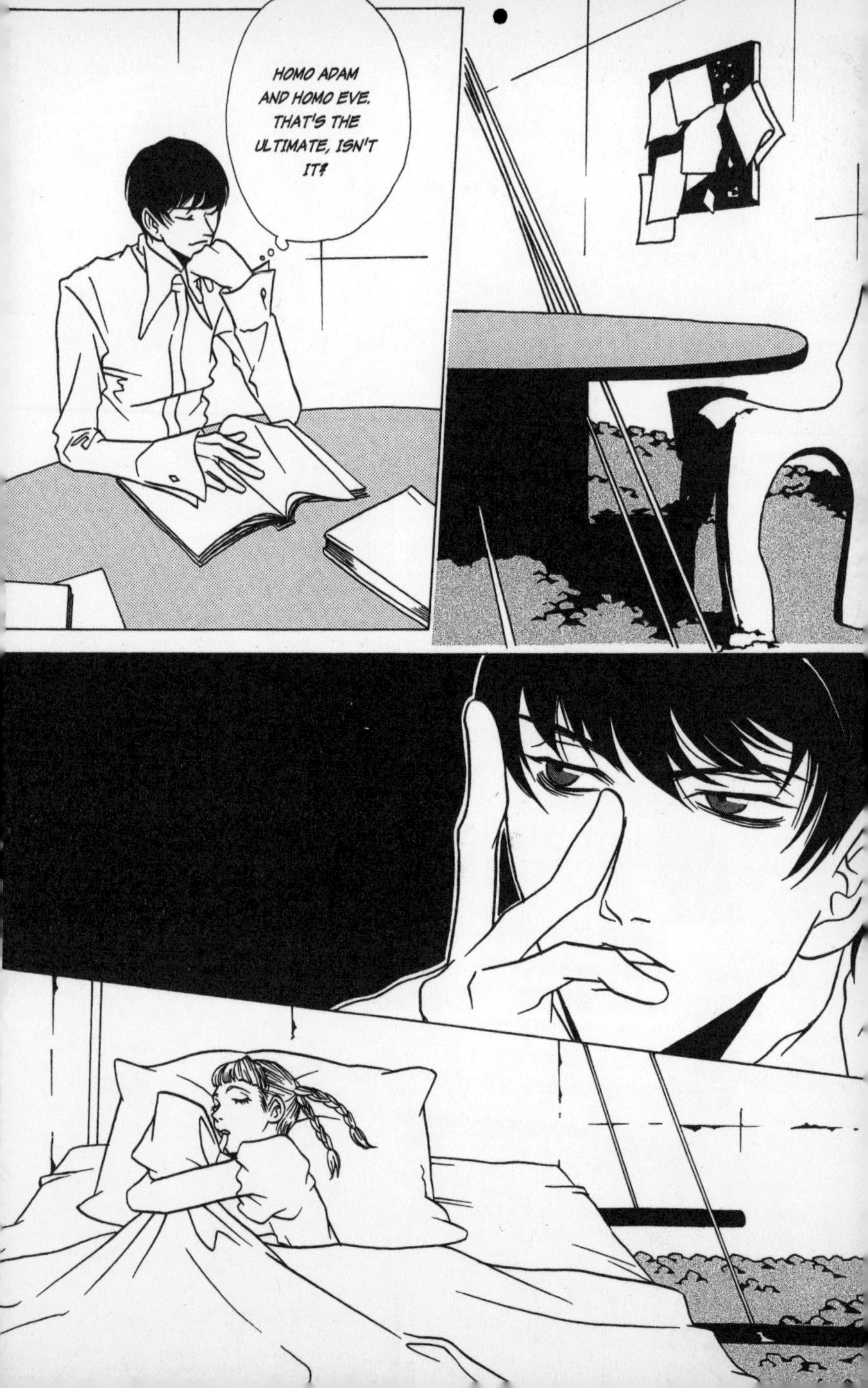
HOMO ADAM AND HOMO EVE. THAT'S THE ULTIMATE, ISN'T IT?

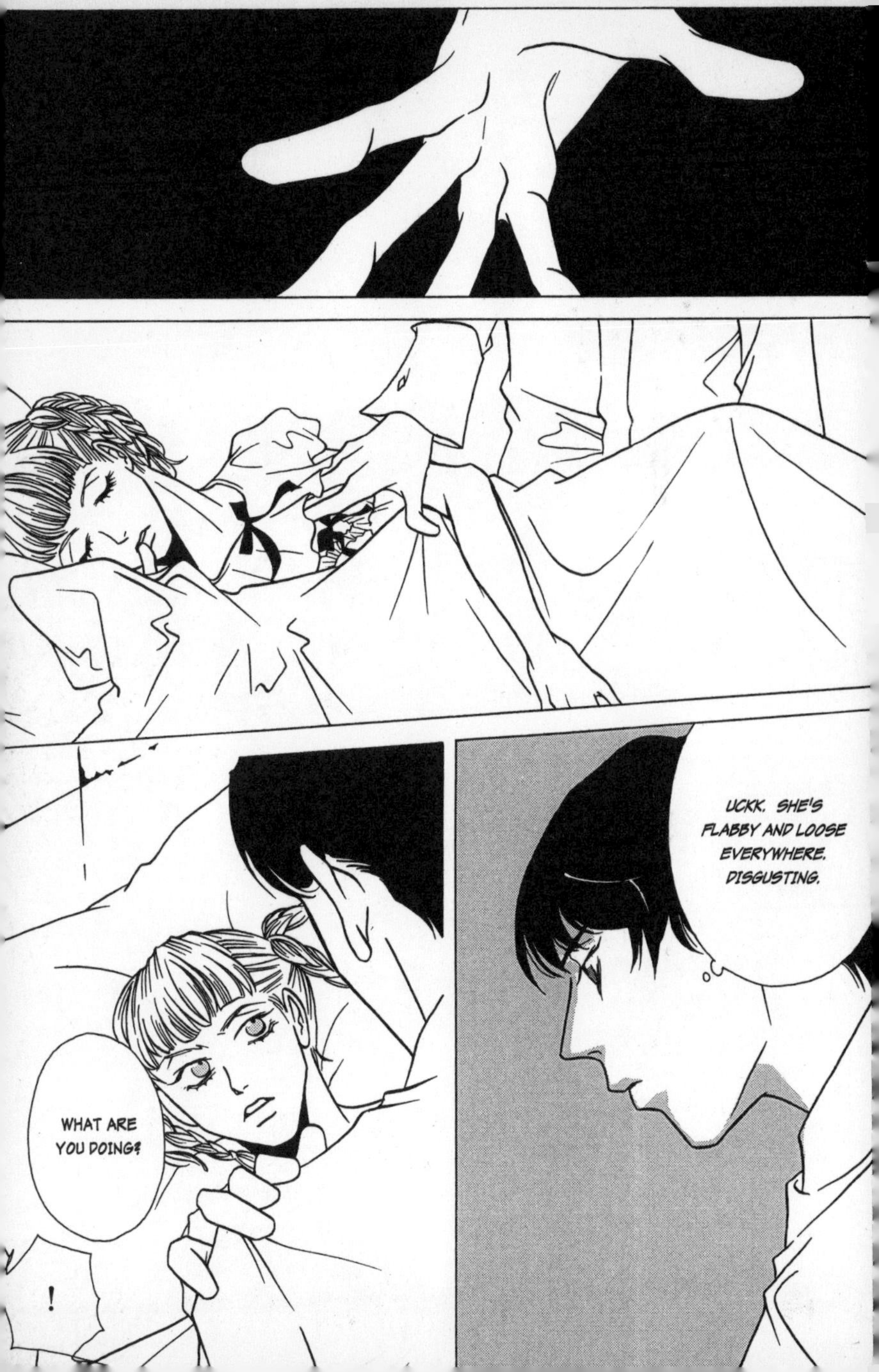
UCKK. SHE'S FLABBY AND LOOSE EVERYWHERE. DISGUSTING.
!
WHAT ARE YOU DOING?

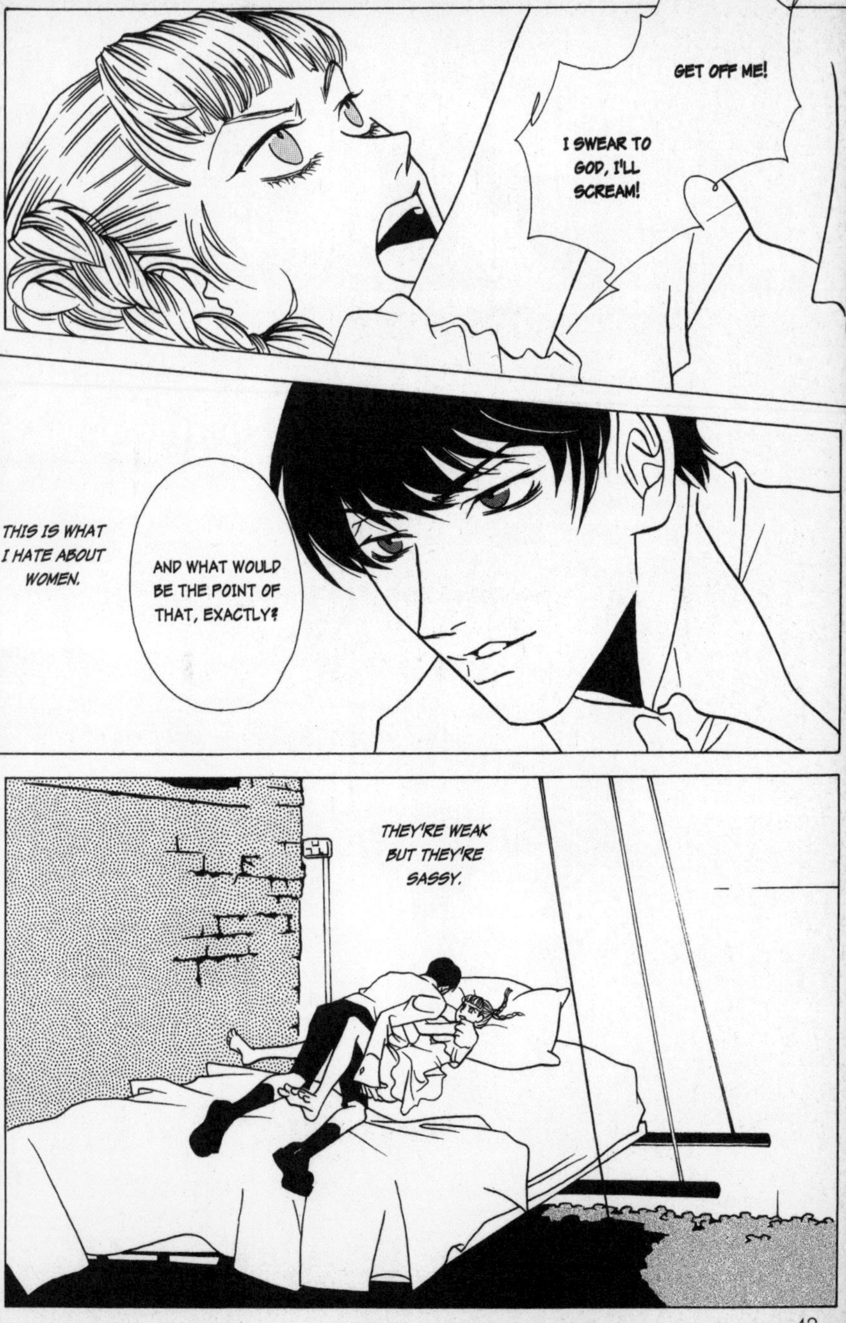
GET OFF ME!
I SWEAR TO GOD, I'LL SCREAM!
AND WHAT WOULD BE THE POINT OF THAT, EXACTLY?
THIS IS WHAT I HATE ABOUT WOMEN.
THEY'RE WEAK BUT THEY'RE SASSY.

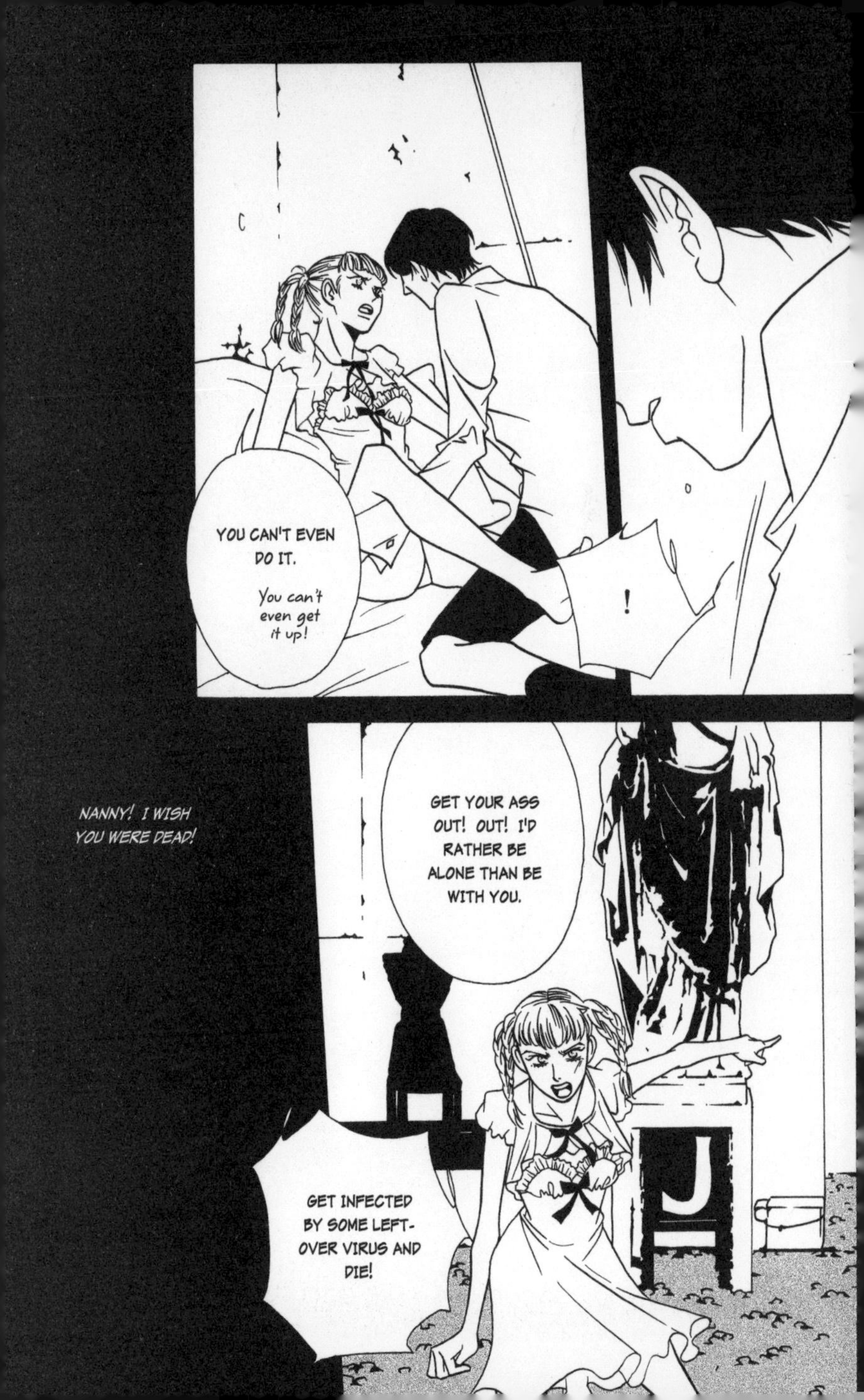
!
YOU CAN'T EVEN DO IT.
You can't even get it up!
GET YOUR ASS OUT! OUT! I'D RATHER BE ALONE THAN BE WITH YOU.
GET INFECTED BY SOME LEFT-OVER VIRUS AND DIE!
NANNY! I WISH YOU WERE DEAD!

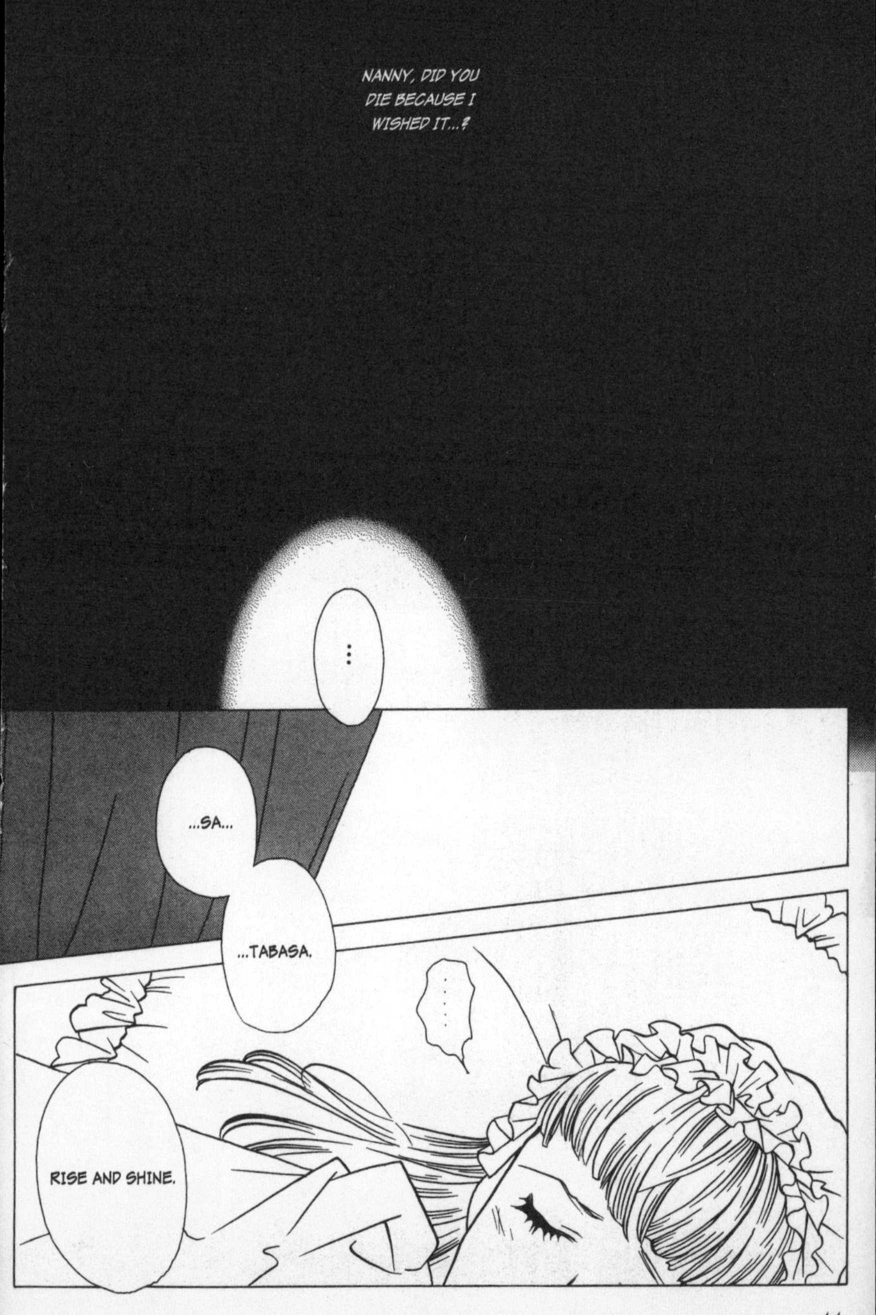
NANNY, DID YOU DIE BECAUSE I WISHED IT...?
...
...SA...
...TABASA.
......
RISE AND SHINE.

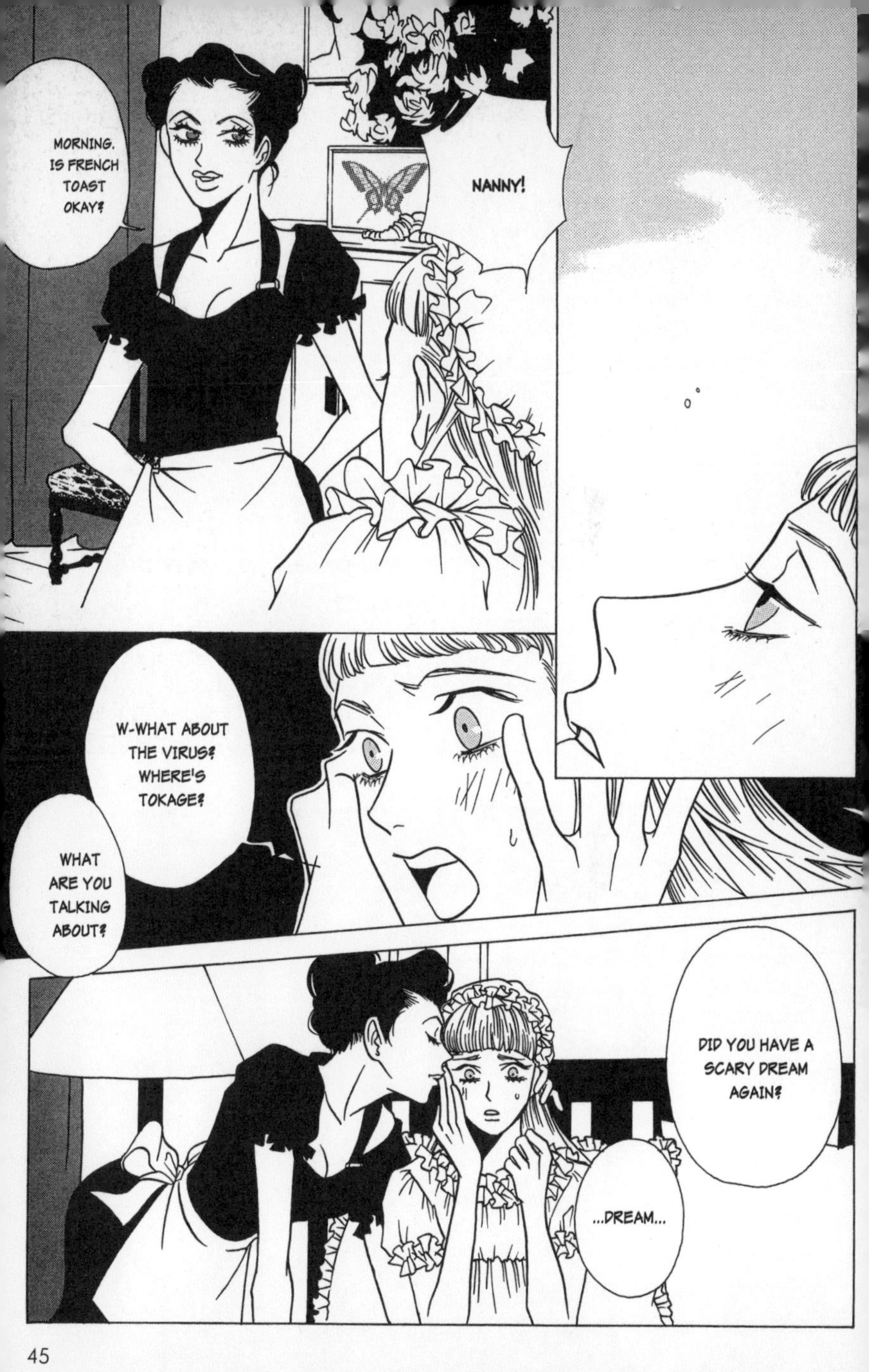
NANNY!
MORNING. IS FRENCH TOAST OKAY?
W-WHAT ABOUT THE VIRUS? WHERE'S TOKAGE?
WHAT ARE YOU TALKING ABOUT?
DID YOU HAVE A SCARY DREAM AGAIN?
...DREAM...

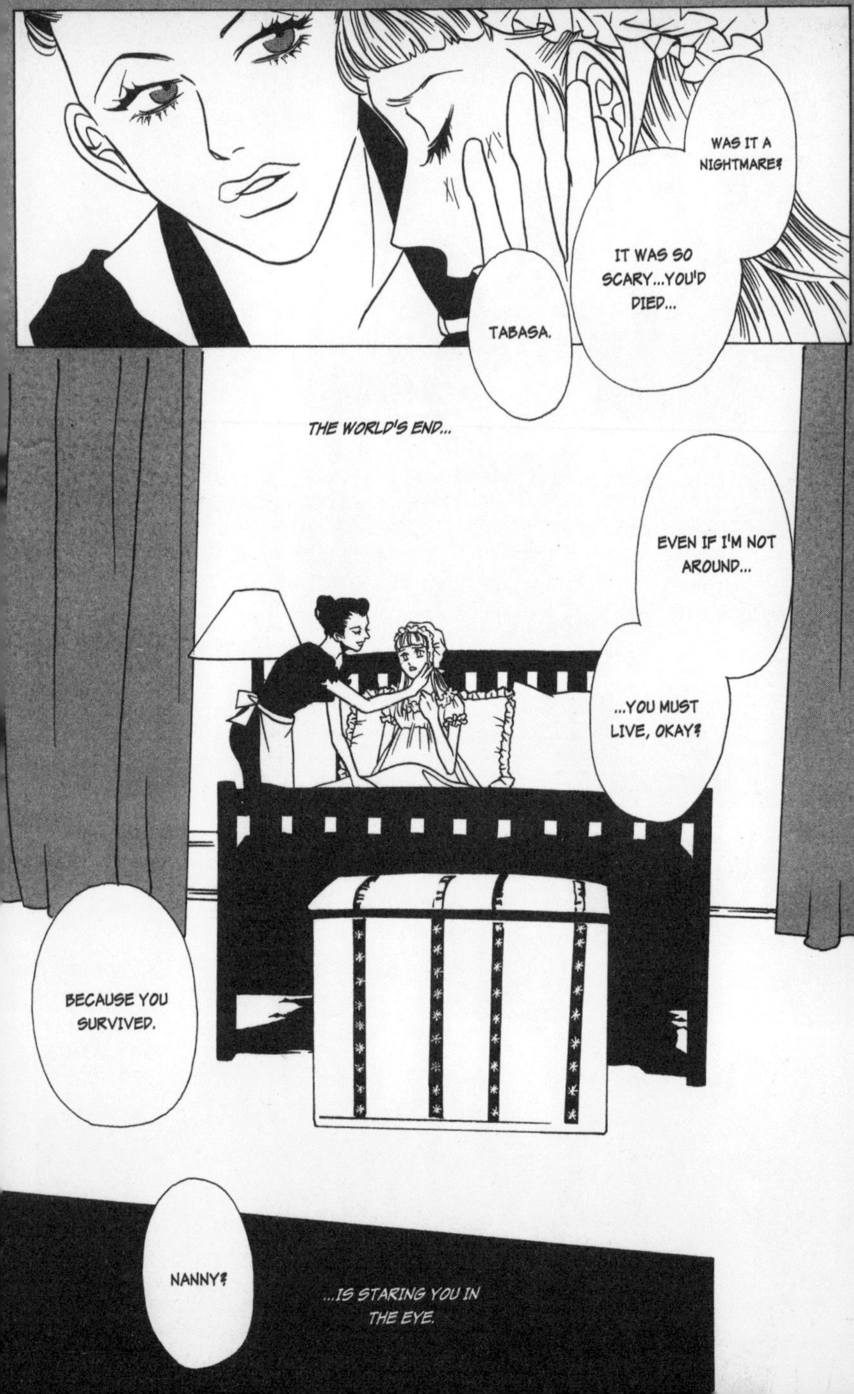
WAS IT A NIGHTMARE?
IT WAS SO SCARY...YOU'D DIED...
TABASA.
THE WORLD'S END...
EVEN IF I'M NOT AROUND...
...YOU MUST LIVE, OKAY?
BECAUSE YOU SURVIVED.
...IS STARING YOU IN THE EYE.
NANNY?

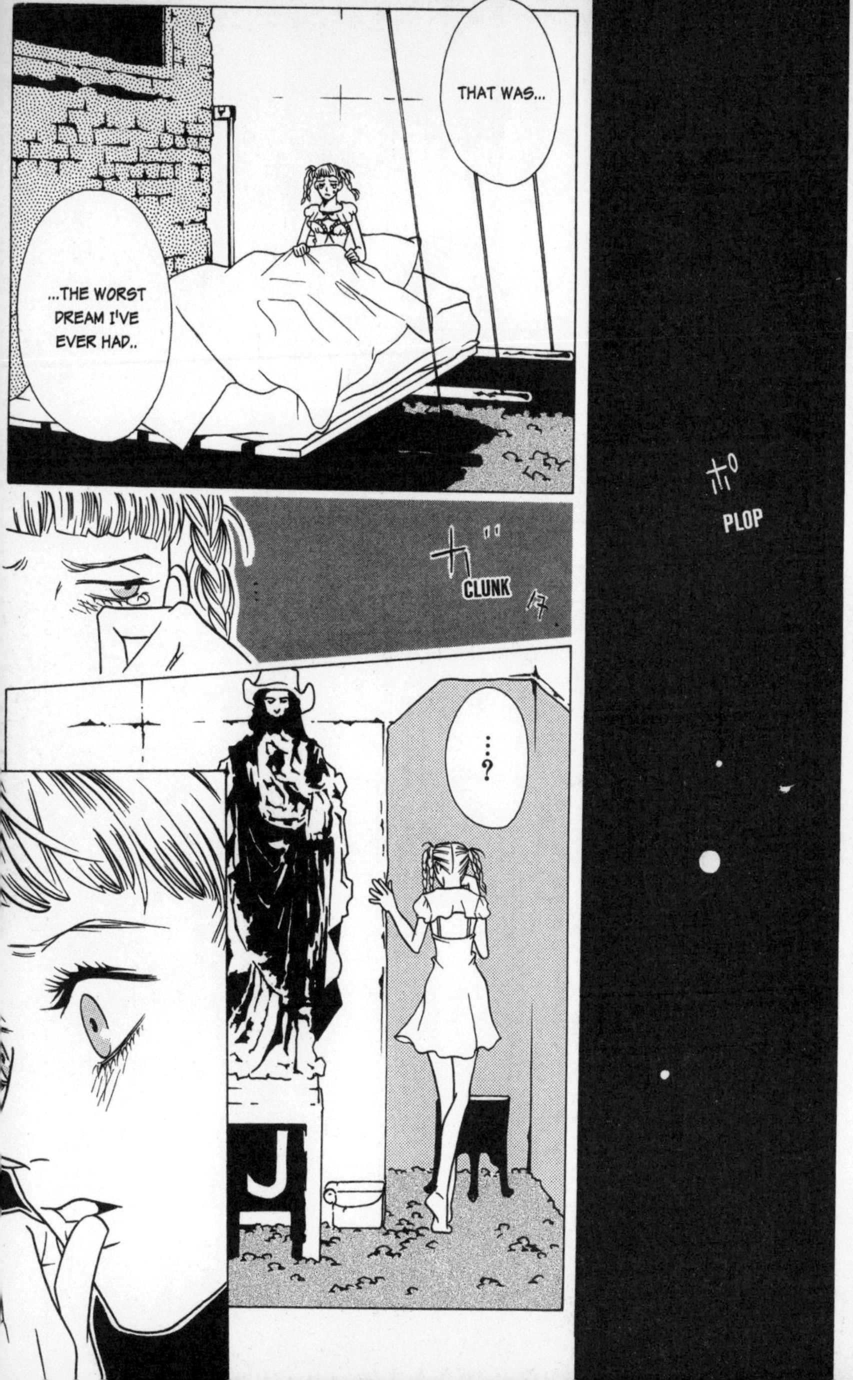
ポ
PLOP
THAT WAS...
...THE WORST DREAM I'VE EVER HAD..
ガ
CLUNK
タ
...?

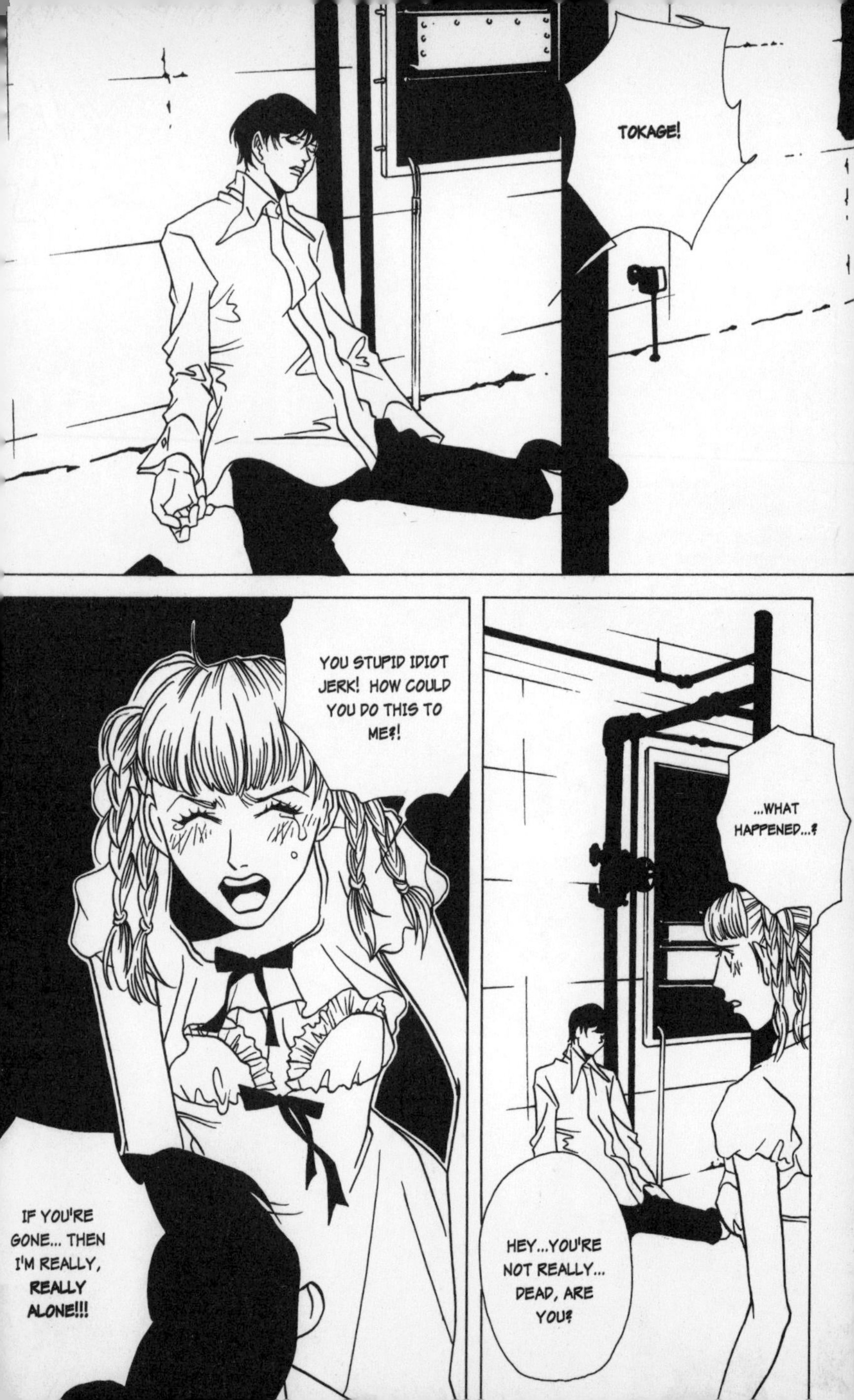
TOKAGE!
...WHAT HAPPENED...?
HEY...YOU'RE NOT REALLY... DEAD, ARE YOU?
YOU STUPID IDIOT JERK! HOW COULD YOU DO THIS TO ME?!
IF YOU'RE GONE... THEN I'M REALLY, REALLY ALONE!!!

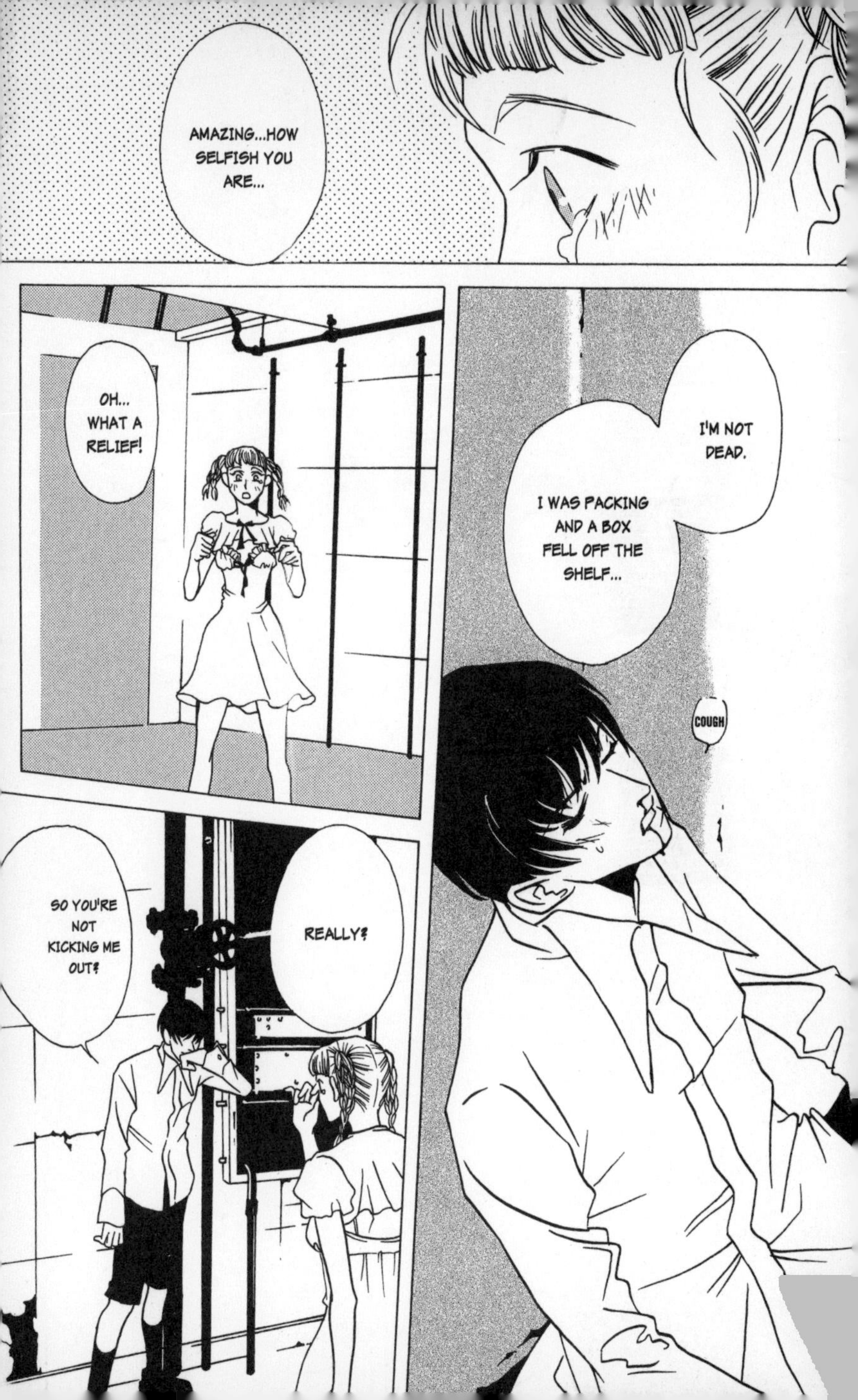
AMAZING...HOW SELFISH YOU ARE...
I'M NOT DEAD.
I WAS PACKING AND A BOX FELL OFF THE SHELF...
COUGH
OH... WHAT A RELIEF!
REALLY?
SO YOU'RE NOT KICKING ME OUT?

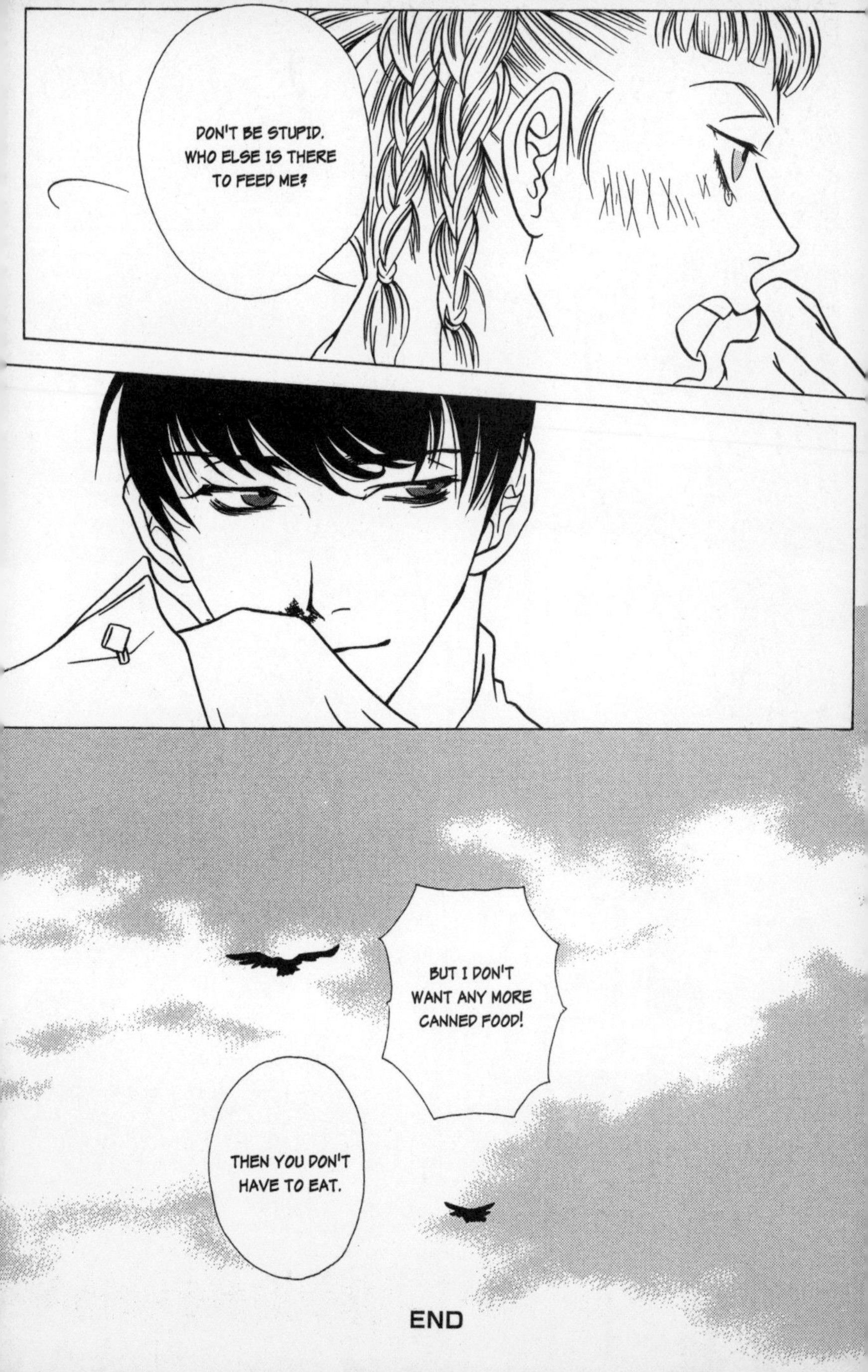
DON'T BE STUPID. WHO ELSE IS THERE TO FEED ME?
BUT I DON'T WANT ANY MORE CANNED FOOD!
THEN YOU DON'T HAVE TO EAT.
END

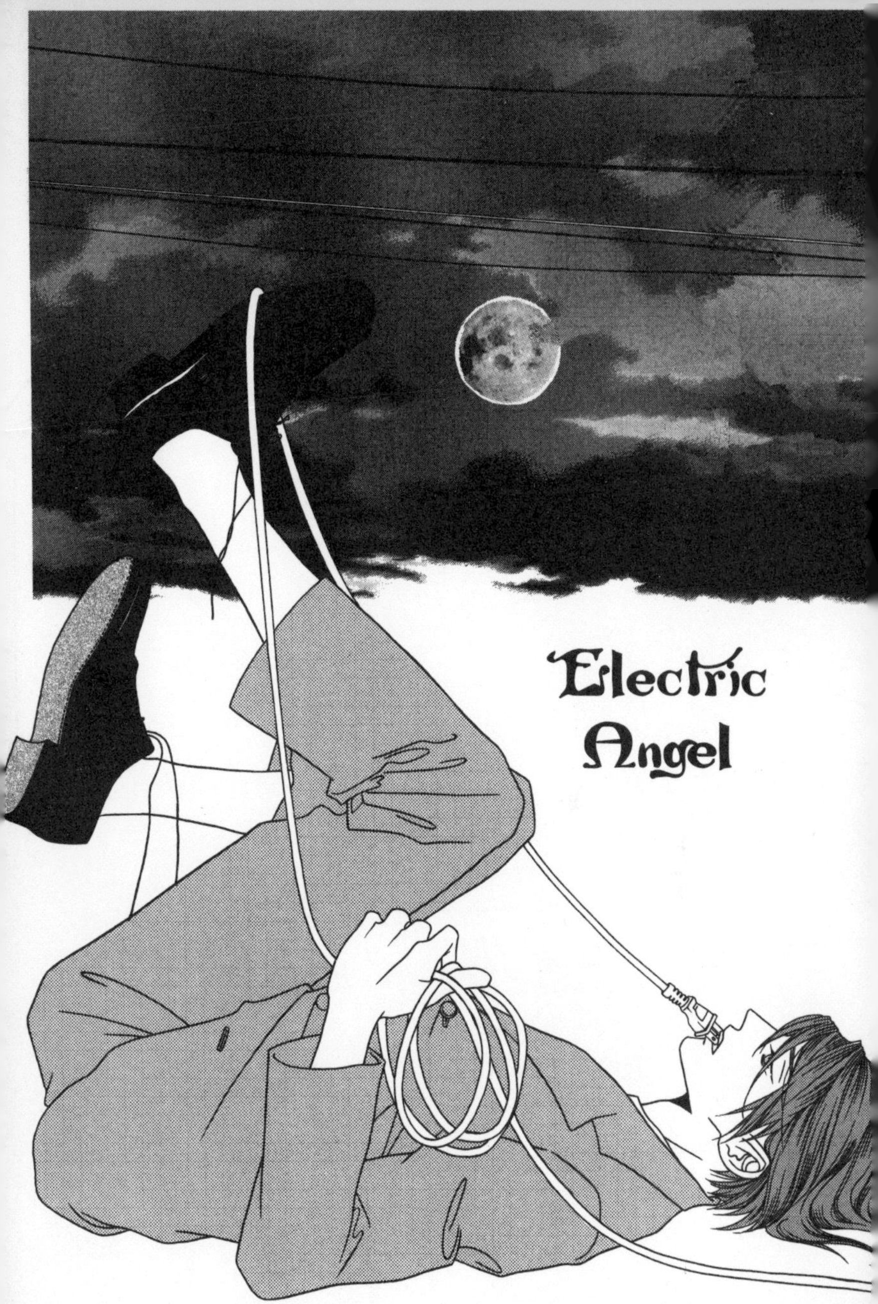
Electric
Angel

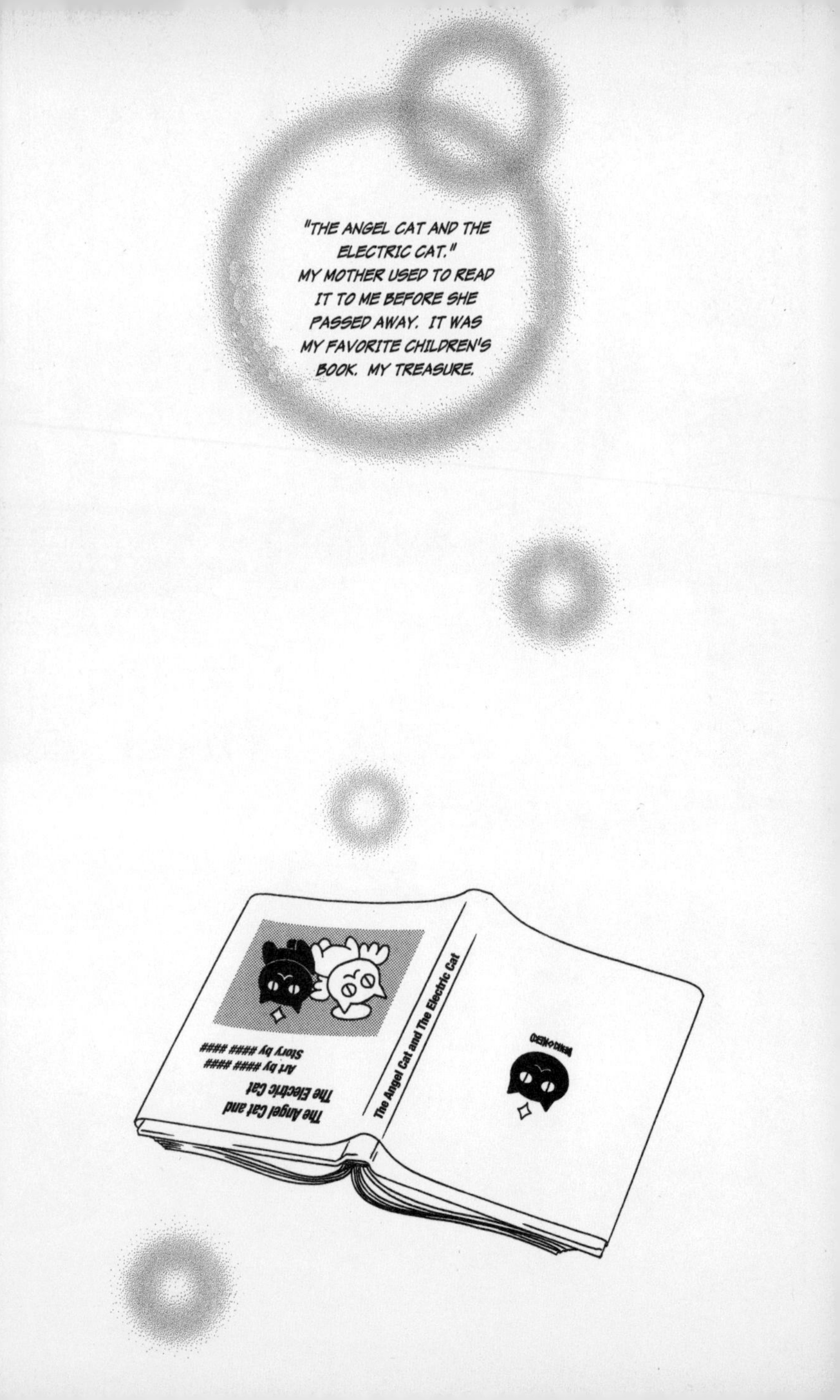
"THE ANGEL CAT AND THE ELECTRIC CAT." MY MOTHER USED TO READ IT TO ME BEFORE SHE PASSED AWAY. IT WAS MY FAVORITE CHILDREN'S BOOK. MY TREASURE.
The Angel Cat and The Electric Cat
The Angel Cat and The Electric Cat
Art by #### ####
Story by #### ####

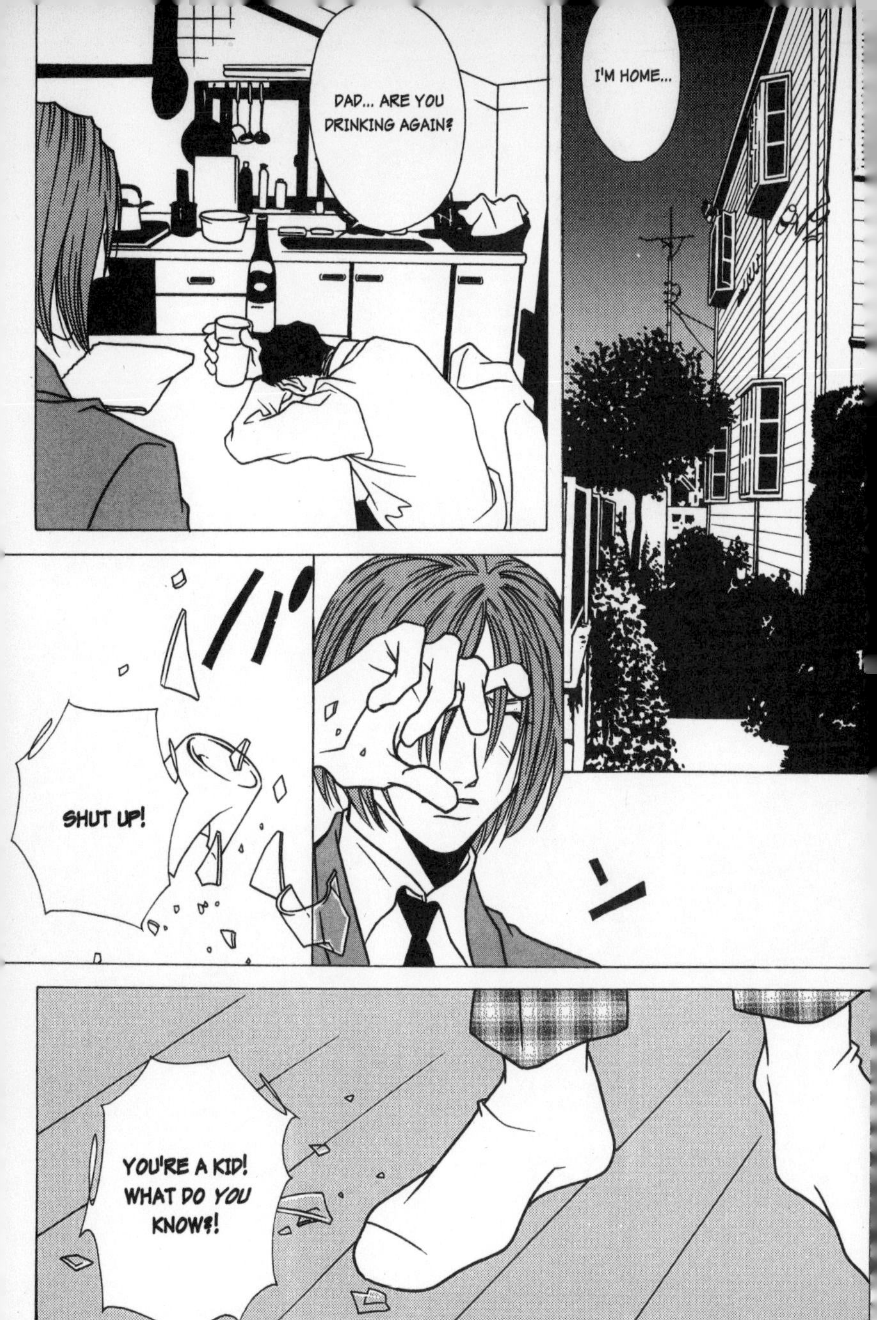
I'M HOME...
DAD... ARE YOU DRINKING AGAIN?
SHUT UP!
YOU'RE A KID! WHAT DO *YOU* KNOW?!

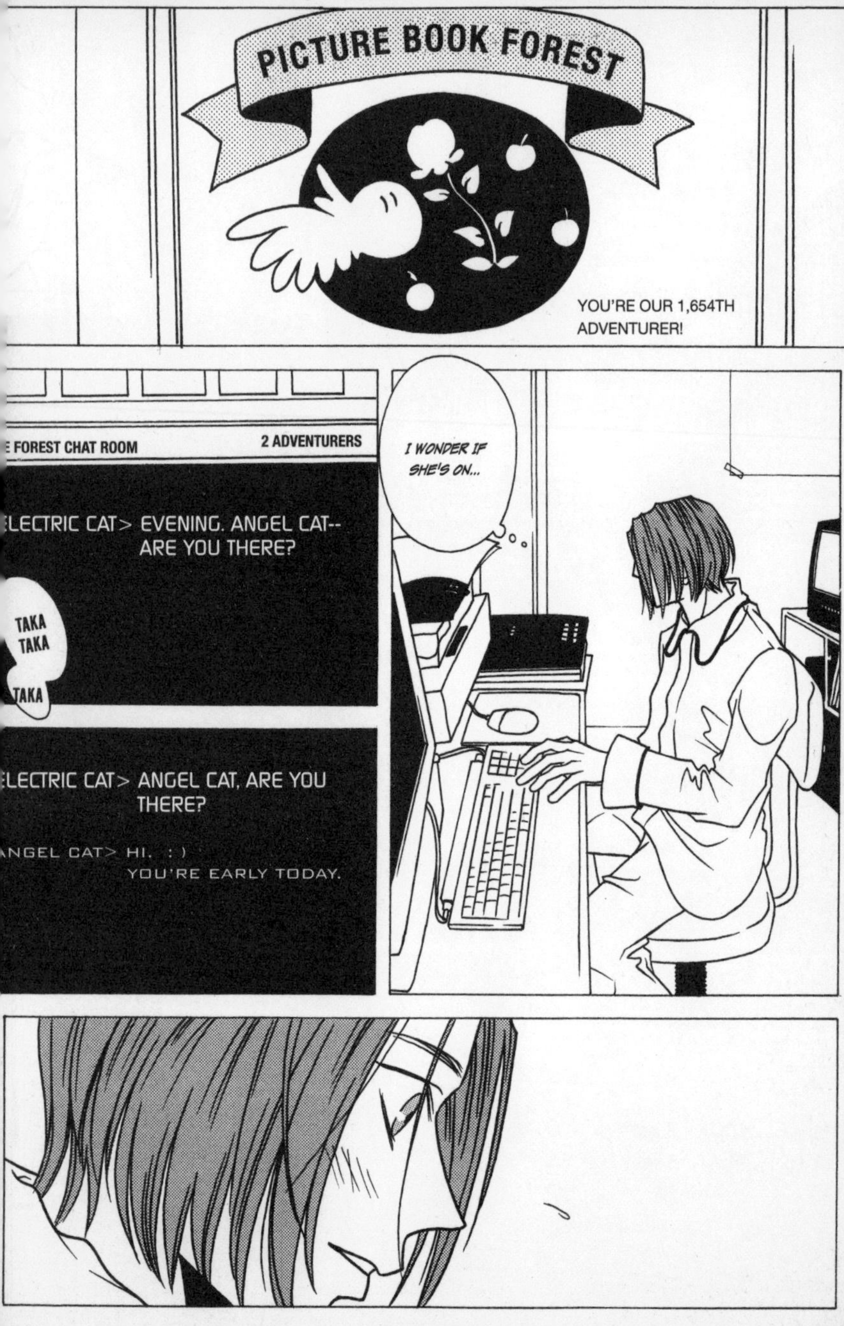
PICTURE BOOK FOREST
YOU'RE OUR 1,654TH ADVENTURER!
I WONDER IF SHE'S ON...
FOREST CHAT ROOM
2 ADVENTURERS
ELECTRIC CAT> EVENING. ANGEL CAT-- ARE YOU THERE?
TAKA TAKA TAKA
ELECTRIC CAT> ANGEL CAT, ARE YOU THERE?
ANGEL CAT> HI. :)
YOU'RE EARLY TODAY.

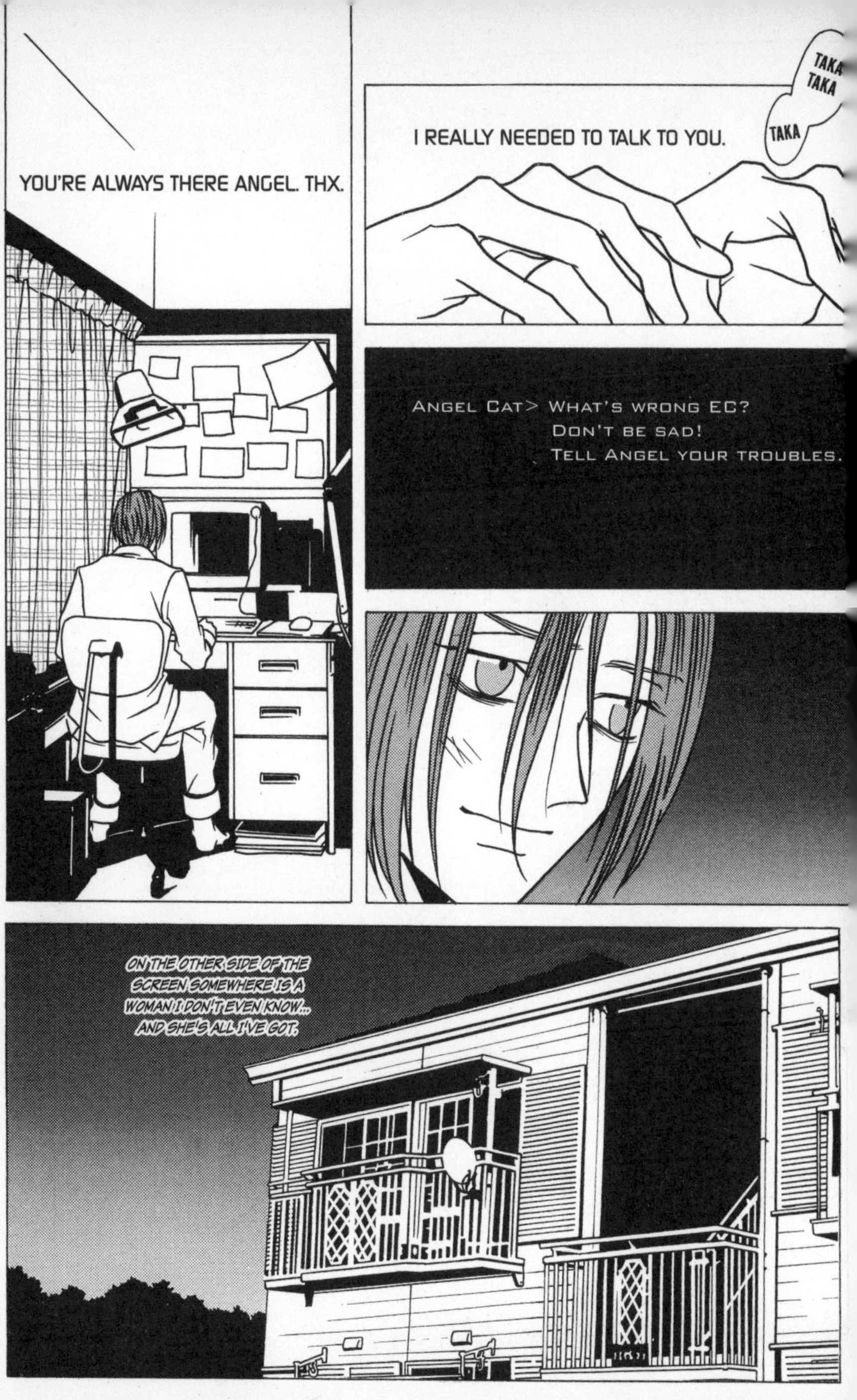
TAKA TAKA
TAKA
I REALLY NEEDED TO TALK TO YOU.
ANGEL CAT> WHAT'S WRONG EC? DON'T BE SAD! TELL ANGEL YOUR TROUBLES.
YOU'RE ALWAYS THERE ANGEL. THX.
ON THE OTHER SIDE OF THE SCREEN SOMEWHERE IS A WOMAN I DON'T EVEN KNOW... AND SHE'S ALL I'VE GOT.

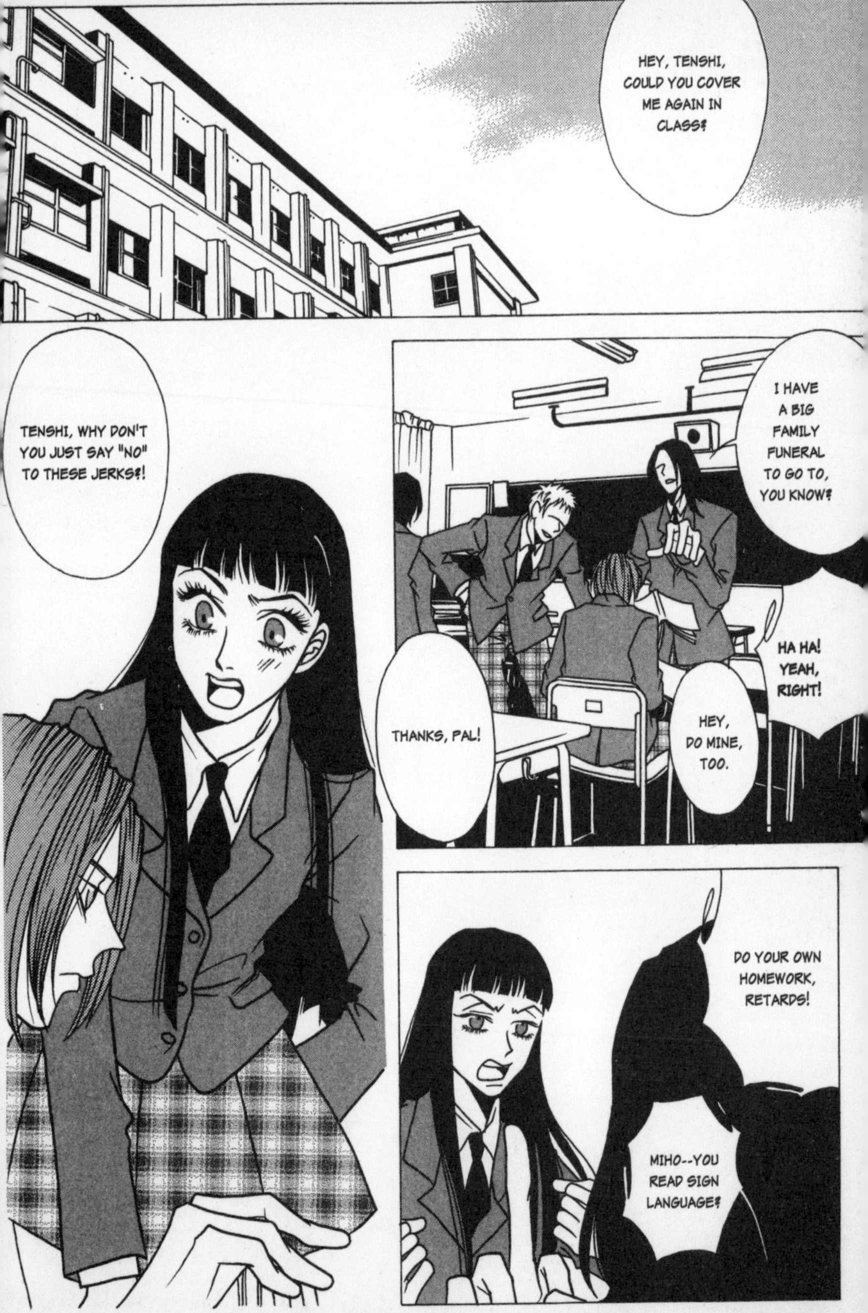
HEY, TENSHI, COULD YOU COVER ME AGAIN IN CLASS?
I HAVE A BIG FAMILY FUNERAL TO GO TO, YOU KNOW?
HA HA! YEAH, RIGHT!
HEY, DO MINE, TOO.
THANKS, PAL!
DO YOUR OWN HOMEWORK, RETARDS!
MIHO--YOU READ SIGN LANGUAGE?
TENSHI, WHY DON'T YOU JUST SAY "NO" TO THESE JERKS?!

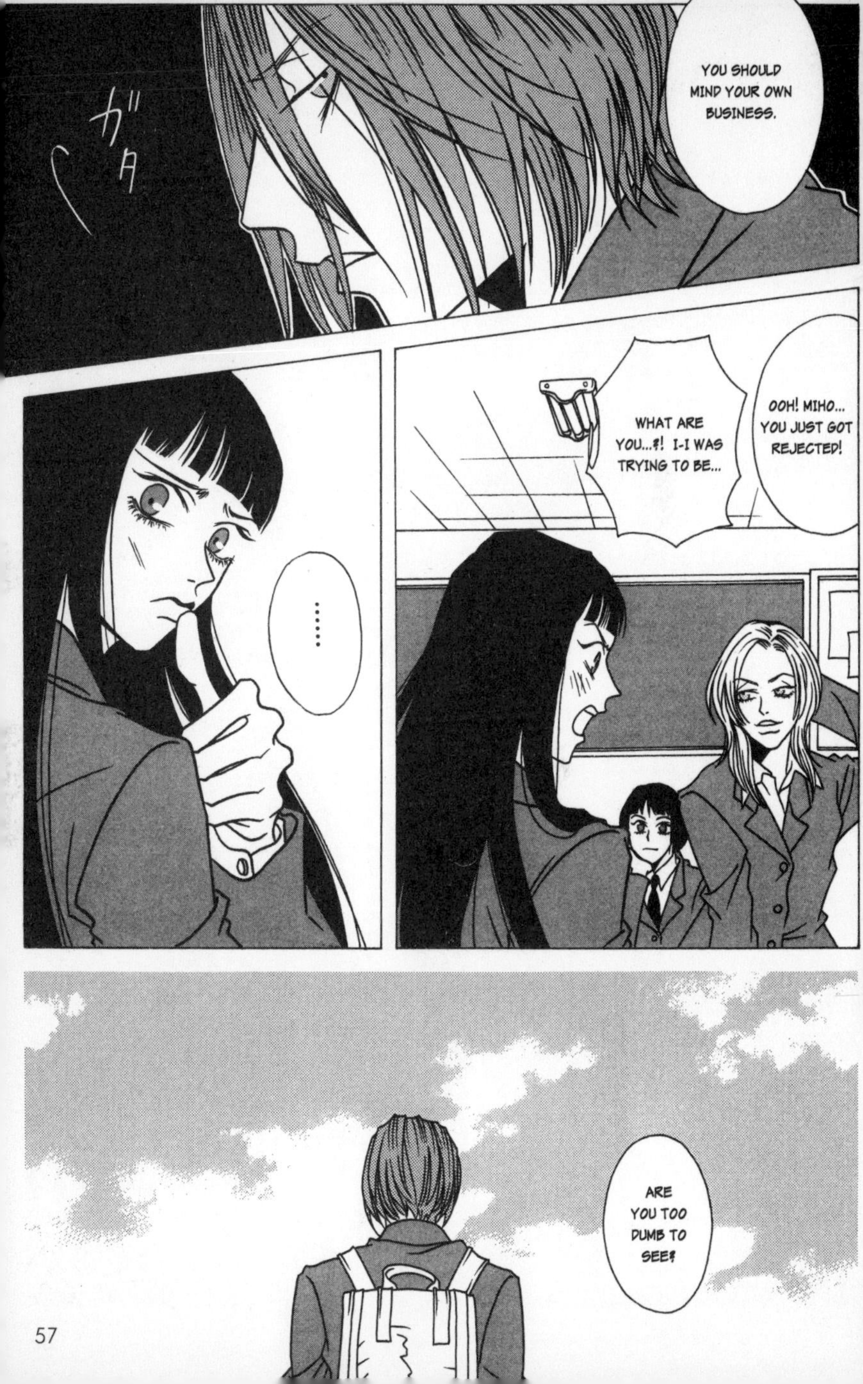
YOU SHOULD MIND YOUR OWN BUSINESS.
ガタ
OOH! MIHO... YOU JUST GOT REJECTED!
WHAT ARE YOU...?! I-I WAS TRYING TO BE...
......
ARE YOU TOO DUMB TO SEE?

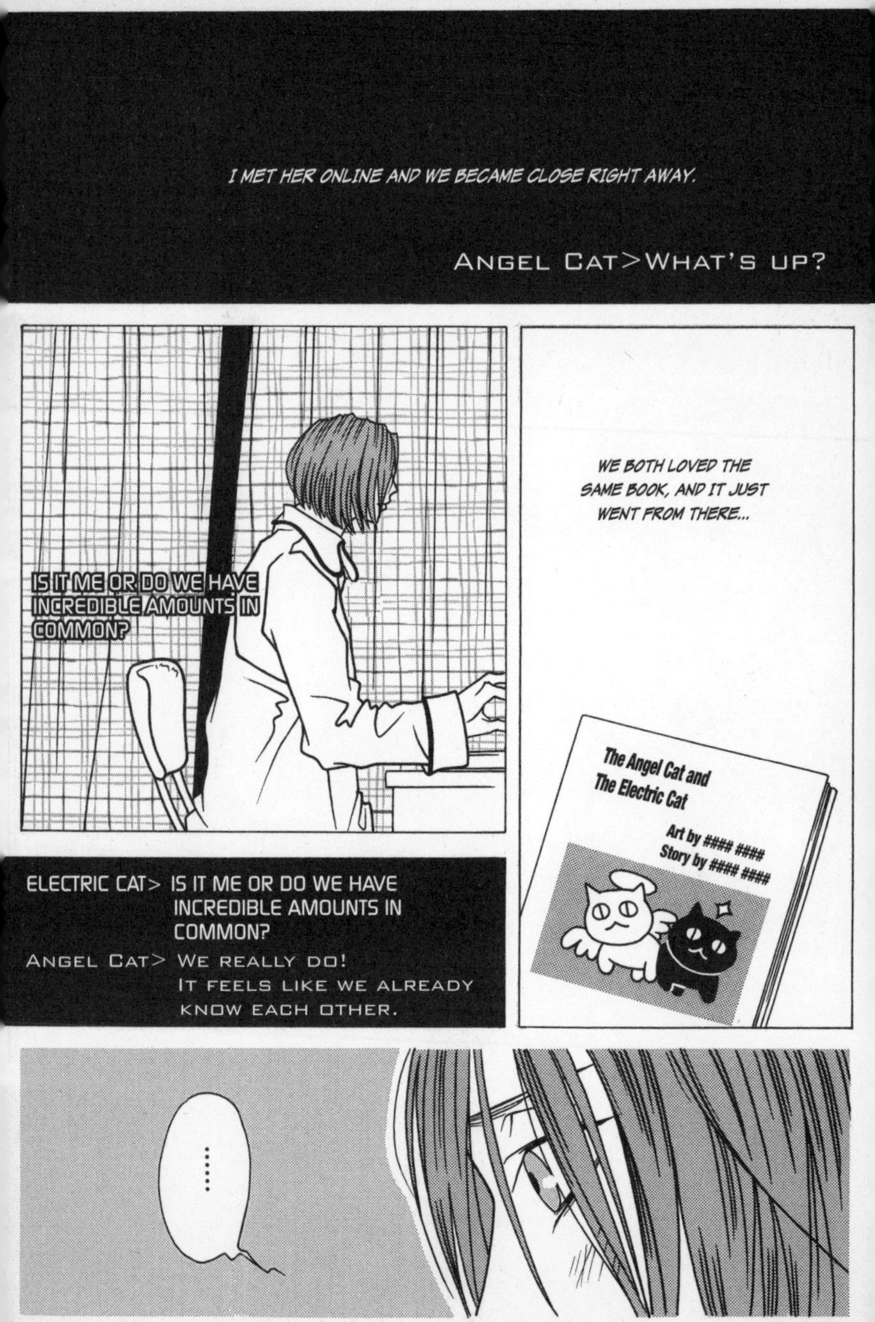
I MET HER ONLINE AND WE BECAME CLOSE RIGHT AWAY.
ANGEL CAT>WHAT'S UP?
WE BOTH LOVED THE SAME BOOK, AND IT JUST WENT FROM THERE...
The Angel Cat and The Electric Cat
Art by #### ####
Story by #### ####
IS IT ME OR DO WE HAVE INCREDIBLE AMOUNTS IN COMMON?
ELECTRIC CAT> IS IT ME OR DO WE HAVE INCREDIBLE AMOUNTS IN COMMON?
ANGEL CAT> WE REALLY DO! IT FEELS LIKE WE ALREADY KNOW EACH OTHER.
......

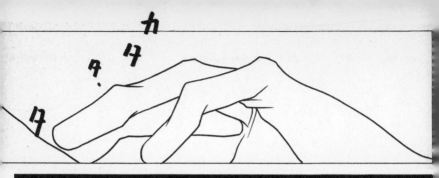

ELECTRIC CAT> I'D LIKE TO TALK 2U IN PERSON.

ANGEL CAT> ME2, I'D ENJOY MEETING YOU SOMETIME.

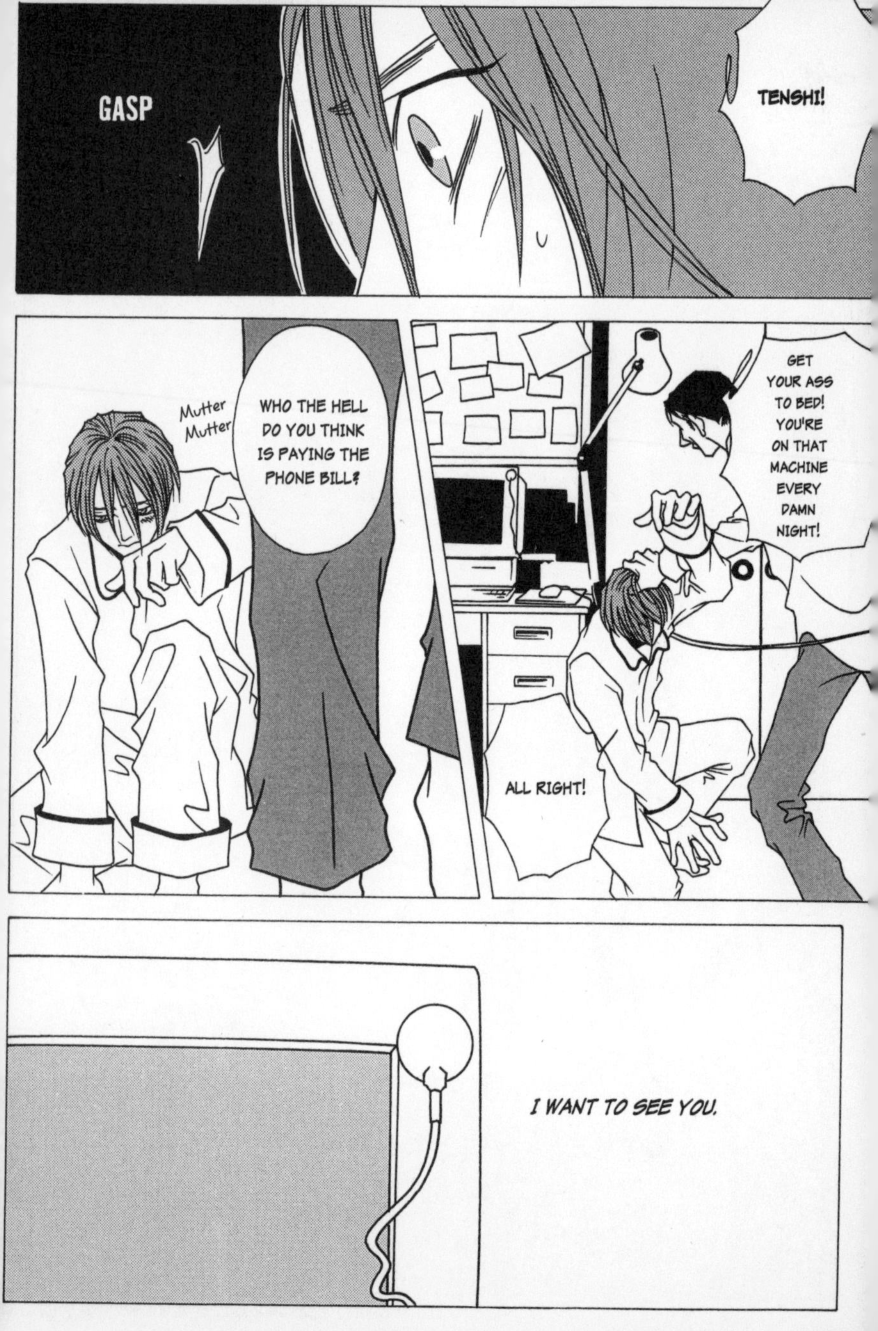
TENSHI!
GASP
GET YOUR ASS TO BED! YOU'RE ON THAT MACHINE EVERY DAMN NIGHT!
ALL RIGHT!
WHO THE HELL DO YOU THINK IS PAYING THE PHONE BILL?
Mutter Mutter
I WANT TO SEE YOU.

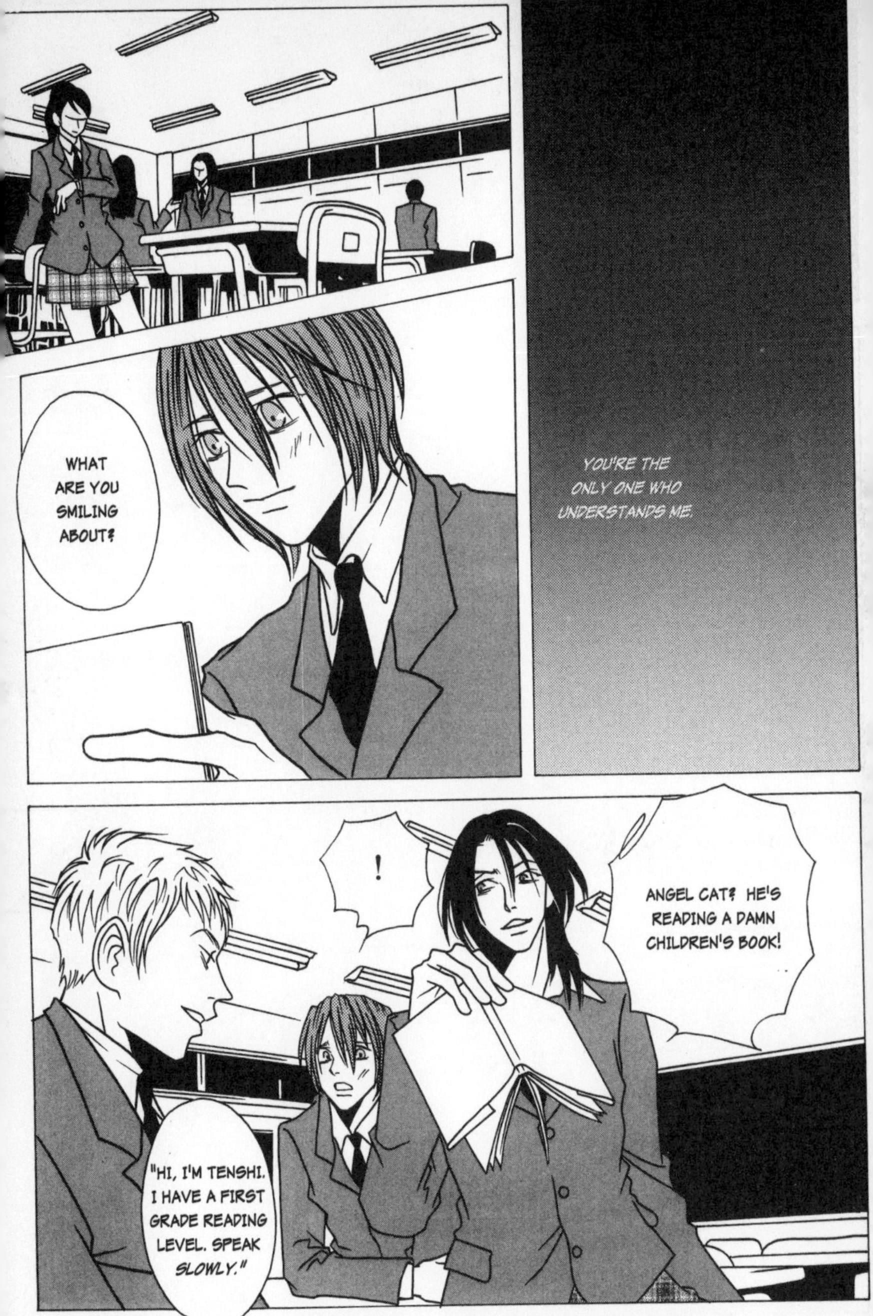
YOU'RE THE ONLY ONE WHO UNDERSTANDS ME.
WHAT ARE YOU SMILING ABOUT?
ANGEL CAT? HE'S READING A DAMN CHILDREN'S BOOK!
!
"HI, I'M TENSHI. I HAVE A FIRST GRADE READING LEVEL. SPEAK *SLOWLY.*"

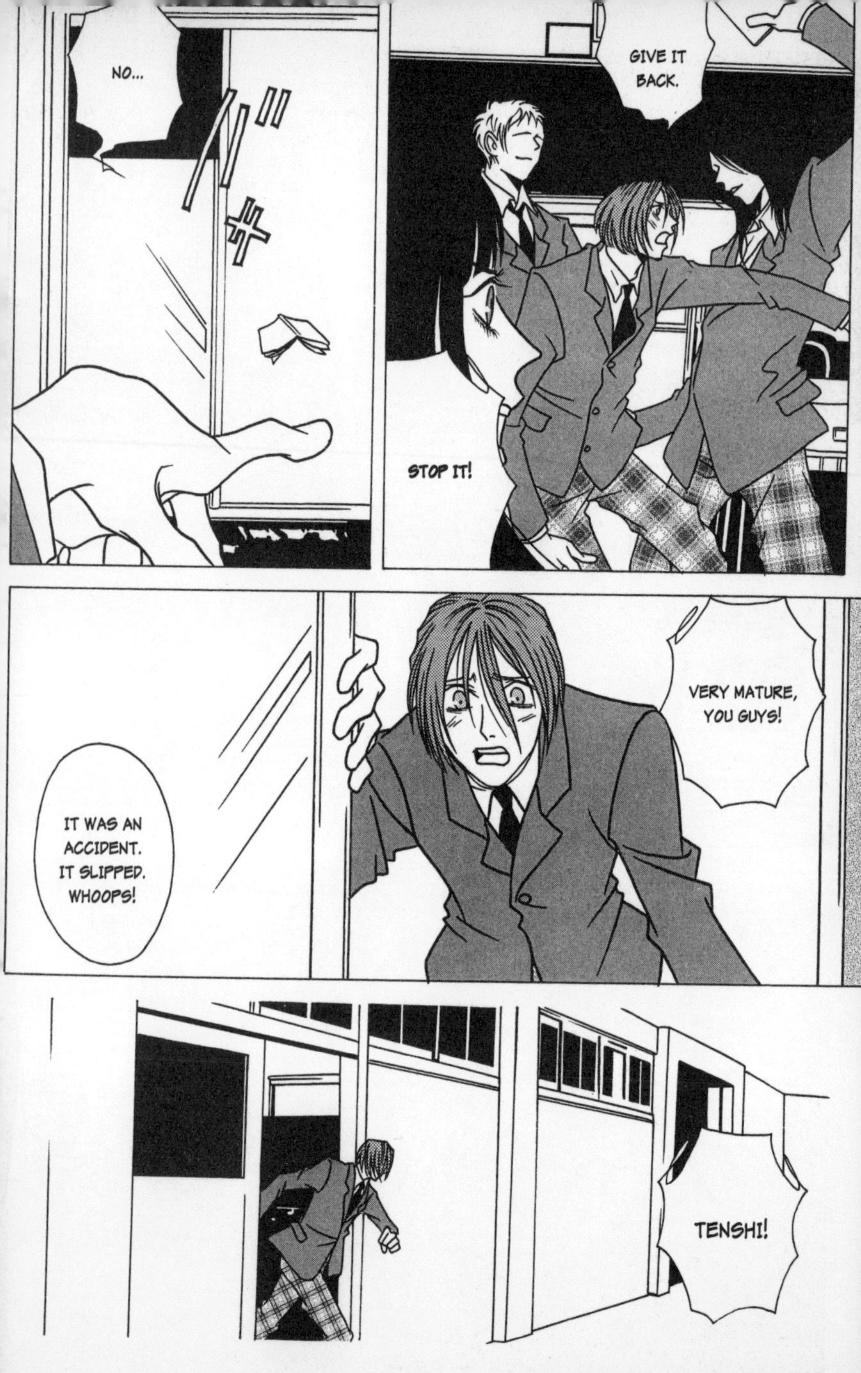
GIVE IT BACK.
STOP IT!
NO...
VERY MATURE, YOU GUYS!
IT WAS AN ACCIDENT. IT SLIPPED. WHOOPS!
TENSHI!

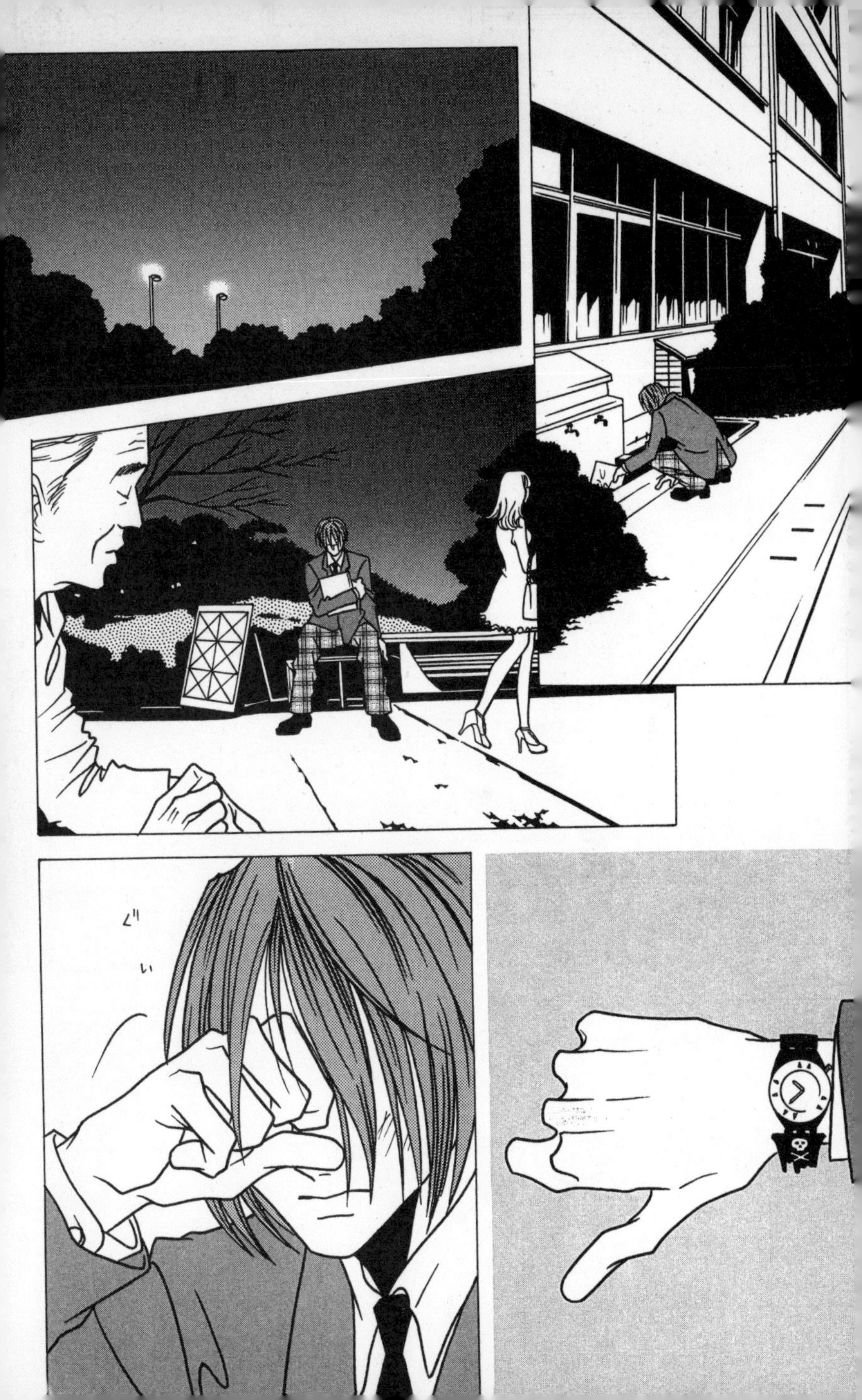
ぐい

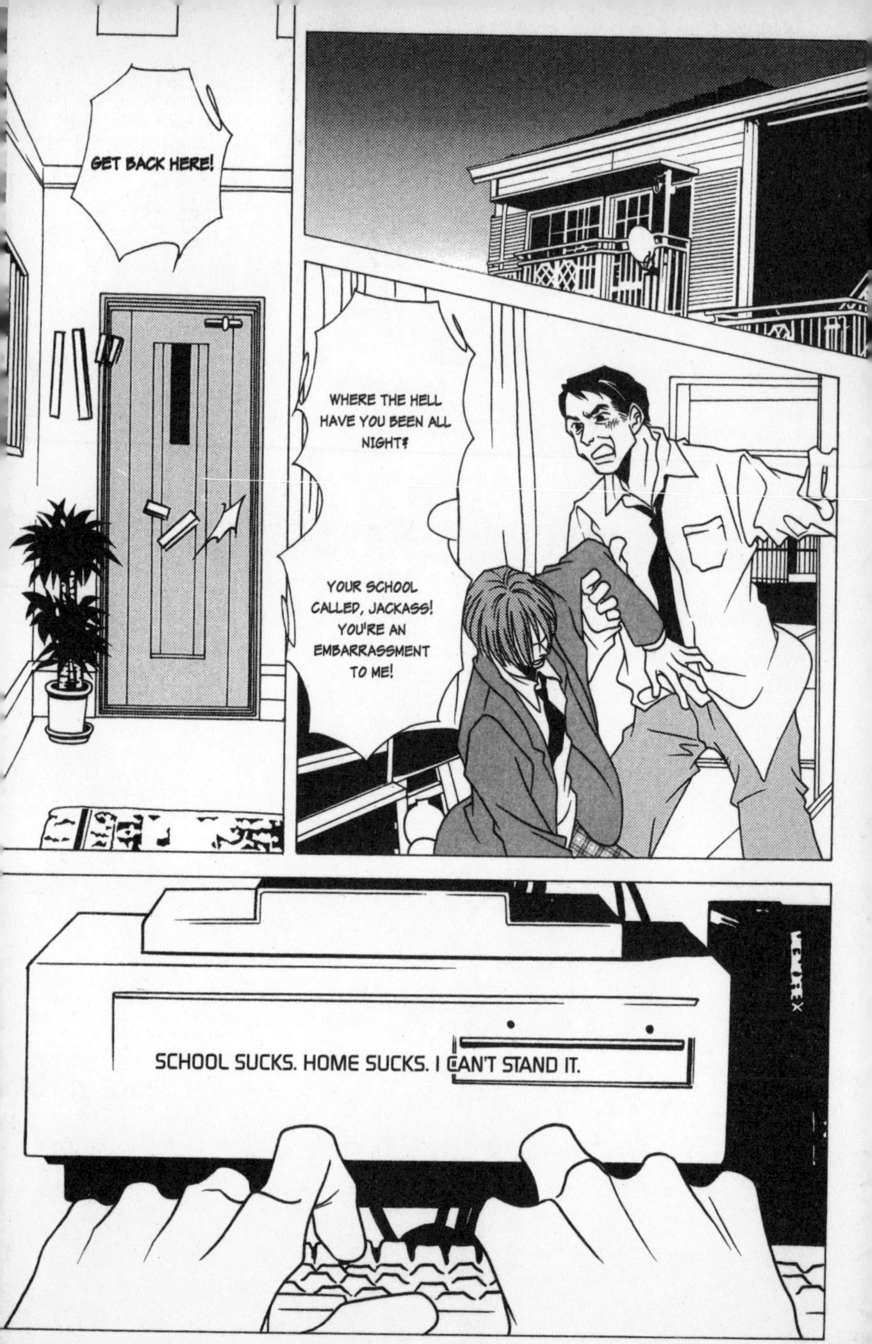
WHERE THE HELL HAVE YOU BEEN ALL NIGHT?!
YOUR SCHOOL CALLED, JACKASS! YOU'RE AN EMBARRASSMENT TO ME!
GET BACK HERE!
SCHOOL SUCKS. HOME SUCKS. I CAN'T STAND IT.

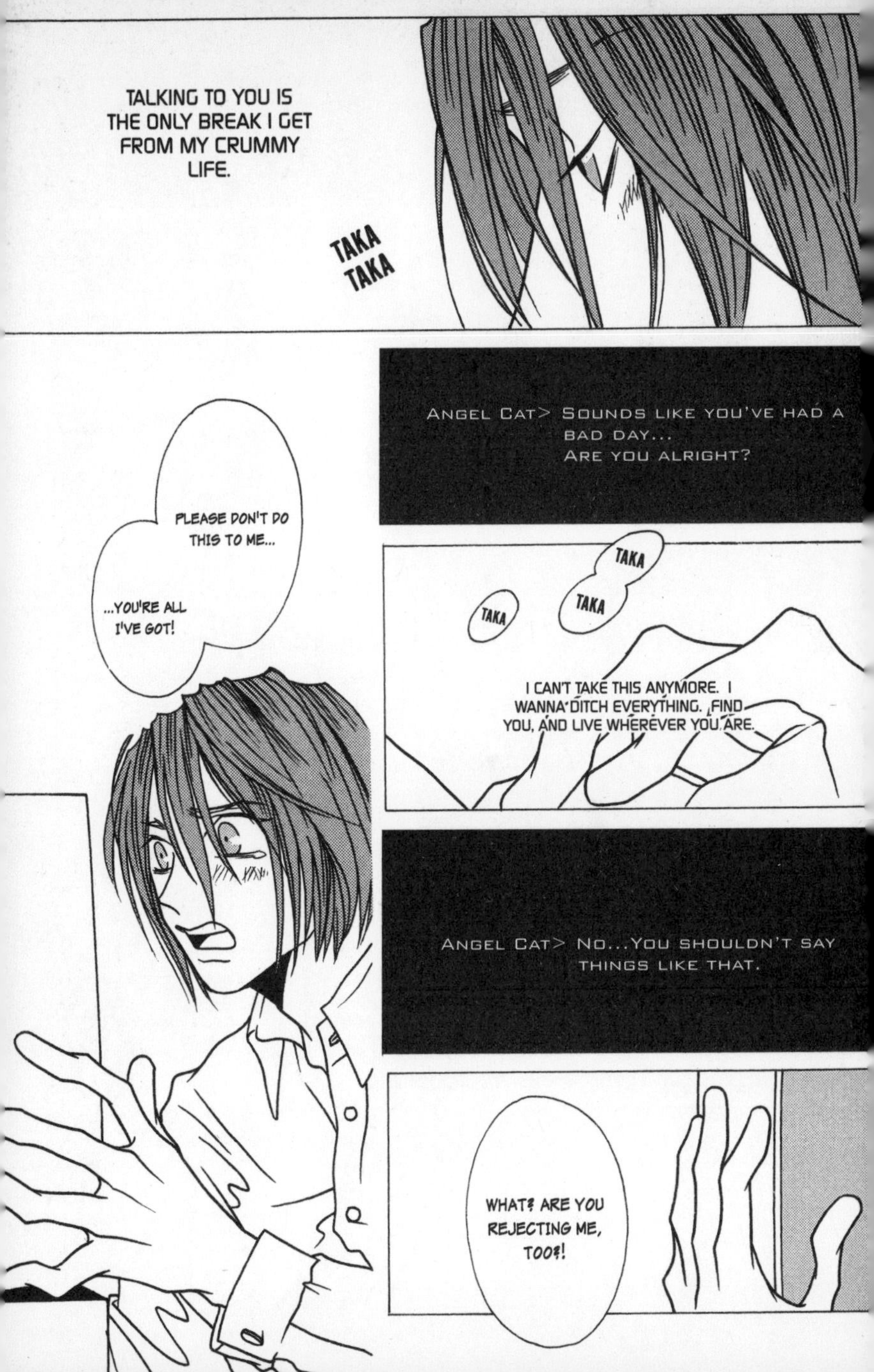
TALKING TO YOU IS THE ONLY BREAK I GET FROM MY CRUMMY LIFE.
TAKA TAKA
ANGEL CAT> SOUNDS LIKE YOU'VE HAD A BAD DAY... ARE YOU ALRIGHT?
TAKA
TAKA
TAKA
I CAN'T TAKE THIS ANYMORE. I WANNA DITCH EVERYTHING, FIND YOU, AND LIVE WHEREVER YOU ARE.
ANGEL CAT> NO...YOU SHOULDN'T SAY THINGS LIKE THAT.
WHAT? ARE YOU REJECTING ME, TOO?!
PLEASE DON'T DO THIS TO ME...
...YOU'RE ALL I'VE GOT!

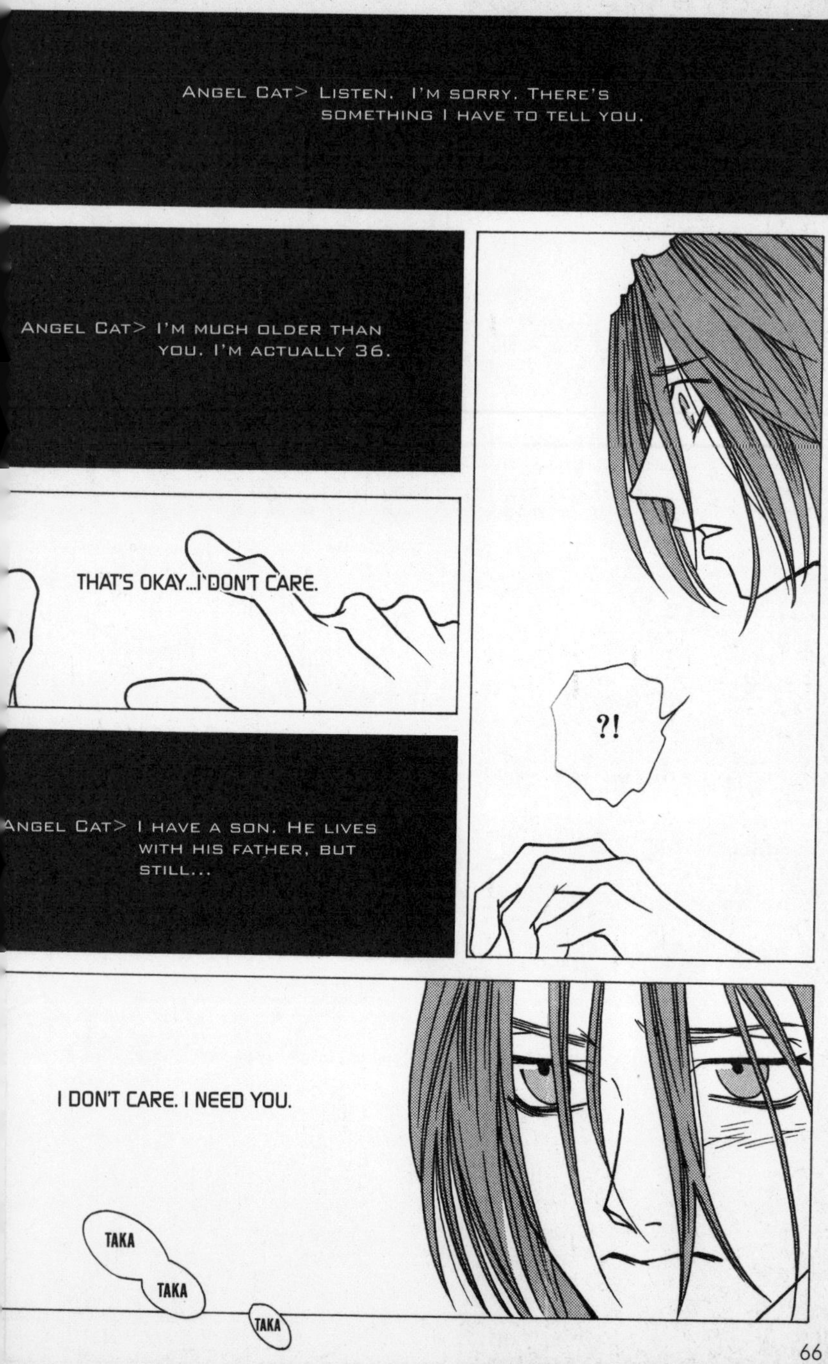
ANGEL CAT> LISTEN. I'M SORRY. THERE'S SOMETHING I HAVE TO TELL YOU.
?!
ANGEL CAT> I'M MUCH OLDER THAN YOU. I'M ACTUALLY 36.
THAT'S OKAY...I DON'T CARE.
ANGEL CAT> I HAVE A SON. HE LIVES WITH HIS FATHER, BUT STILL...
I DON'T CARE. I NEED YOU.
TAKA
TAKA
TAKA

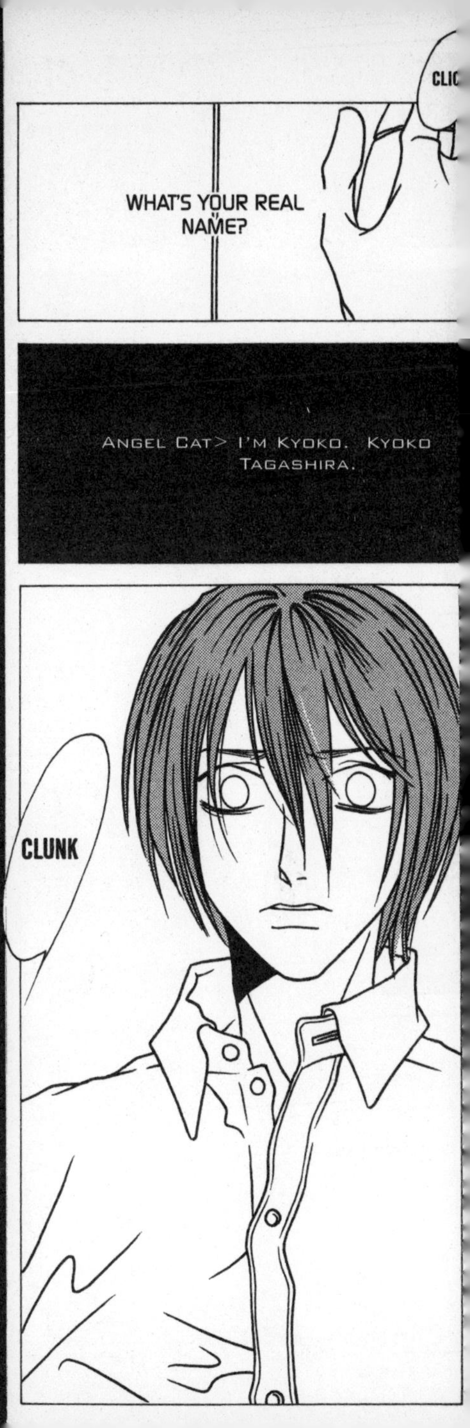
CLIC
WHAT'S YOUR REAL NAME?
ANGEL CAT> I'M KYOKO. KYOKO TAGASHIRA.
CLUNK

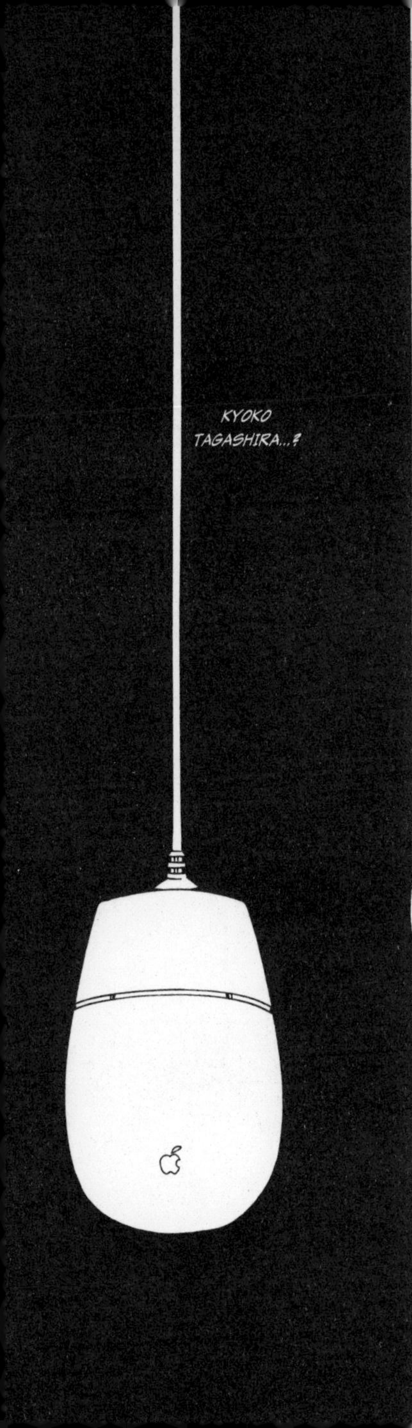
KYOKO TAGASHIRA...?

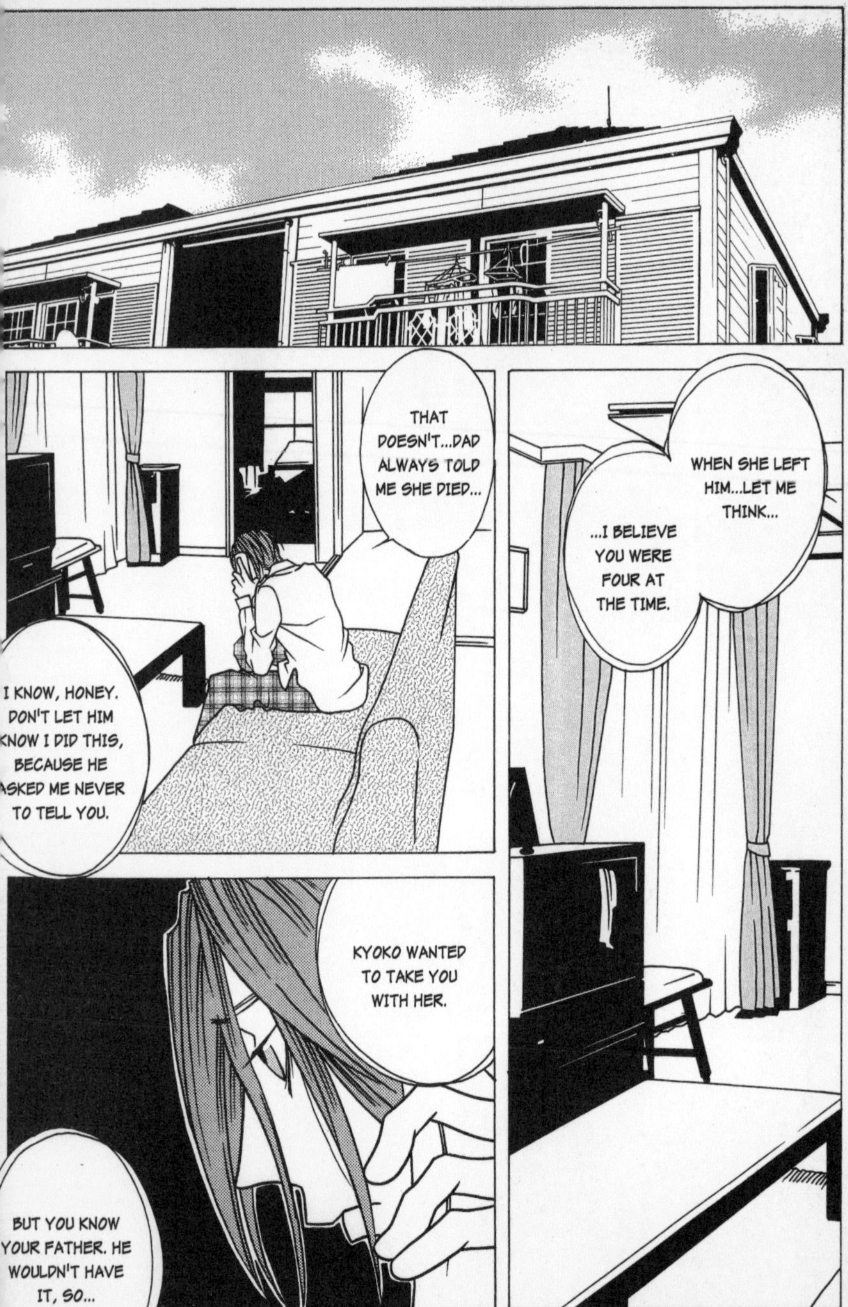
WHEN SHE LEFT HIM...LET ME THINK...
...I BELIEVE YOU WERE FOUR AT THE TIME.
THAT DOESN'T...DAD ALWAYS TOLD ME SHE DIED...
I KNOW, HONEY. DON'T LET HIM KNOW I DID THIS, BECAUSE HE ASKED ME NEVER TO TELL YOU.
KYOKO WANTED TO TAKE YOU WITH HER.
BUT YOU KNOW YOUR FATHER. HE WOULDN'T HAVE IT, SO...

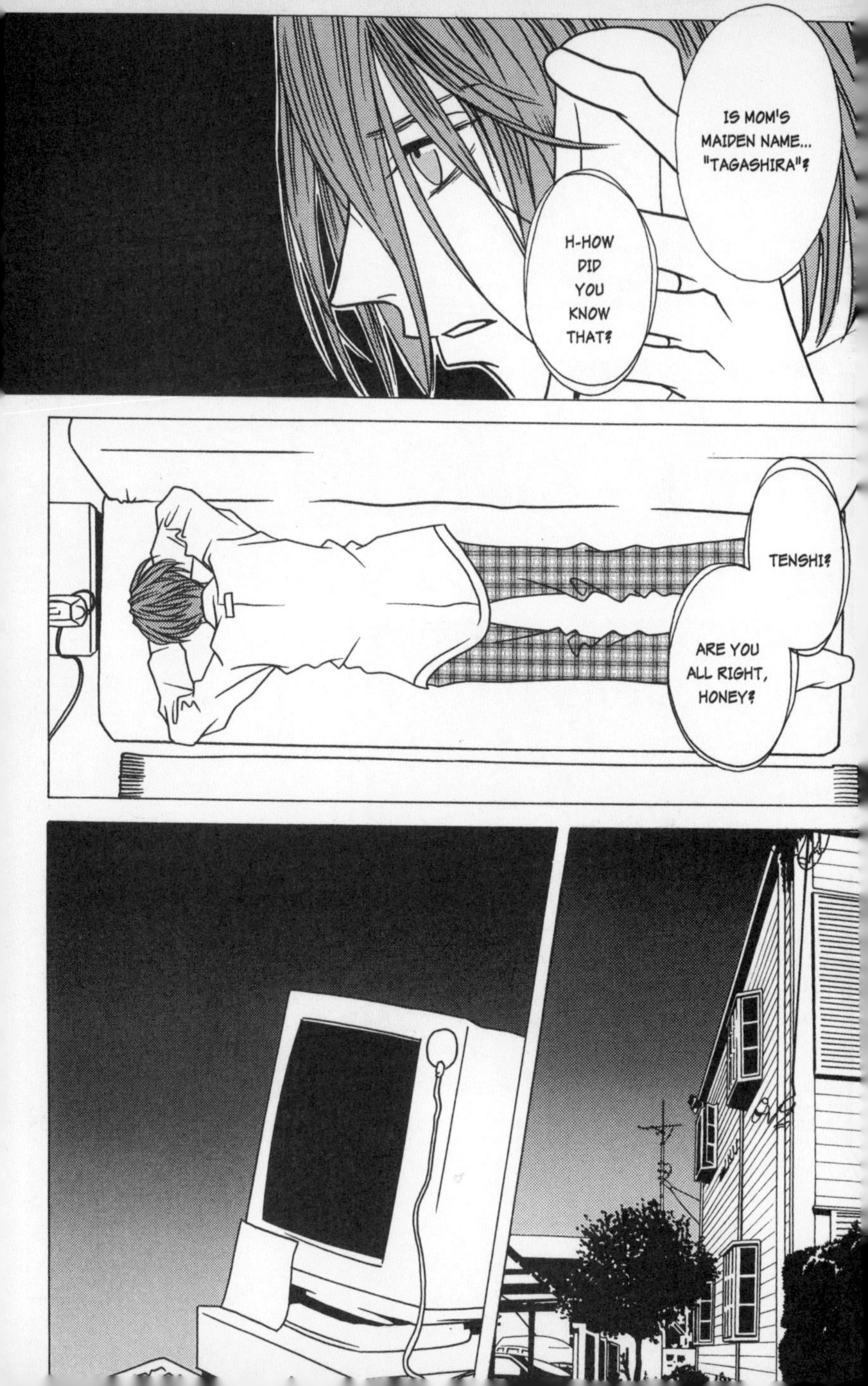
IS MOM'S MAIDEN NAME... "TAGASHIRA"?
H-HOW DID YOU KNOW THAT?
TENSHI?
ARE YOU ALL RIGHT, HONEY?

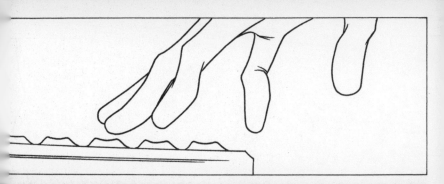

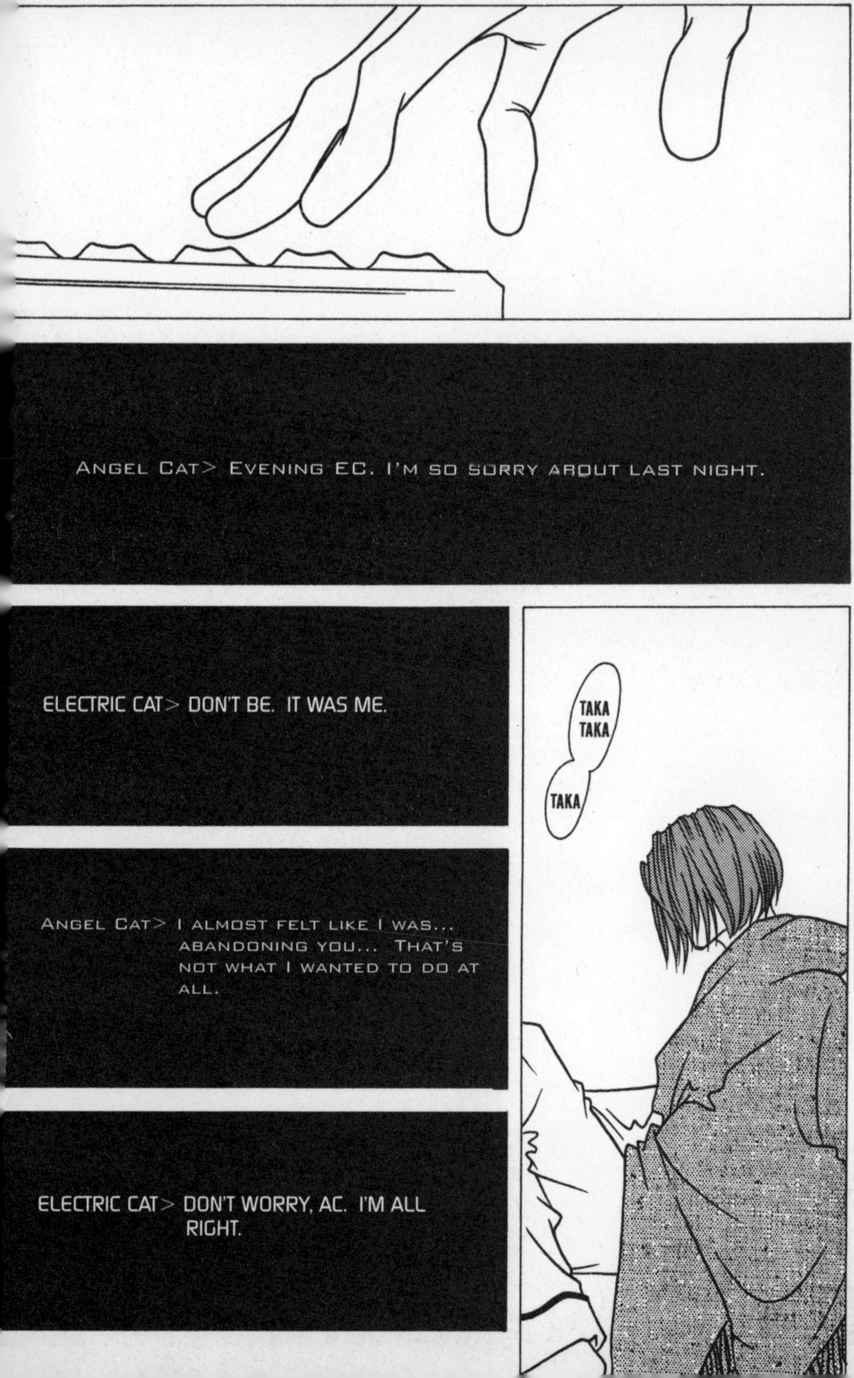

ANGEL CAT> EVENING EC. I'M SO SORRY ABOUT LAST NIGHT.

ELECTRIC CAT> DON'T BE. IT WAS ME.

TAKA
TAKA

TAKA

ANGEL CAT> I ALMOST FELT LIKE I WAS...
ABANDONING YOU... THAT'S
NOT WHAT I WANTED TO DO AT
ALL.

ELECTRIC CAT> DON'T WORRY, AC. I'M ALL
RIGHT.

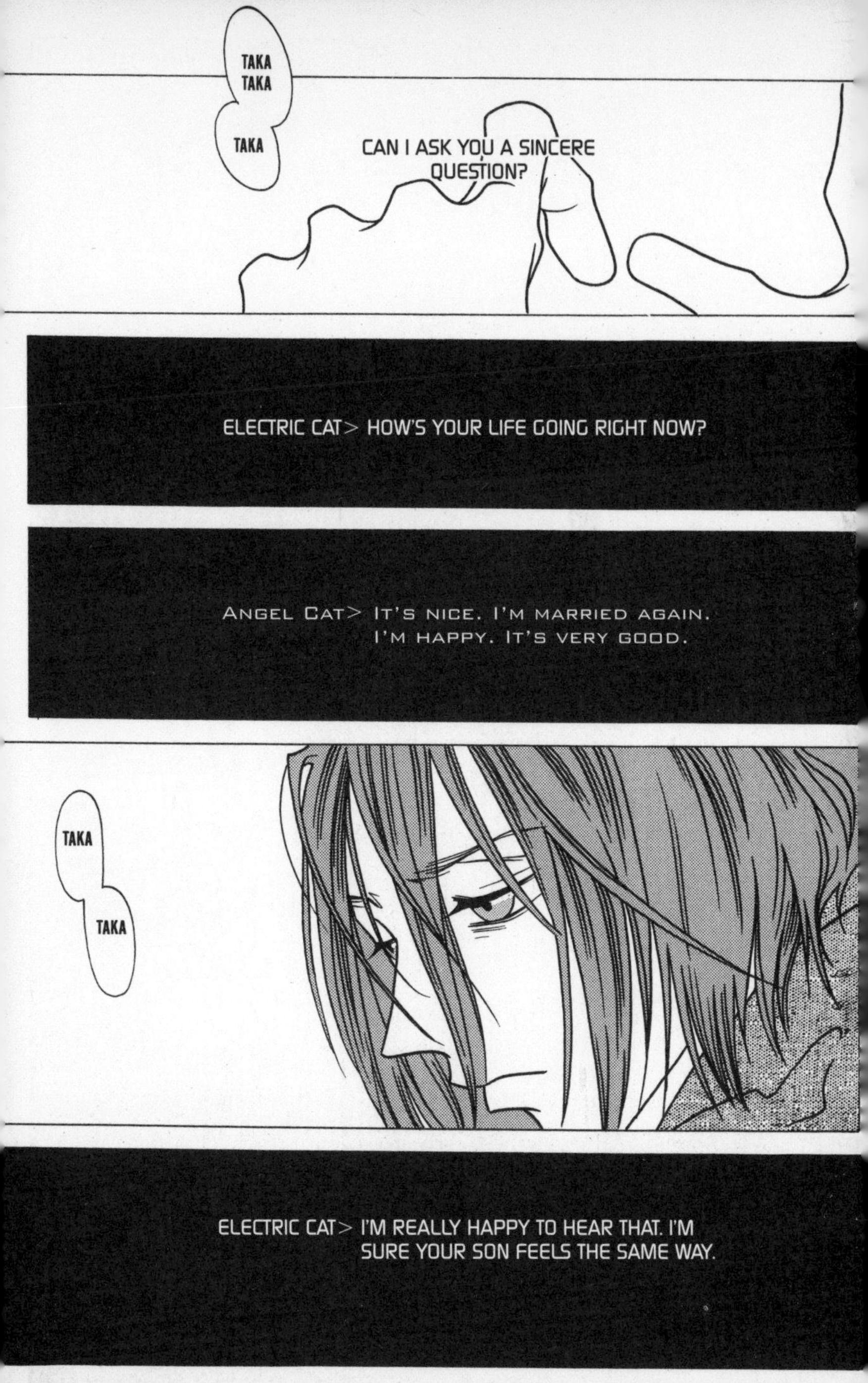
CAN I ASK YOU A SINCERE QUESTION?
TAKA TAKA
TAKA
ELECTRIC CAT> HOW'S YOUR LIFE GOING RIGHT NOW?
ANGEL CAT> IT'S NICE. I'M MARRIED AGAIN. I'M HAPPY. IT'S VERY GOOD.
TAKA
TAKA
ELECTRIC CAT> I'M REALLY HAPPY TO HEAR THAT. I'M SURE YOUR SON FEELS THE SAME WAY.

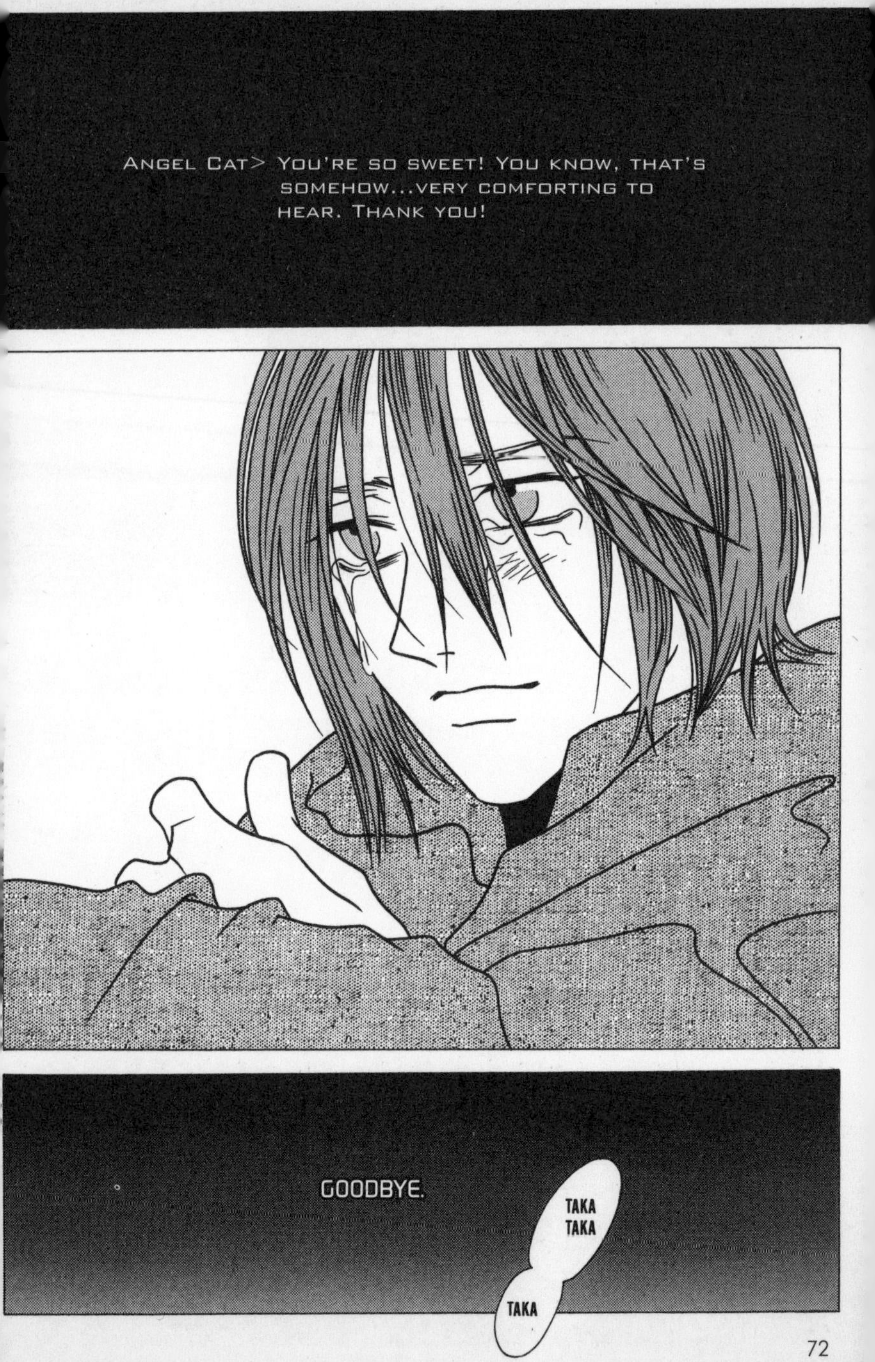
Angel Cat> You're so sweet! You know, that's somehow...very comforting to hear. Thank you!
GOODBYE.
TAKA TAKA
TAKA

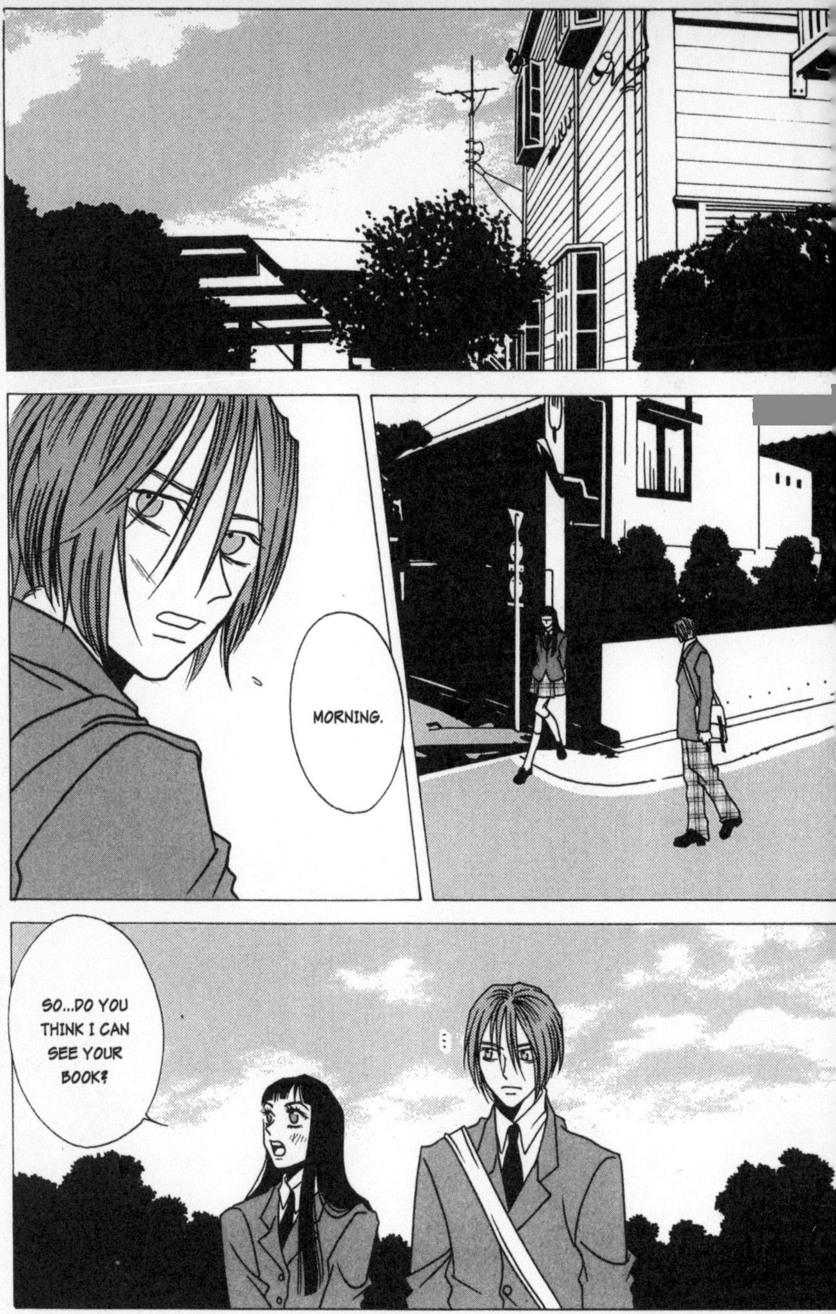
MORNING.
SO...DO YOU THINK I CAN SEE YOUR BOOK?
...

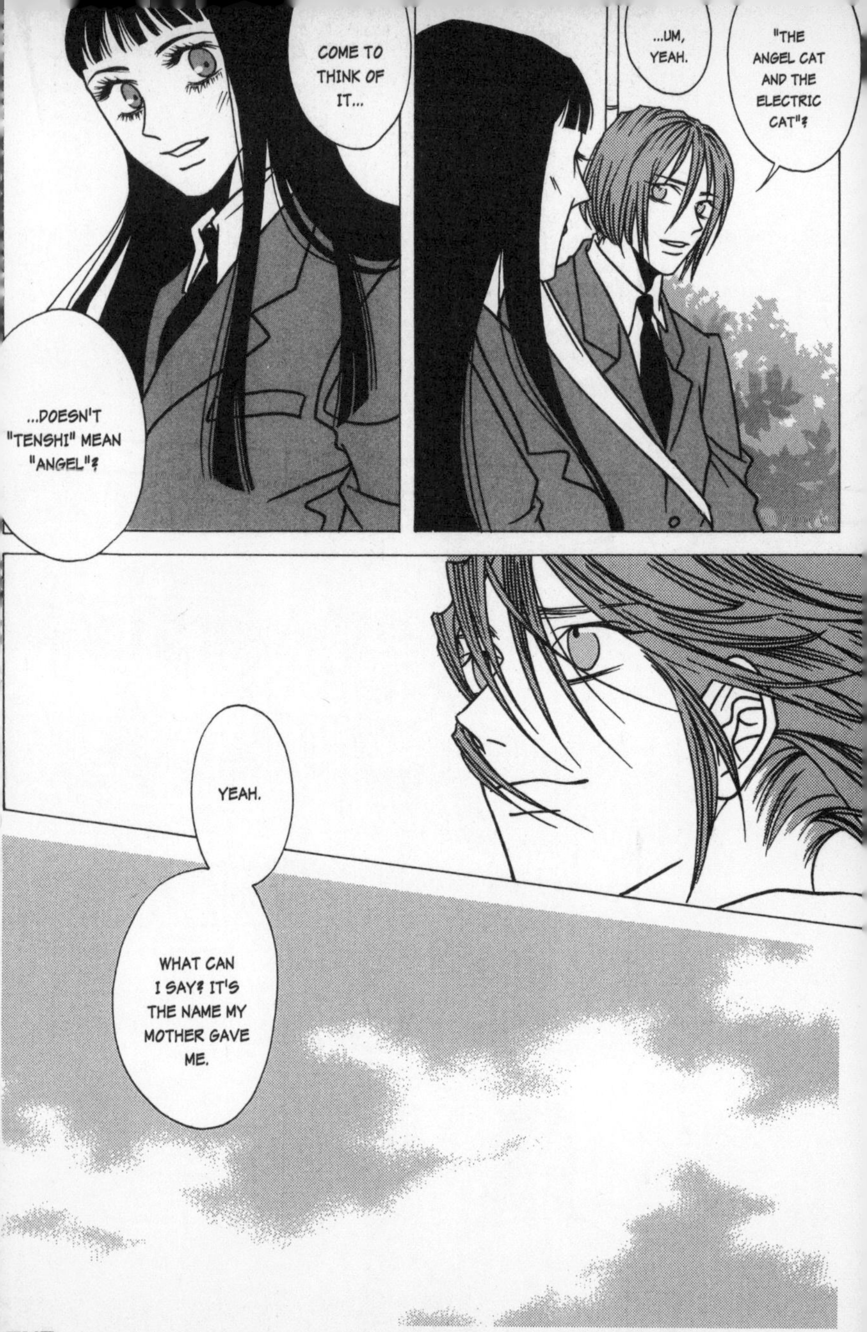
"THE ANGEL CAT AND THE ELECTRIC CAT"?
...UM, YEAH.
COME TO THINK OF IT...
...DOESN'T "TENSHI" MEAN "ANGEL"?
YEAH.
WHAT CAN I SAY? IT'S THE NAME MY MOTHER GAVE ME.

END

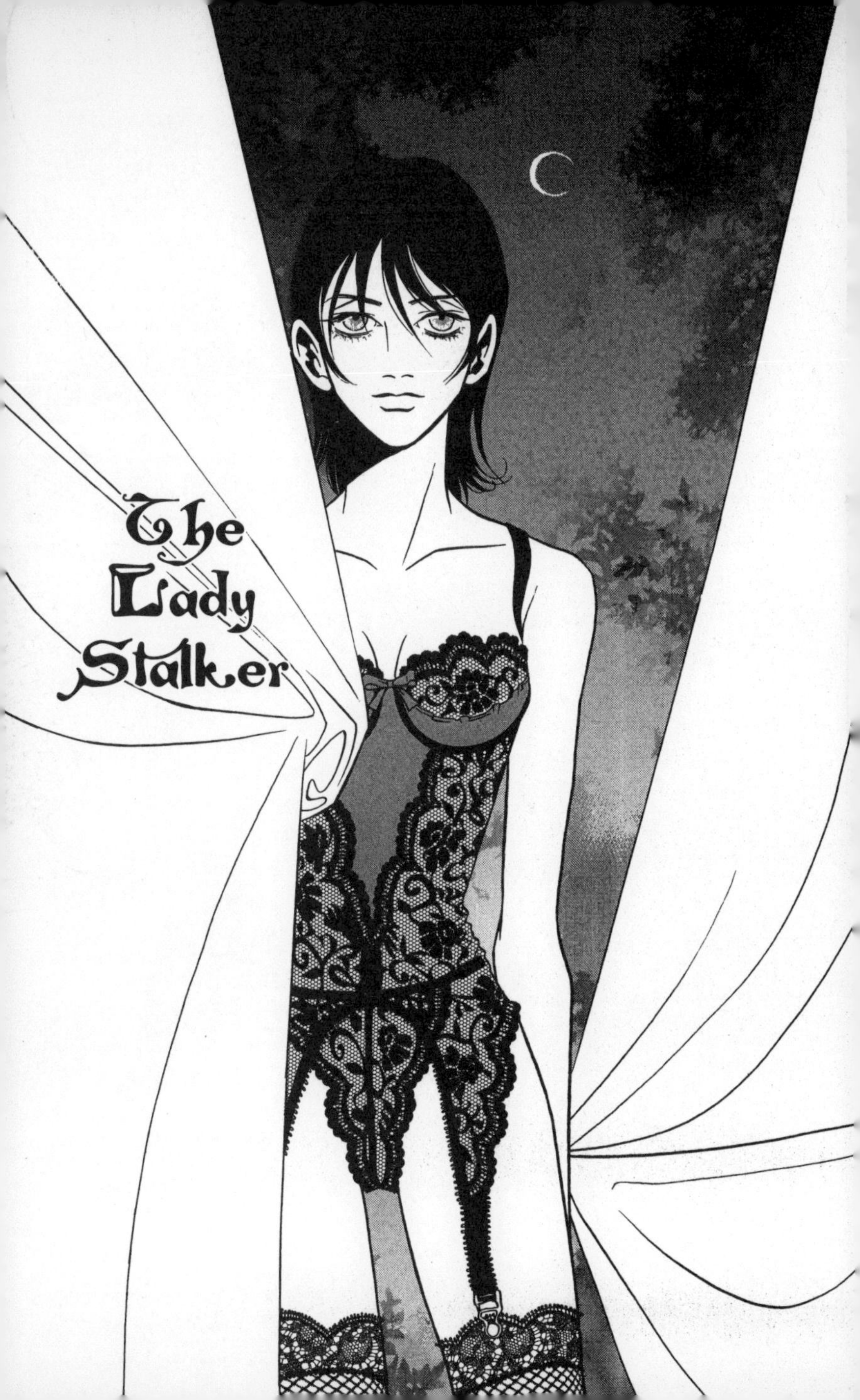
The Lady Stalker

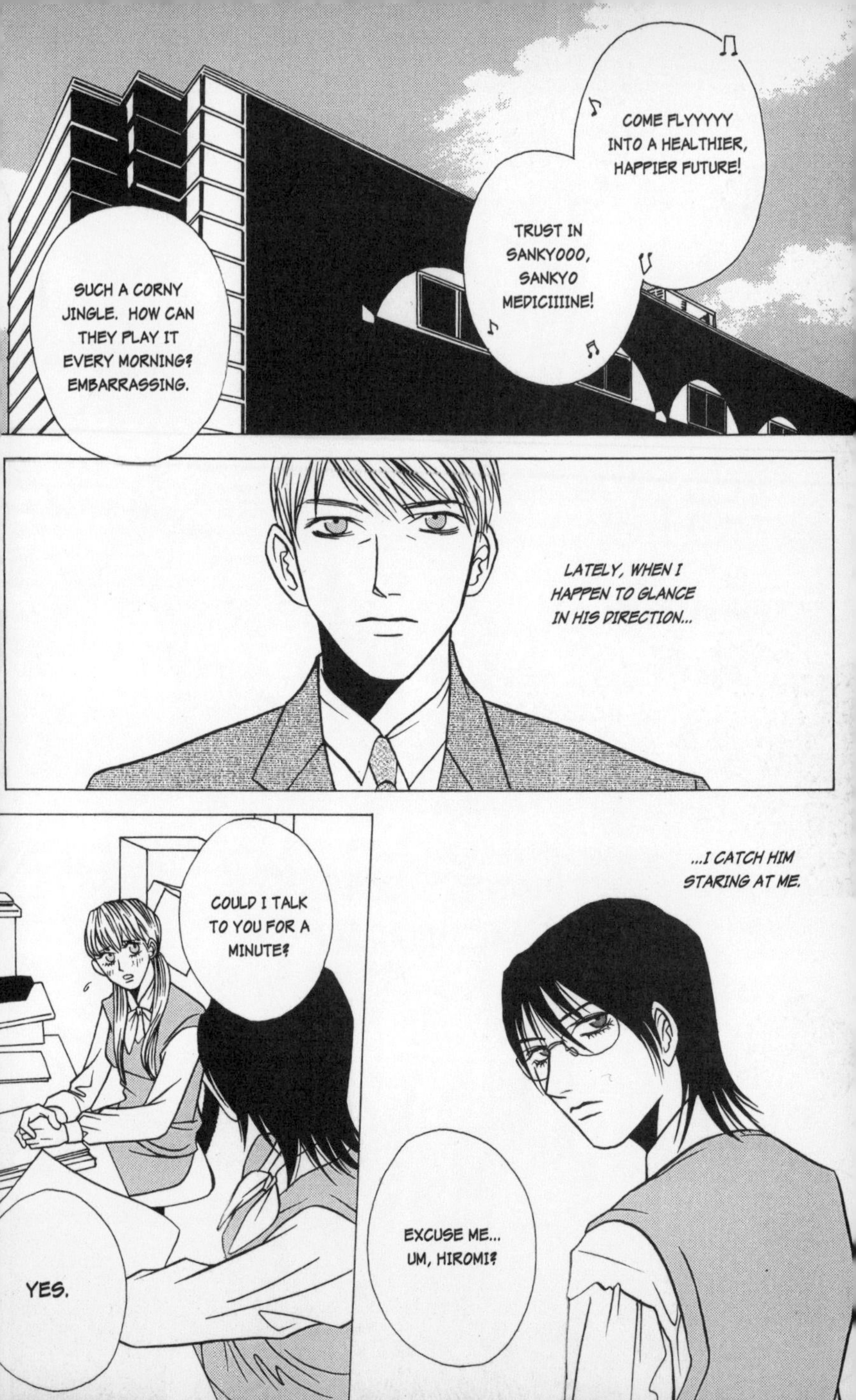
COME FLYYYYY INTO A HEALTHIER, HAPPIER FUTURE!
TRUST IN SANKYOOO, SANKYO MEDICIIIINE!
SUCH A CORNY JINGLE. HOW CAN THEY PLAY IT EVERY MORNING? EMBARRASSING.
LATELY, WHEN I HAPPEN TO GLANCE IN HIS DIRECTION...
...I CATCH HIM STARING AT ME.
EXCUSE ME... UM, HIROMI?
COULD I TALK TO YOU FOR A MINUTE?
YES.

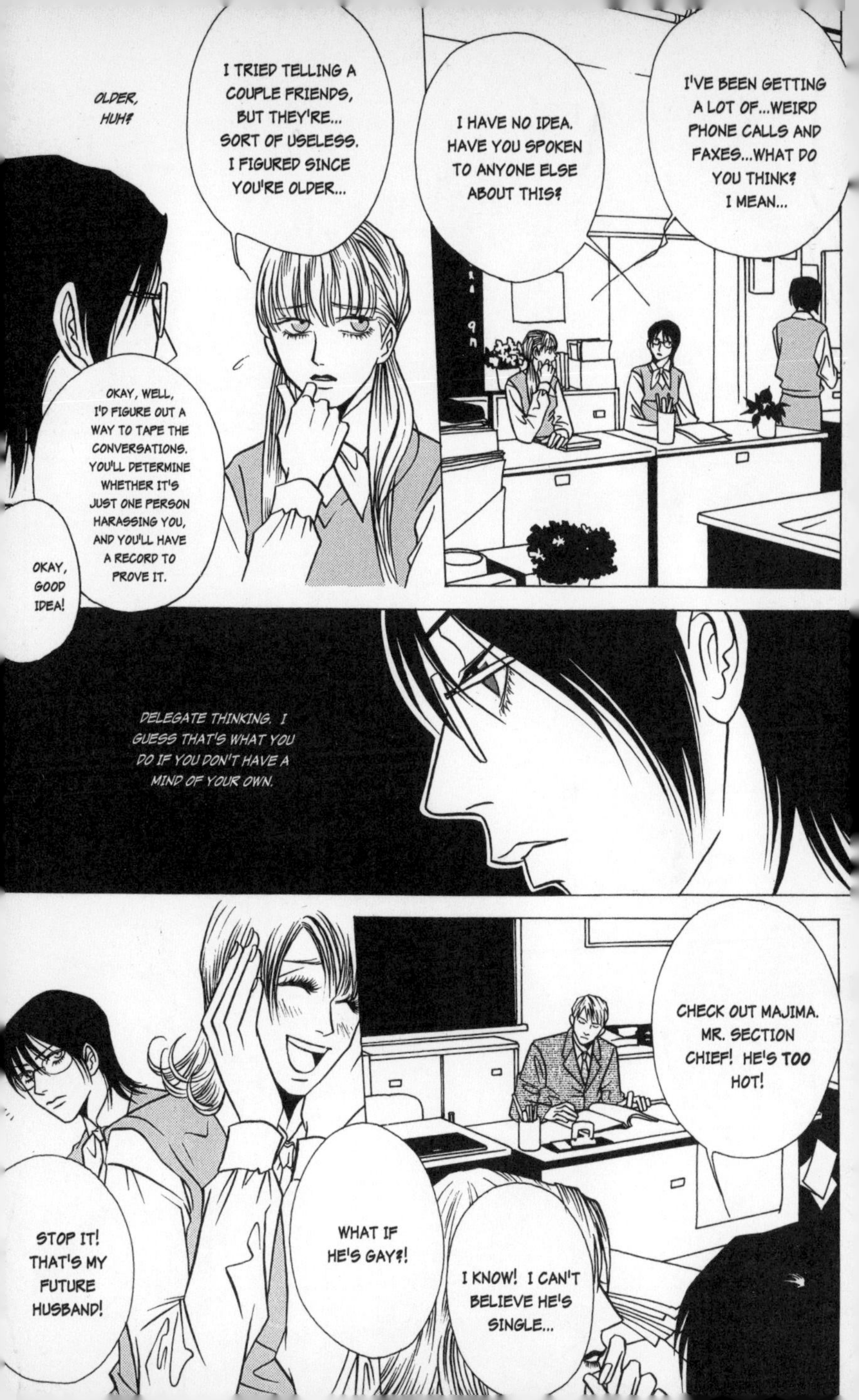
I'VE BEEN GETTING A LOT OF...WEIRD PHONE CALLS AND FAXES...WHAT DO YOU THINK? I MEAN...
I HAVE NO IDEA. HAVE YOU SPOKEN TO ANYONE ELSE ABOUT THIS?
I TRIED TELLING A COUPLE FRIENDS, BUT THEY'RE... SORT OF USELESS. I FIGURED SINCE YOU'RE OLDER...
OLDER, HUH?
OKAY, WELL, I'D FIGURE OUT A WAY TO TAPE THE CONVERSATIONS. YOU'LL DETERMINE WHETHER IT'S JUST ONE PERSON HARASSING YOU, AND YOU'LL HAVE A RECORD TO PROVE IT.
OKAY, GOOD IDEA!
DELEGATE THINKING. I GUESS THAT'S WHAT YOU DO IF YOU DON'T HAVE A MIND OF YOUR OWN.
CHECK OUT MAJIMA. MR. SECTION CHIEF! HE'S TOO HOT!
I KNOW! I CAN'T BELIEVE HE'S SINGLE...
WHAT IF HE'S GAY?!
STOP IT! THAT'S MY FUTURE HUSBAND!

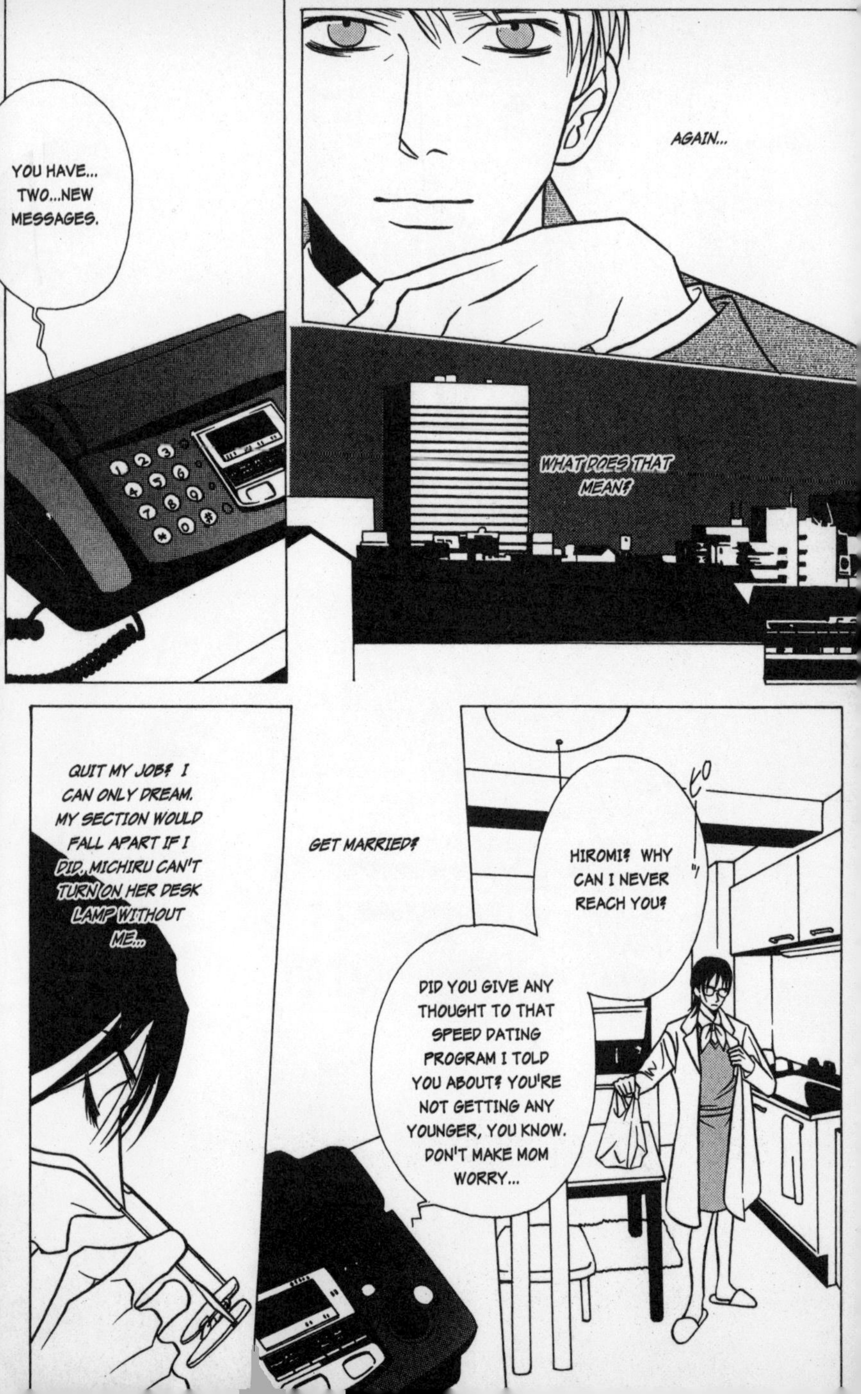
AGAIN...
WHAT DOES THAT MEAN?
YOU HAVE... TWO...NEW MESSAGES.
HIROMI? WHY CAN I NEVER REACH YOU?
DID YOU GIVE ANY THOUGHT TO THAT SPEED DATING PROGRAM I TOLD YOU ABOUT? YOU'RE NOT GETTING ANY YOUNGER, YOU KNOW. DON'T MAKE MOM WORRY...
GET MARRIED?
QUIT MY JOB? I CAN ONLY DREAM. MY SECTION WOULD FALL APART IF I DID. MICHIRU CAN'T TURN ON HER DESK LAMP WITHOUT ME...

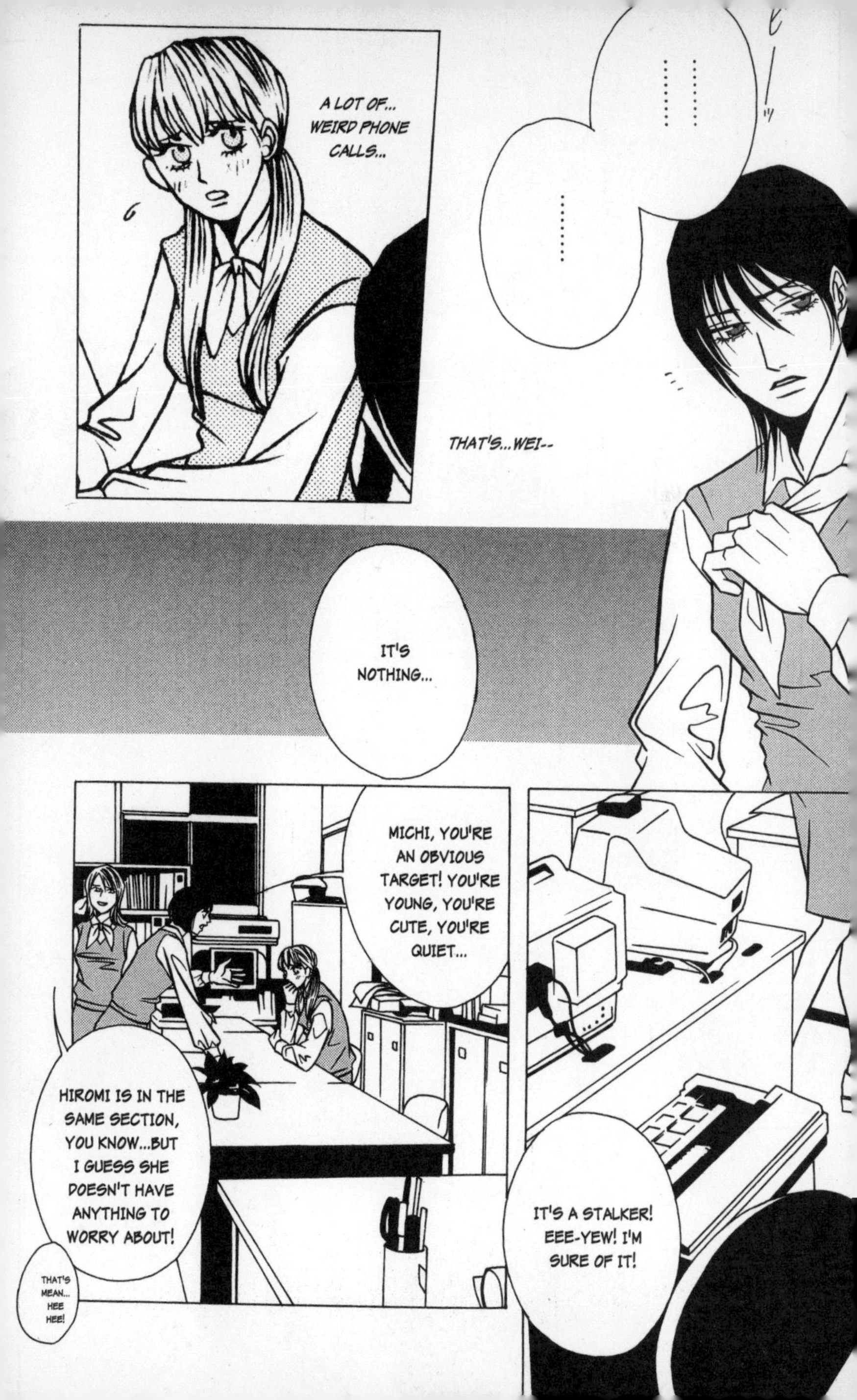
......
......
THAT'S...WEI--
A LOT OF... WEIRD PHONE CALLS...
IT'S NOTHING...
IT'S A STALKER! EEE-YEW! I'M SURE OF IT!
MICHI, YOU'RE AN OBVIOUS TARGET! YOU'RE YOUNG, YOU'RE CUTE, YOU'RE QUIET...
HIROMI IS IN THE SAME SECTION, YOU KNOW...BUT I GUESS SHE DOESN'T HAVE ANYTHING TO WORRY ABOUT!
THAT'S MEAN... HEE HEE!

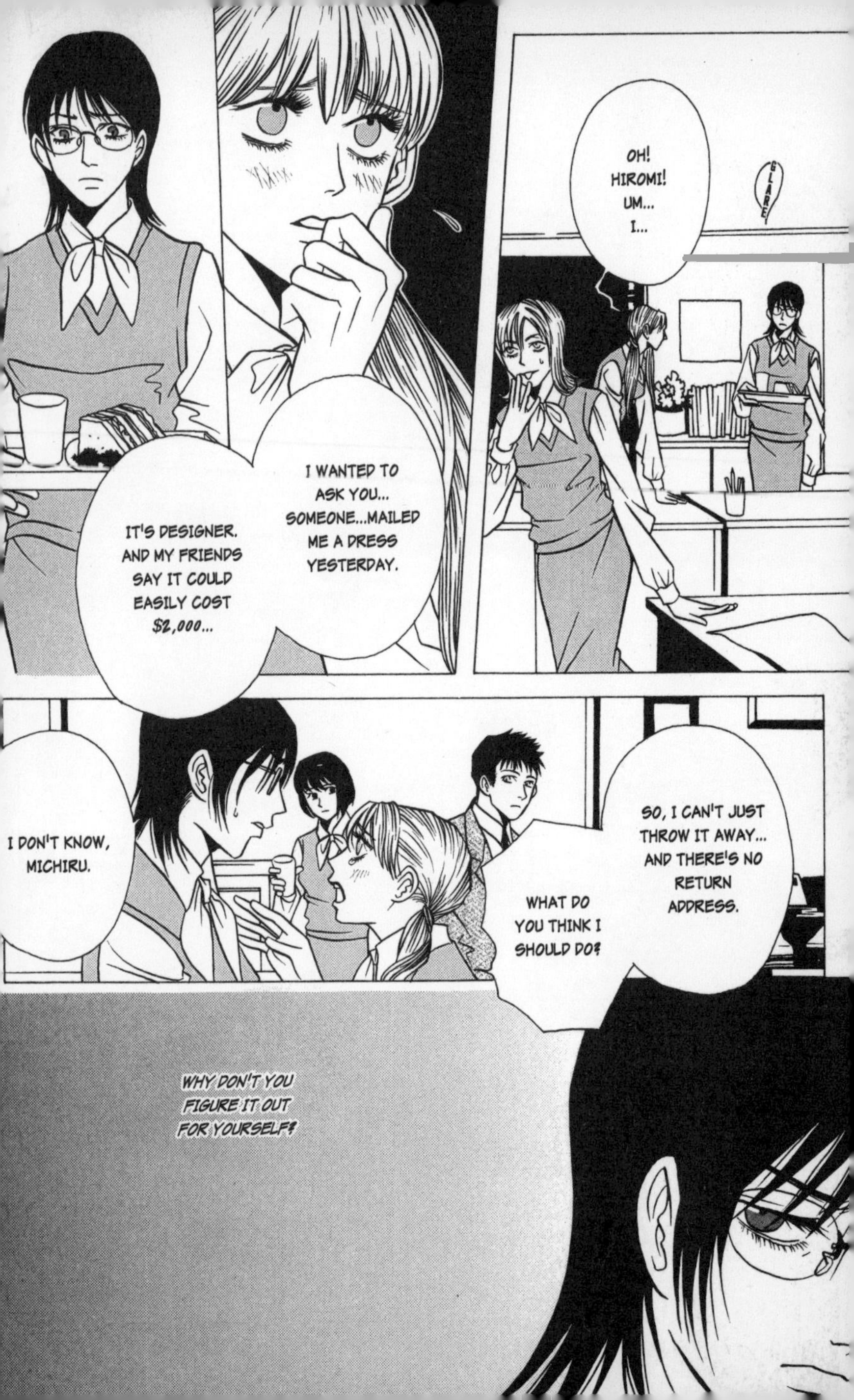
OH! HIROMI! UM... I...
GLARE
I WANTED TO ASK YOU... SOMEONE...MAILED ME A DRESS YESTERDAY.
IT'S DESIGNER. AND MY FRIENDS SAY IT COULD EASILY COST $2,000...
SO, I CAN'T JUST THROW IT AWAY... AND THERE'S NO RETURN ADDRESS.
WHAT DO YOU THINK I SHOULD DO?
I DON'T KNOW, MICHIRU.
WHY DON'T YOU FIGURE IT OUT FOR YOURSELF?

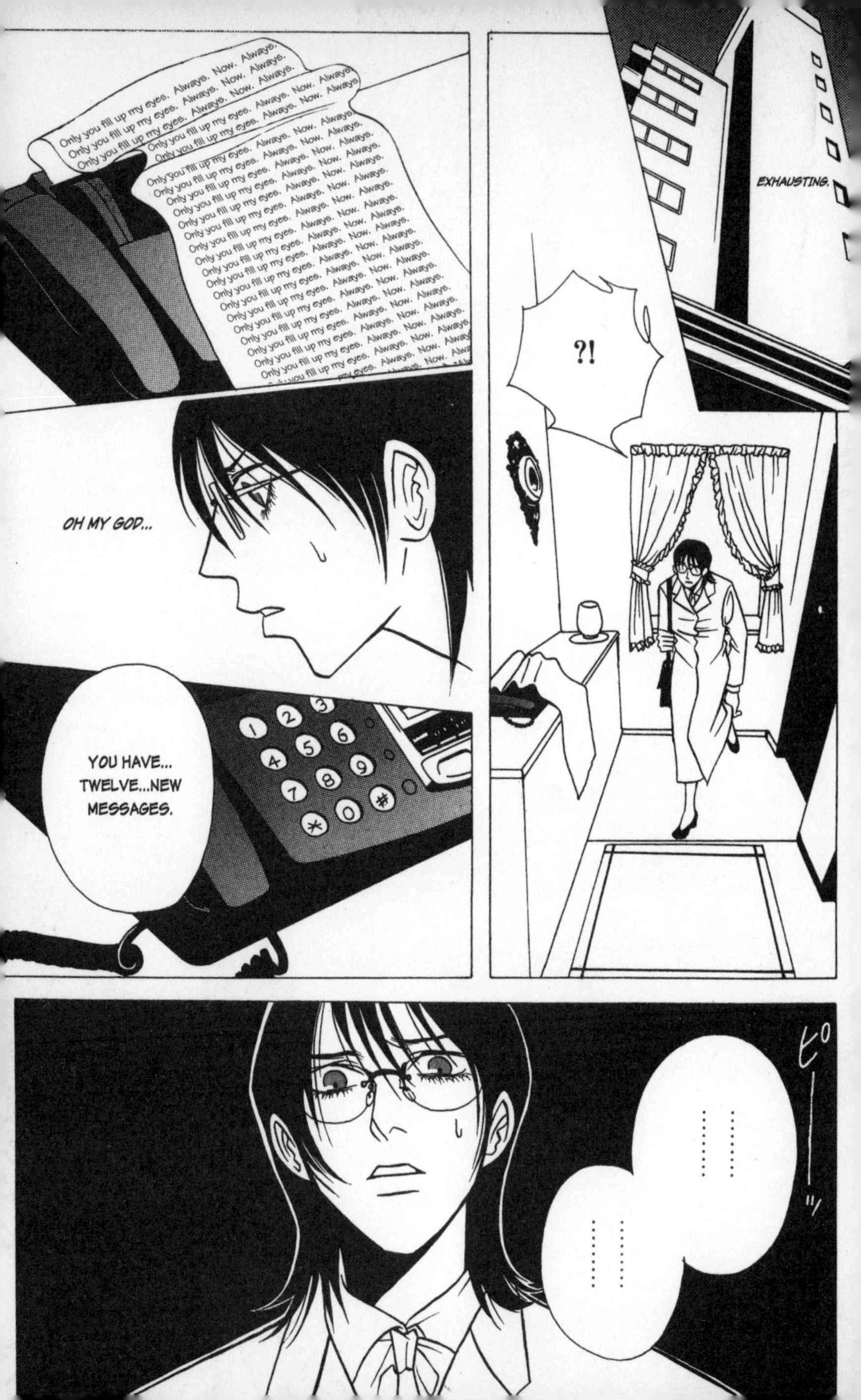
EXHAUSTING.
?!
Only you fill up my eyes. Always. Now. Always.
Only you fill up my eyes. Always. Now. Always.
Only you fill up my eyes. Always. Now. Always.
Only you fill up my eyes. Always. Now. Always.
Only you fill up my eyes. Always. Now. Always.
Only you fill up my eyes. Always. Now. Always.
Only you fill up my eyes. Always. Now. Always.
Only you fill up my eyes. Always. Now. Always.
Only you fill up my eyes. Always. Now. Always.
Only you fill up my eyes. Always. Now. Always.
Only you fill up my eyes. Always. Now. Always.
Only you fill up my eyes. Always. Now. Always.
Only you fill up my eyes. Always. Now. Always.
Only you fill up my eyes. Always. Now. Always.
Only you fill up my eyes. Always. Now. Always.
Only you fill up my eyes. Always. Now. Always.
Only you fill up my eyes. Always. Now. Always.
Only you fill up my eyes. Always. Now. Always.
OH MY GOD...
YOU HAVE... TWELVE...NEW MESSAGES.
ピーッ
......
......

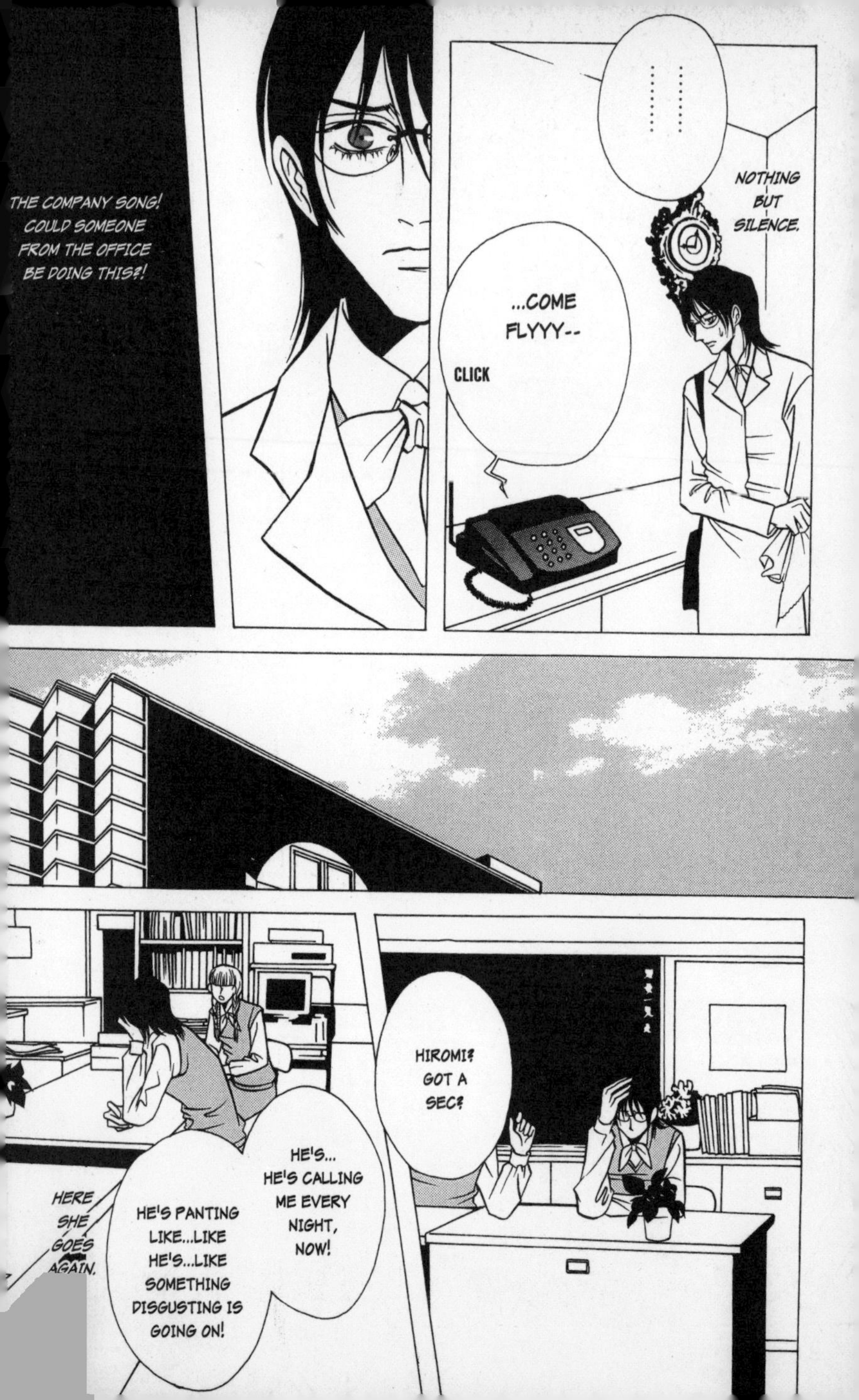
......
NOTHING BUT SILENCE.
...COME FLYYY--
CLICK
THE COMPANY SONG! COULD SOMEONE FROM THE OFFICE BE DOING THIS?!
HIROMI? GOT A SEC?
HE'S... HE'S CALLING ME EVERY NIGHT, NOW!
HE'S PANTING LIKE...LIKE HE'S...LIKE SOMETHING DISGUSTING IS GOING ON!
HERE SHE GOES AGAIN.

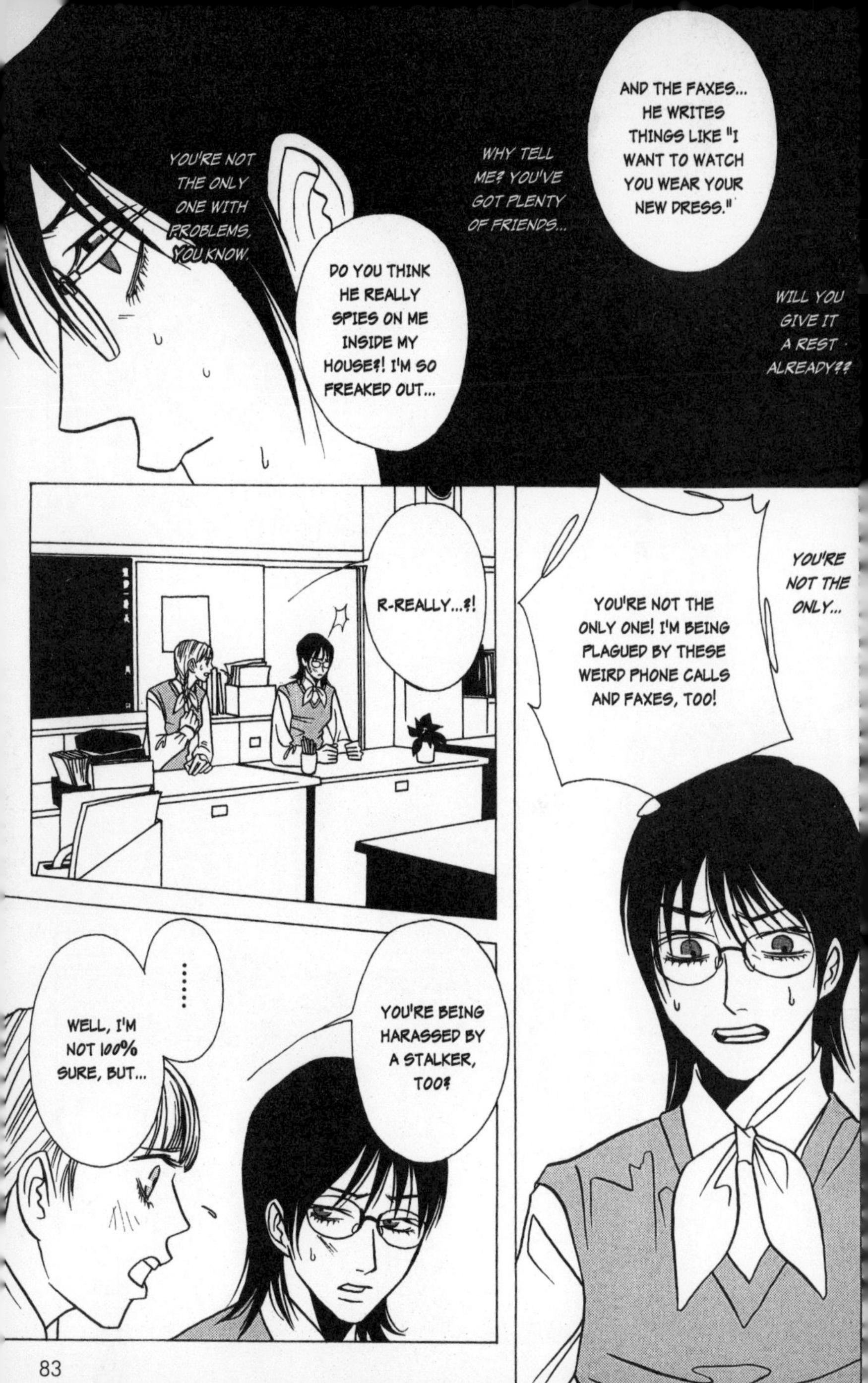
AND THE FAXES... HE WRITES THINGS LIKE "I WANT TO WATCH YOU WEAR YOUR NEW DRESS."
WILL YOU GIVE IT A REST ALREADY??
WHY TELL ME? YOU'VE GOT PLENTY OF FRIENDS...
DO YOU THINK HE REALLY SPIES ON ME INSIDE MY HOUSE?! I'M SO FREAKED OUT...
YOU'RE NOT THE ONLY ONE WITH PROBLEMS, YOU KNOW.
YOU'RE NOT THE ONLY...
YOU'RE NOT THE ONLY ONE! I'M BEING PLAGUED BY THESE WEIRD PHONE CALLS AND FAXES, TOO!
R-REALLY...?!
YOU'RE BEING HARASSED BY A STALKER, TOO?
......
WELL, I'M NOT 100% SURE, BUT...

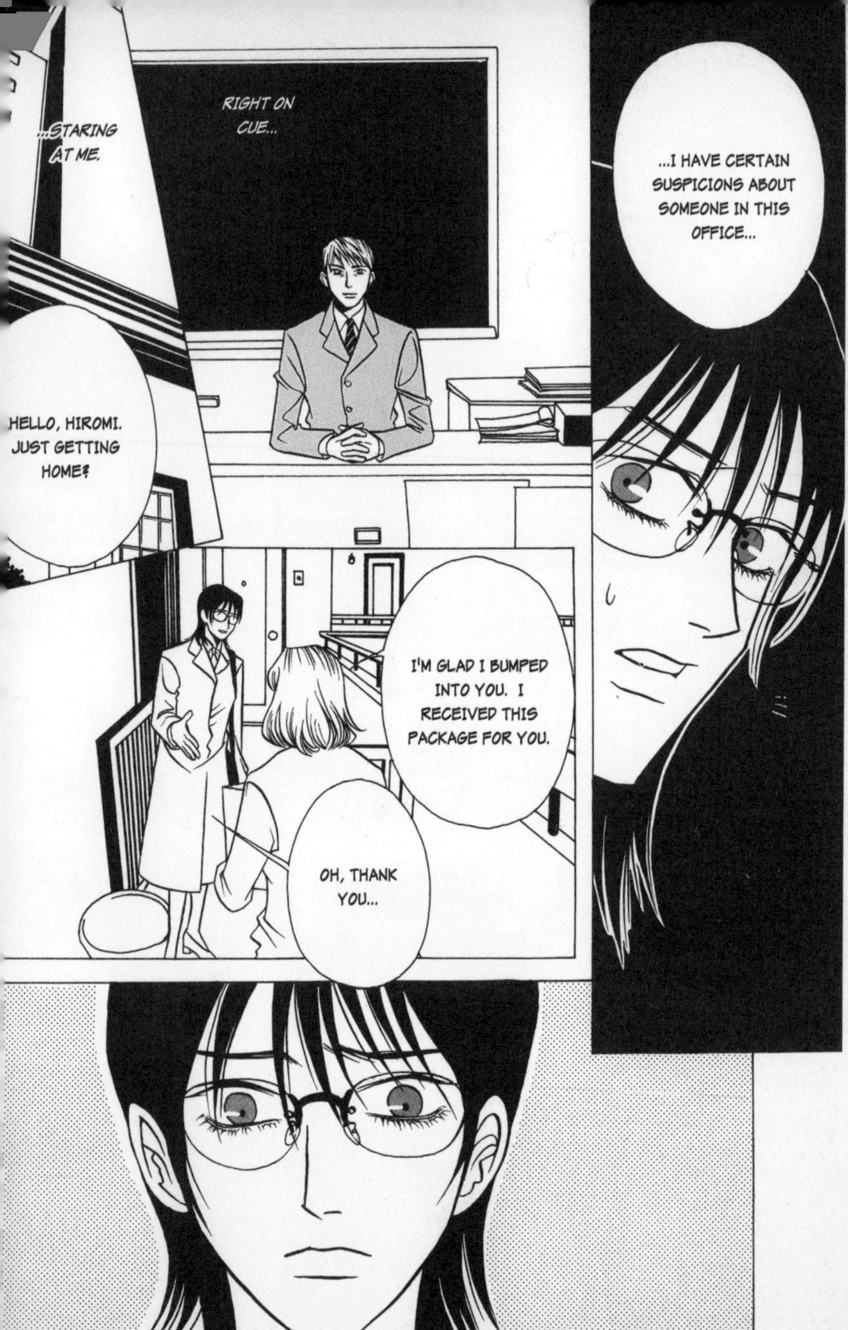
...I HAVE CERTAIN SUSPICIONS ABOUT SOMEONE IN THIS OFFICE...
RIGHT ON CUE...
...STARING AT ME.
HELLO, HIROMI. JUST GETTING HOME?
I'M GLAD I BUMPED INTO YOU. I RECEIVED THIS PACKAGE FOR YOU.
OH, THANK YOU...

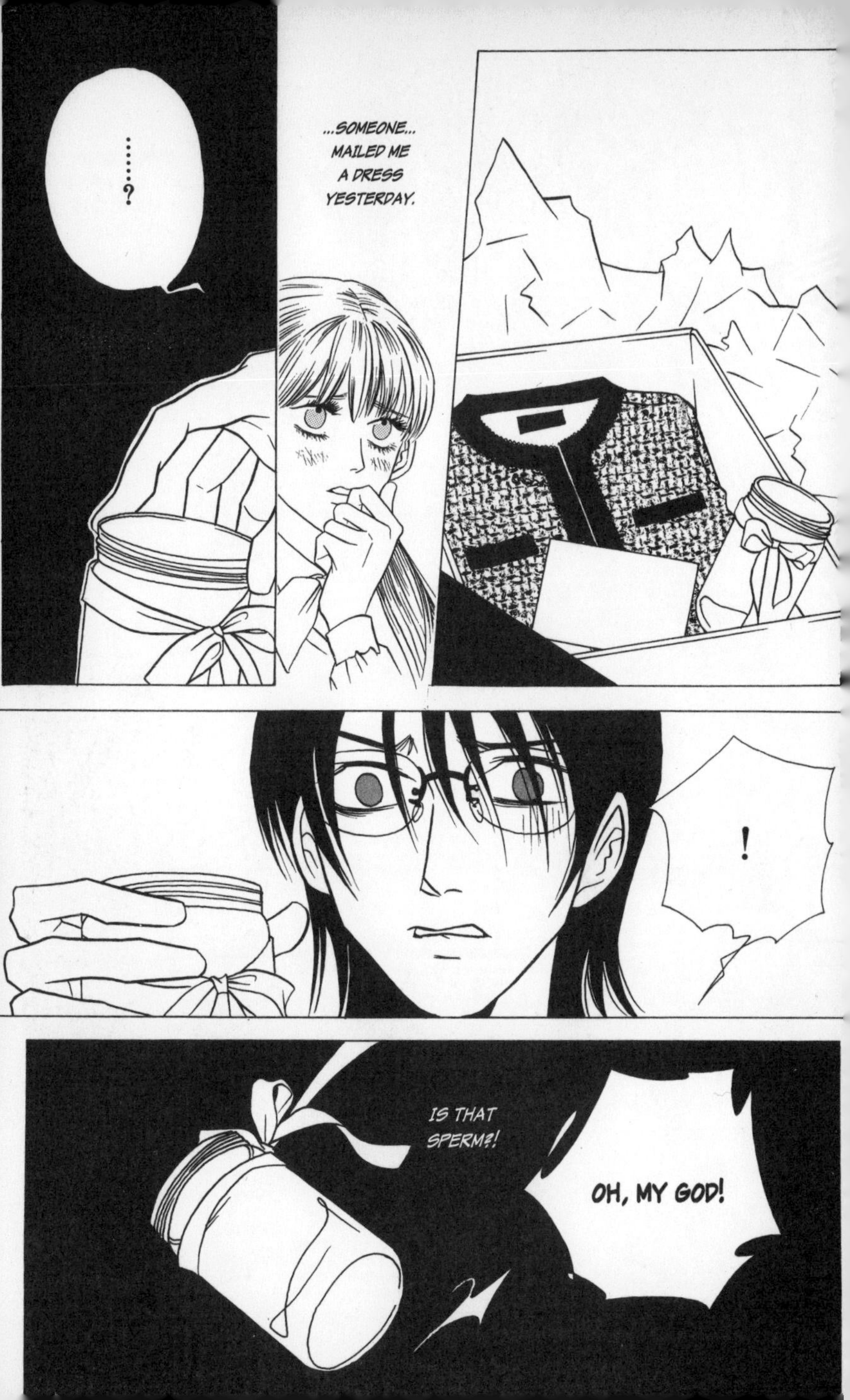
...SOMEONE... MAILED ME A DRESS YESTERDAY.
......?
!
OH, MY GOD!
IS THAT SPERM?!

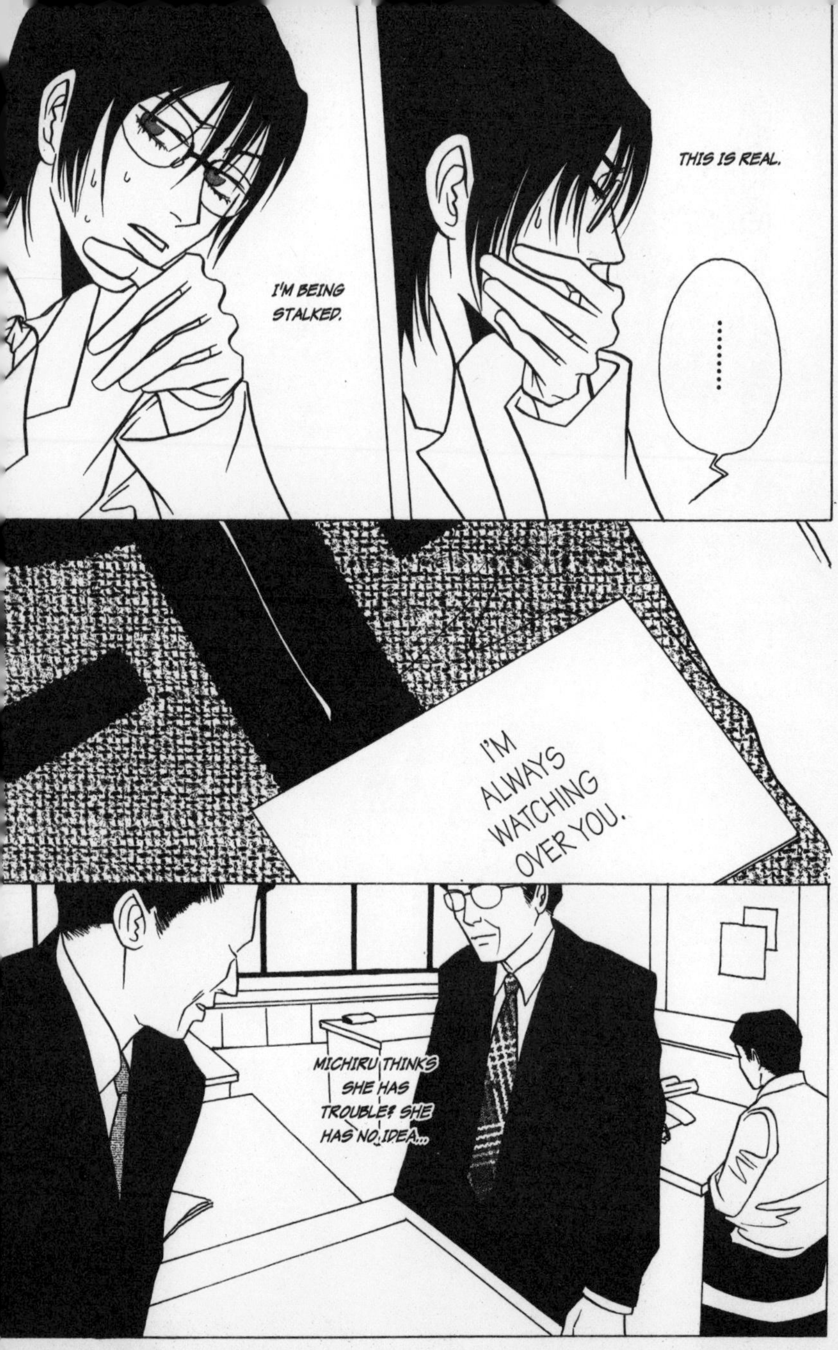
THIS IS REAL.
……
I'M BEING STALKED.
I'M ALWAYS WATCHING OVER YOU.
MICHIRU THINKS SHE HAS TROUBLE? SHE HAS NO IDEA...

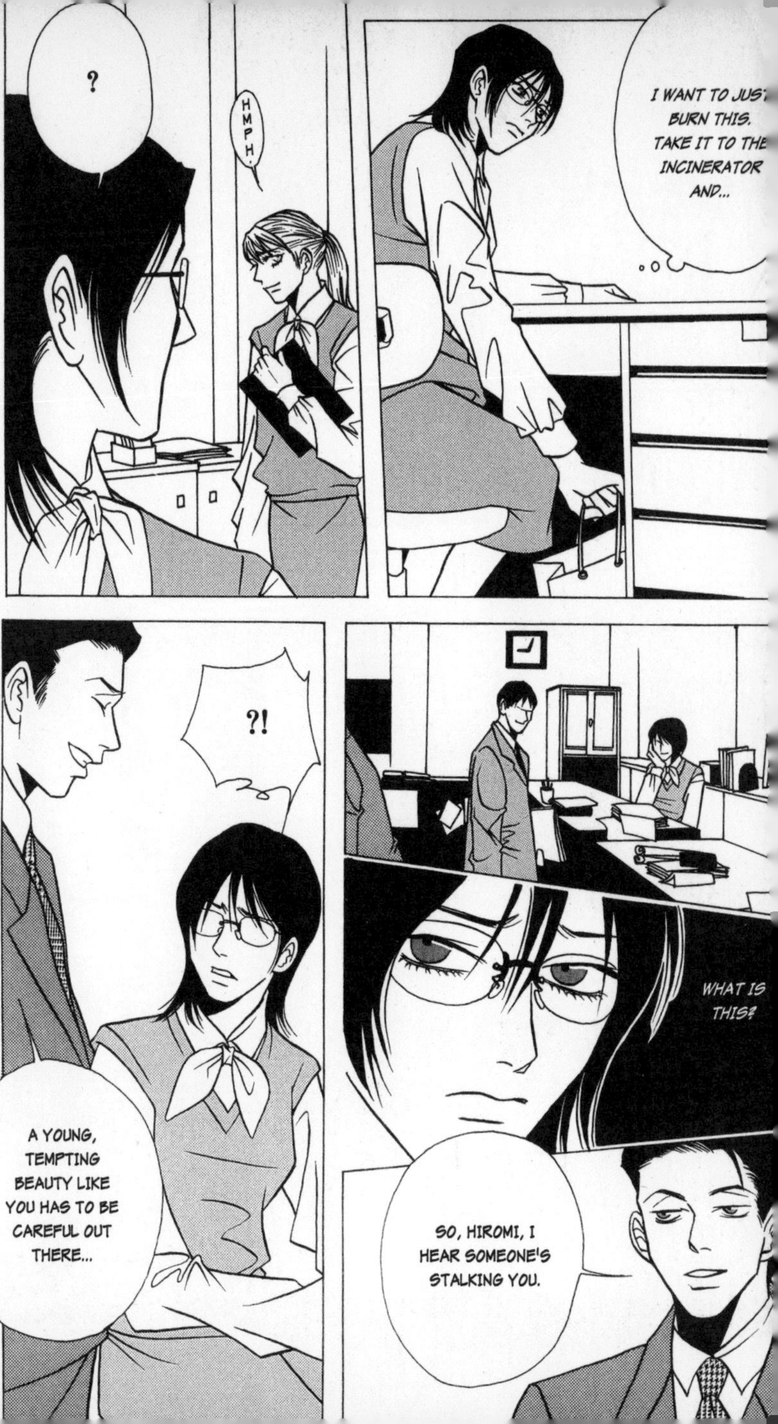
I WANT TO JUST BURN THIS. TAKE IT TO THE INCINERATOR AND...
HMPH.
?
WHAT IS THIS?
SO, HIROMI, I HEAR SOMEONE'S STALKING YOU.
?!
A YOUNG, TEMPTING BEAUTY LIKE YOU HAS TO BE CAREFUL OUT THERE...
(Snort) Heh heh!

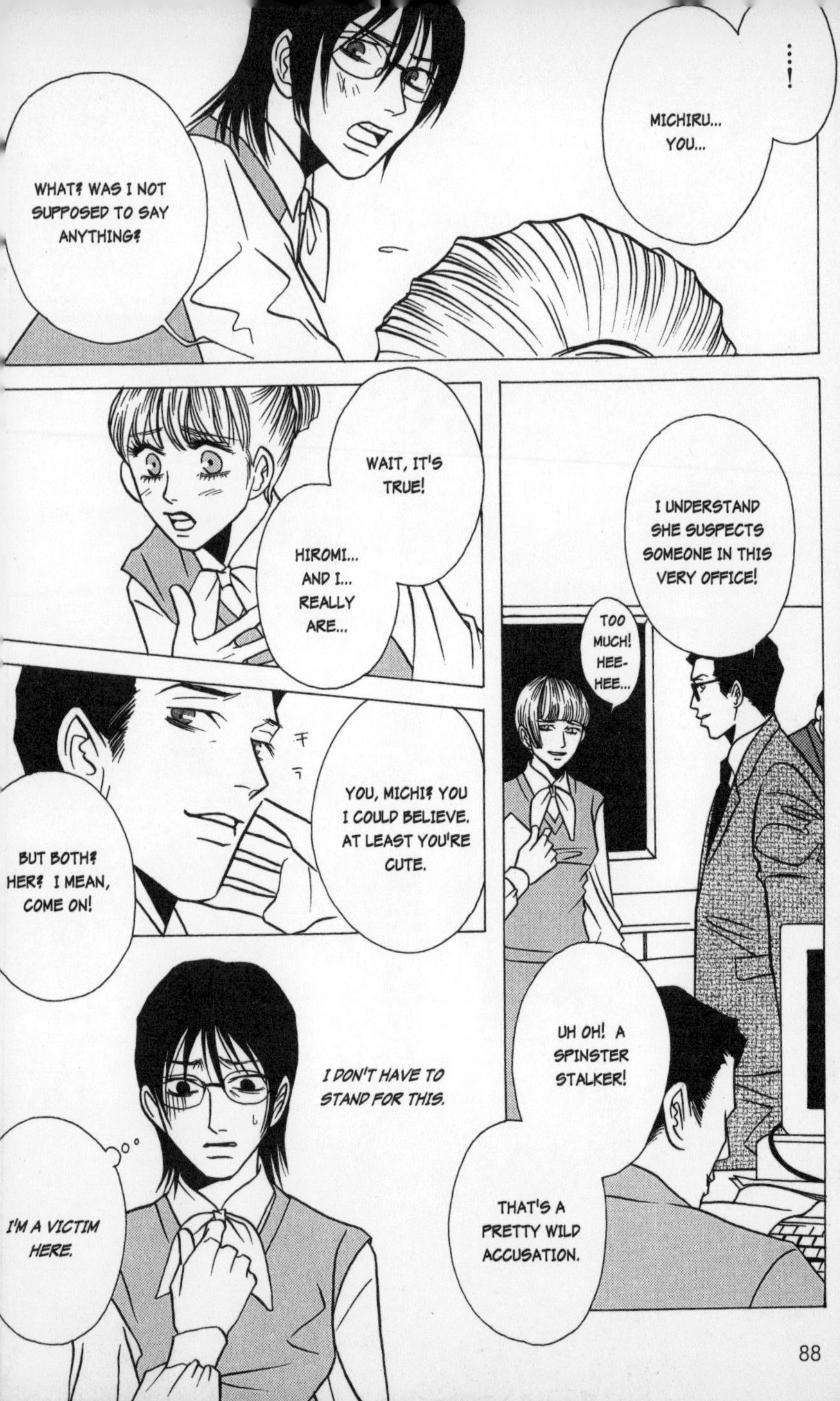
...!
MICHIRU... YOU...
WHAT? WAS I NOT SUPPOSED TO SAY ANYTHING?
I UNDERSTAND SHE SUSPECTS SOMEONE IN THIS VERY OFFICE!
TOO MUCH! HEE-HEE...
UH OH! A SPINSTER STALKER!
THAT'S A PRETTY WILD ACCUSATION.
WAIT, IT'S TRUE!
HIROMI... AND I... REALLY ARE...
YOU, MICHI? YOU I COULD BELIEVE. AT LEAST YOU'RE CUTE.
BUT BOTH? HER? I MEAN, COME ON!
I DON'T HAVE TO STAND FOR THIS.
I'M A VICTIM HERE.

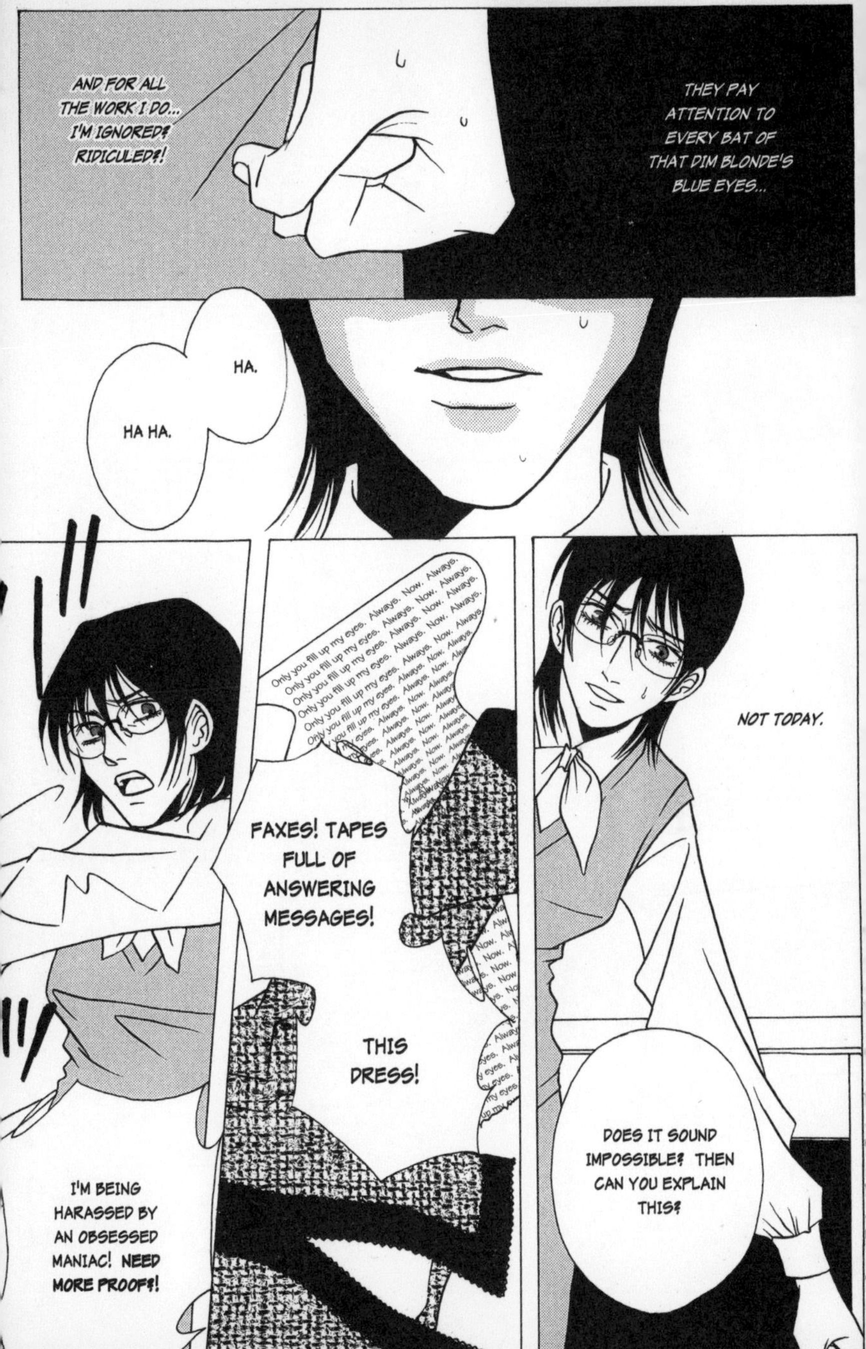
THEY PAY ATTENTION TO EVERY BAT OF THAT DIM BLONDE'S BLUE EYES...
AND FOR ALL THE WORK I DO... I'M IGNORED? RIDICULED?!
HA.
HA HA.
NOT TODAY.
DOES IT SOUND IMPOSSIBLE? THEN CAN YOU EXPLAIN THIS?
Only you fill up my eyes. Always. Now. Always.
FAXES! TAPES FULL OF ANSWERING MESSAGES!
THIS DRESS!
I'M BEING HARASSED BY AN OBSESSED MANIAC! NEED MORE PROOF?!

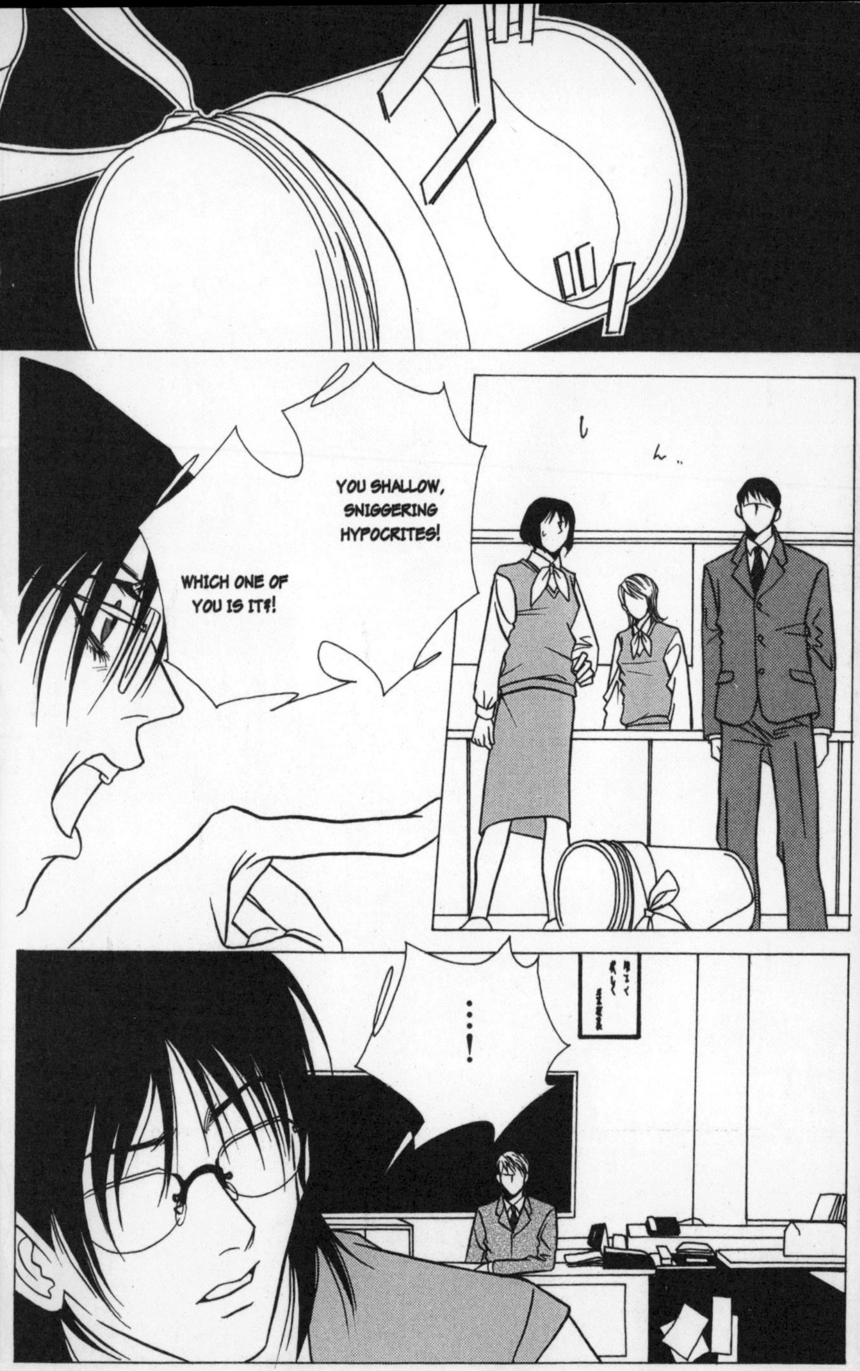
しん..
YOU SHALLOW, SNIGGERING HYPOCRITES!
WHICH ONE OF YOU IS IT?!
...!

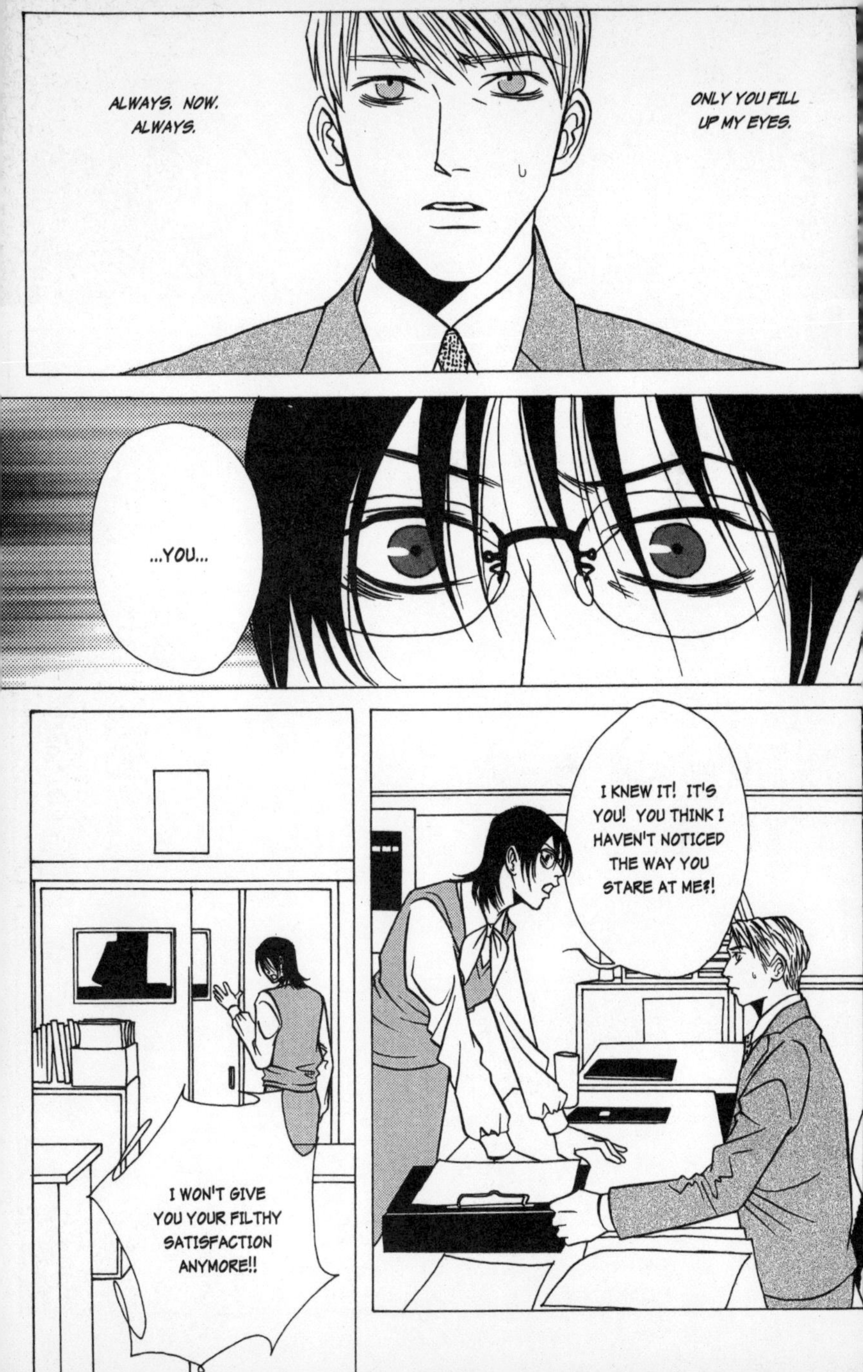
ONLY YOU FILL UP MY EYES.
ALWAYS. NOW. ALWAYS.
...YOU...
I KNEW IT! IT'S YOU! YOU THINK I HAVEN'T NOTICED THE WAY YOU STARE AT ME?!
I WON'T GIVE YOU YOUR FILTHY SATISFACTION ANYMORE!!

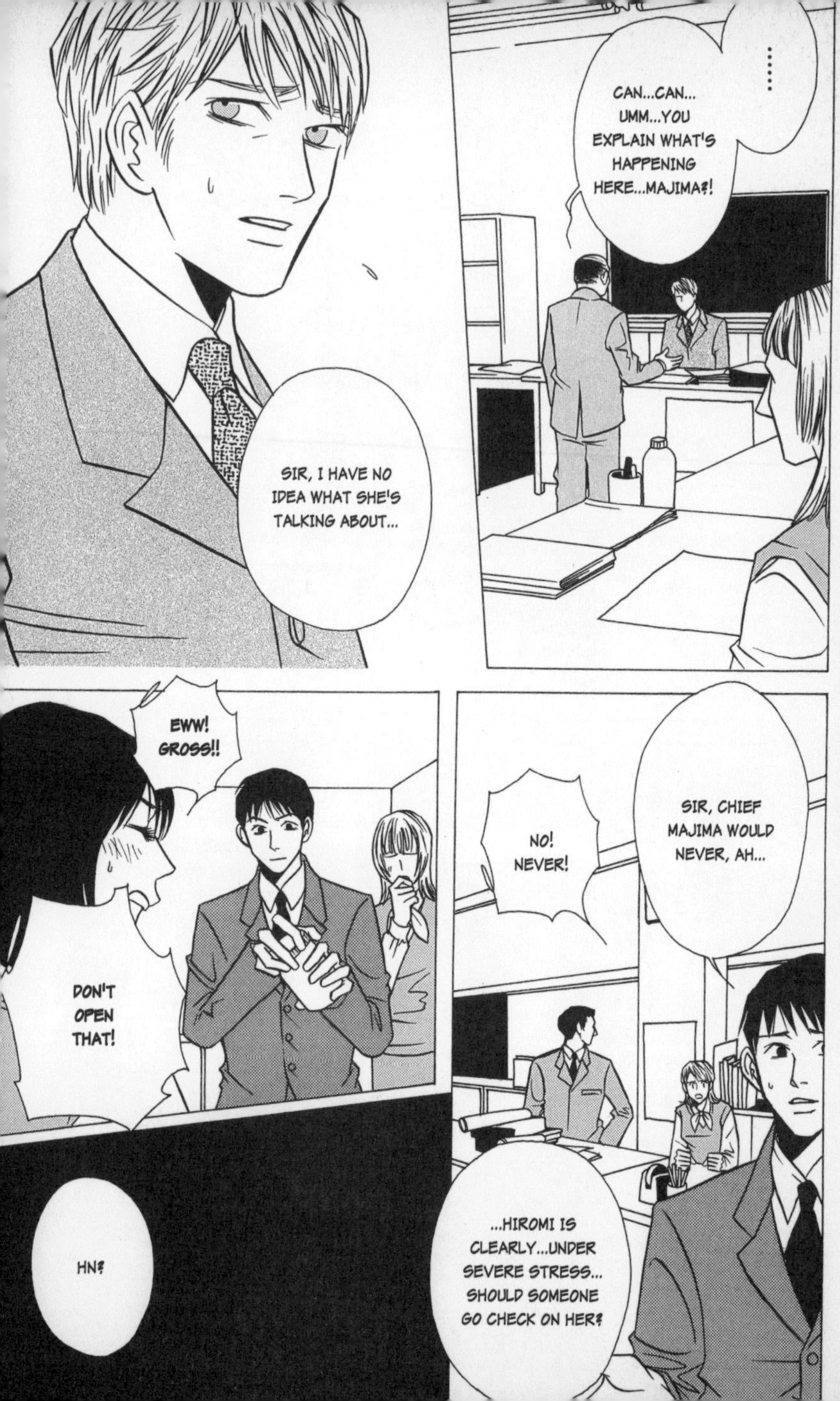
......
CAN...CAN... UMM...YOU EXPLAIN WHAT'S HAPPENING HERE...MAJIMA?!
SIR, I HAVE NO IDEA WHAT SHE'S TALKING ABOUT...
SIR, CHIEF MAJIMA WOULD NEVER, AH...
NO! NEVER!
...HIROMI IS CLEARLY...UNDER SEVERE STRESS... SHOULD SOMEONE GO CHECK ON HER?
EWW! GROSS!!
DON'T OPEN THAT!
HN?

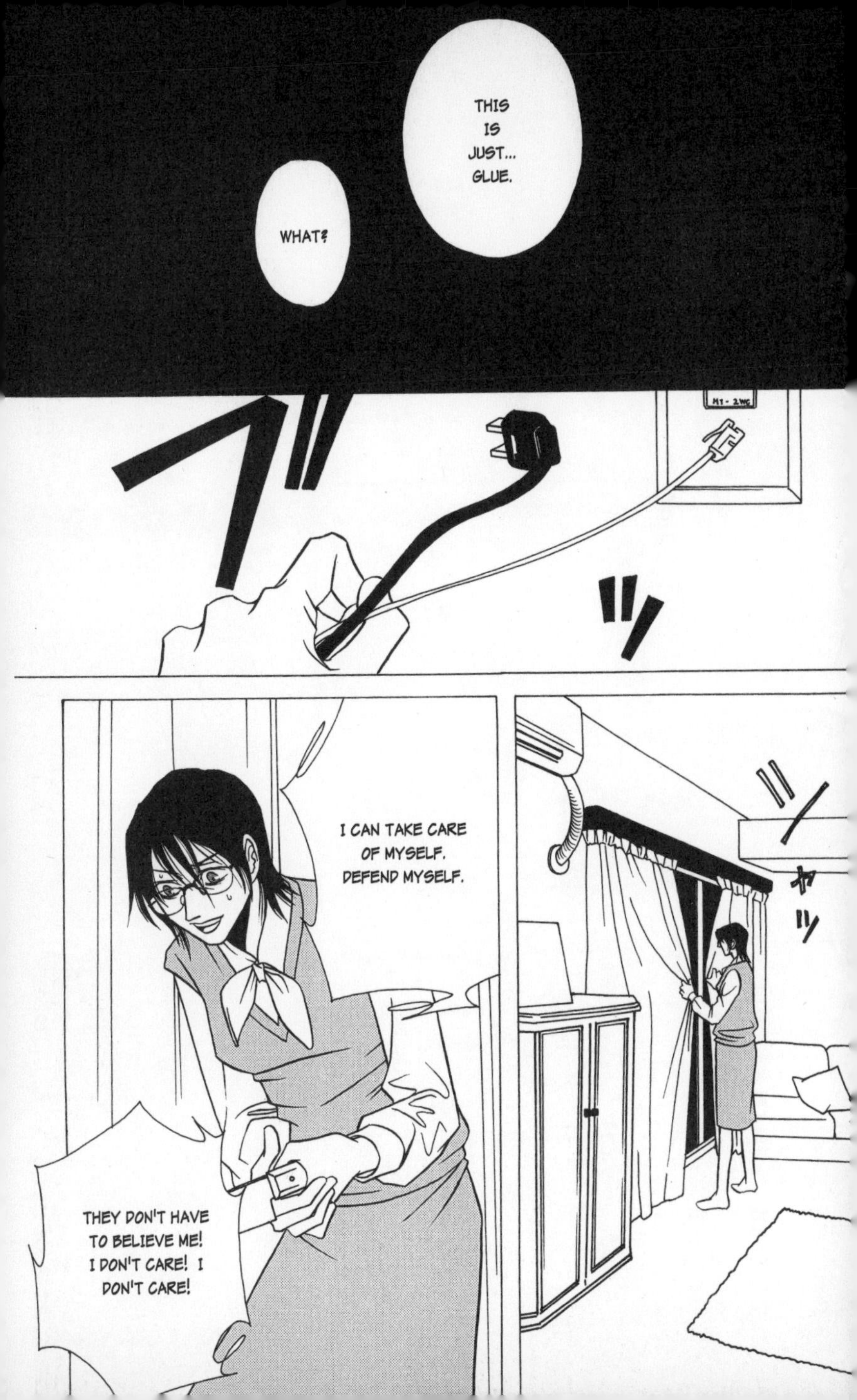
THIS IS JUST... GLUE.
WHAT?
I CAN TAKE CARE OF MYSELF. DEFEND MYSELF.
THEY DON'T HAVE TO BELIEVE ME! I DON'T CARE! I DON'T CARE!

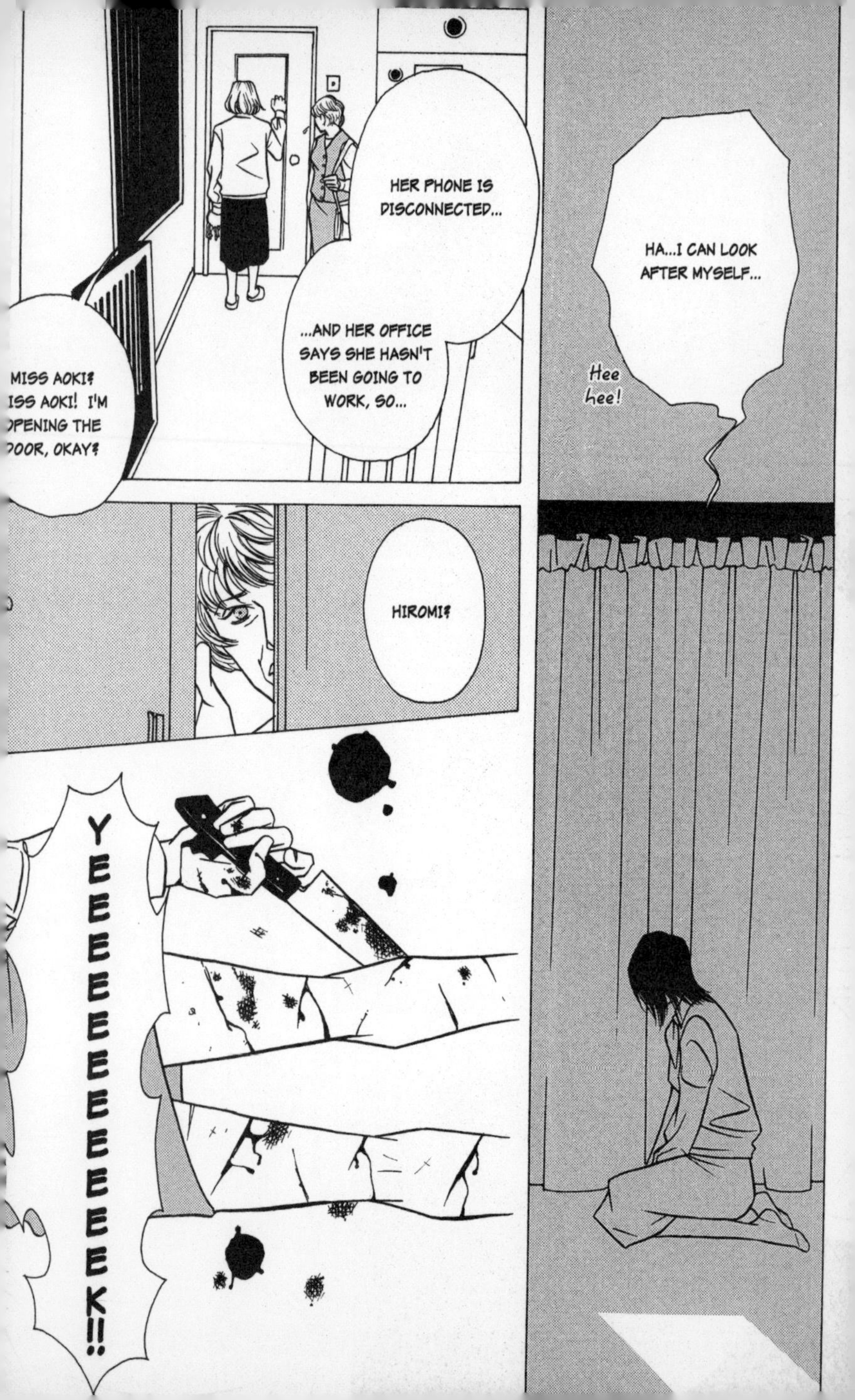
HA...I CAN LOOK AFTER MYSELF...
Hee hee!
HER PHONE IS DISCONNECTED...
...AND HER OFFICE SAYS SHE HASN'T BEEN GOING TO WORK, SO...
MISS AOKI?
ISS AOKI! I'M
PENING THE
OOR, OKAY?
HIROMI?
YEEEEEEEEEEEEEEK!!

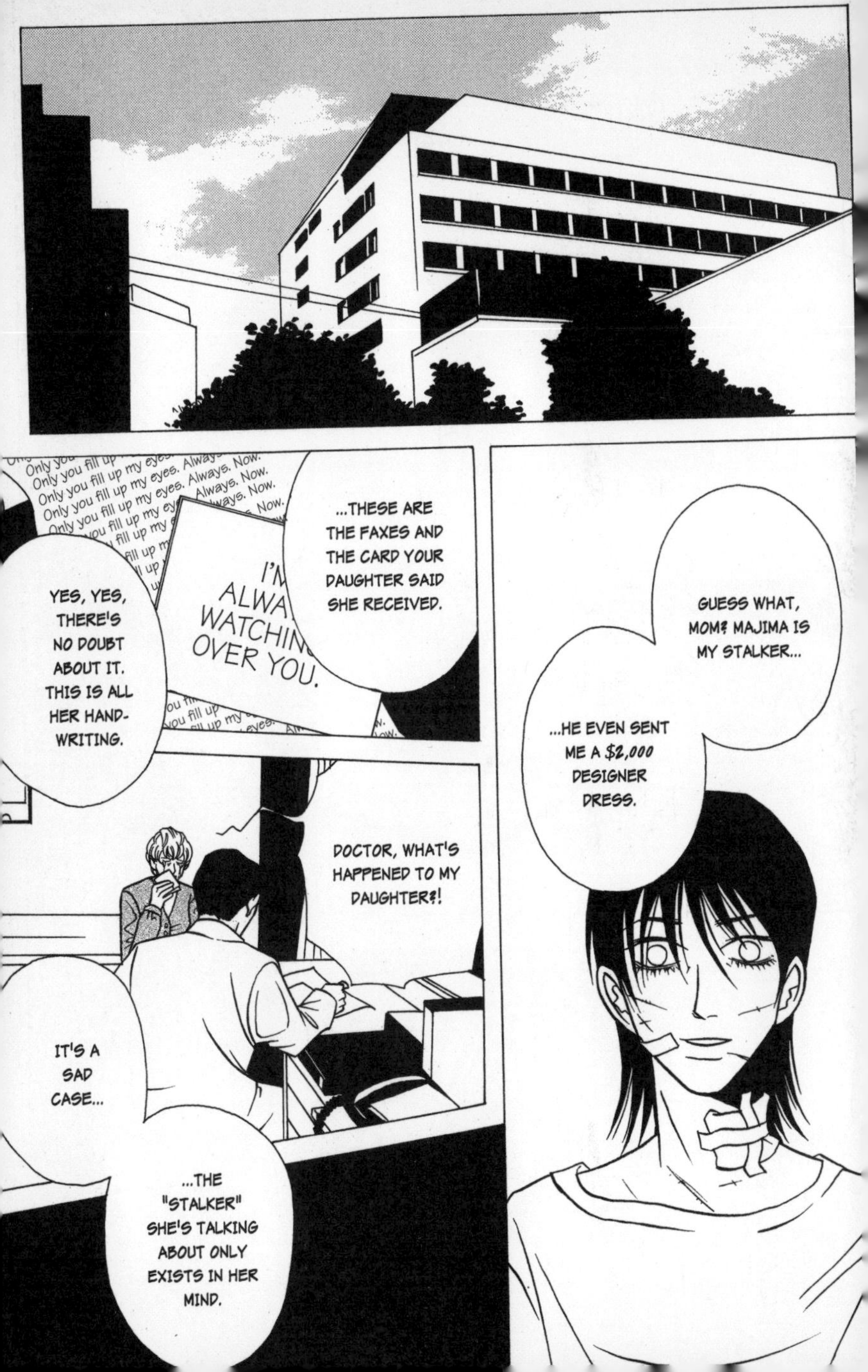
GUESS WHAT, MOM? MAJIMA IS MY STALKER...
...HE EVEN SENT ME A $2,000 DESIGNER DRESS.
Only you fill up my eyes. Always. Now.
Only you fill up my eyes. Always. Now.
Only you fill up my eyes. Always. Now.
...THESE ARE THE FAXES AND THE CARD YOUR DAUGHTER SAID SHE RECEIVED.
OVER YOU.
YES, YES, THERE'S NO DOUBT ABOUT IT. THIS IS ALL HER HAND-WRITING.
DOCTOR, WHAT'S HAPPENED TO MY DAUGHTER?!
IT'S A SAD CASE...
...THE "STALKER" SHE'S TALKING ABOUT ONLY EXISTS IN HER MIND.

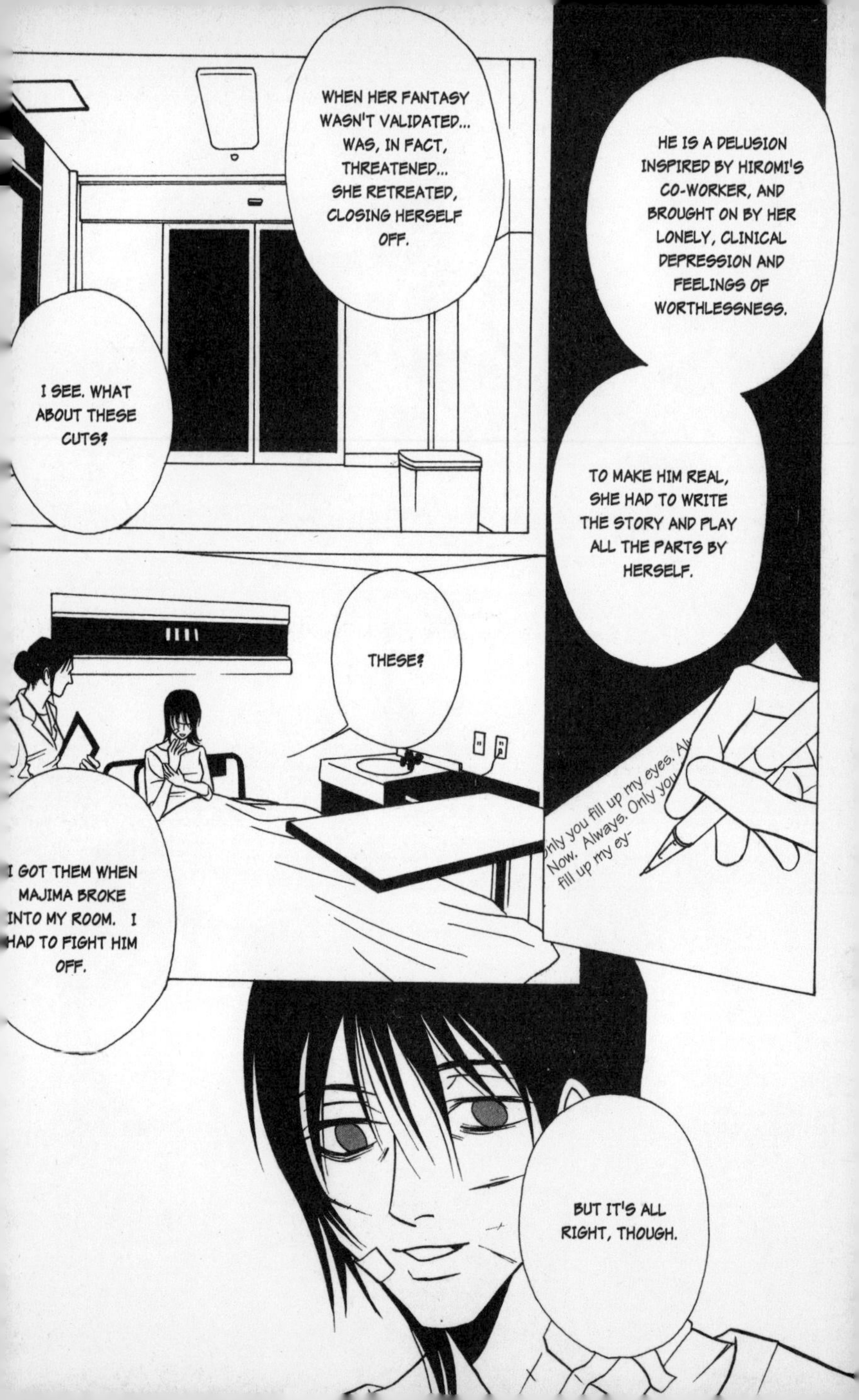

HE IS A DELUSION INSPIRED BY HIROMI'S CO-WORKER, AND BROUGHT ON BY HER LONELY, CLINICAL DEPRESSION AND FEELINGS OF WORTHLESSNESS.
TO MAKE HIM REAL, SHE HAD TO WRITE THE STORY AND PLAY ALL THE PARTS BY HERSELF.
nly you fill up my eyes. Al
Now. Always. Only you
fill up my ey-
WHEN HER FANTASY WASN'T VALIDATED... WAS, IN FACT, THREATENED... SHE RETREATED, CLOSING HERSELF OFF.
I SEE. WHAT ABOUT THESE CUTS?
THESE?
I GOT THEM WHEN MAJIMA BROKE INTO MY ROOM. I HAD TO FIGHT HIM OFF.
BUT IT'S ALL RIGHT, THOUGH.

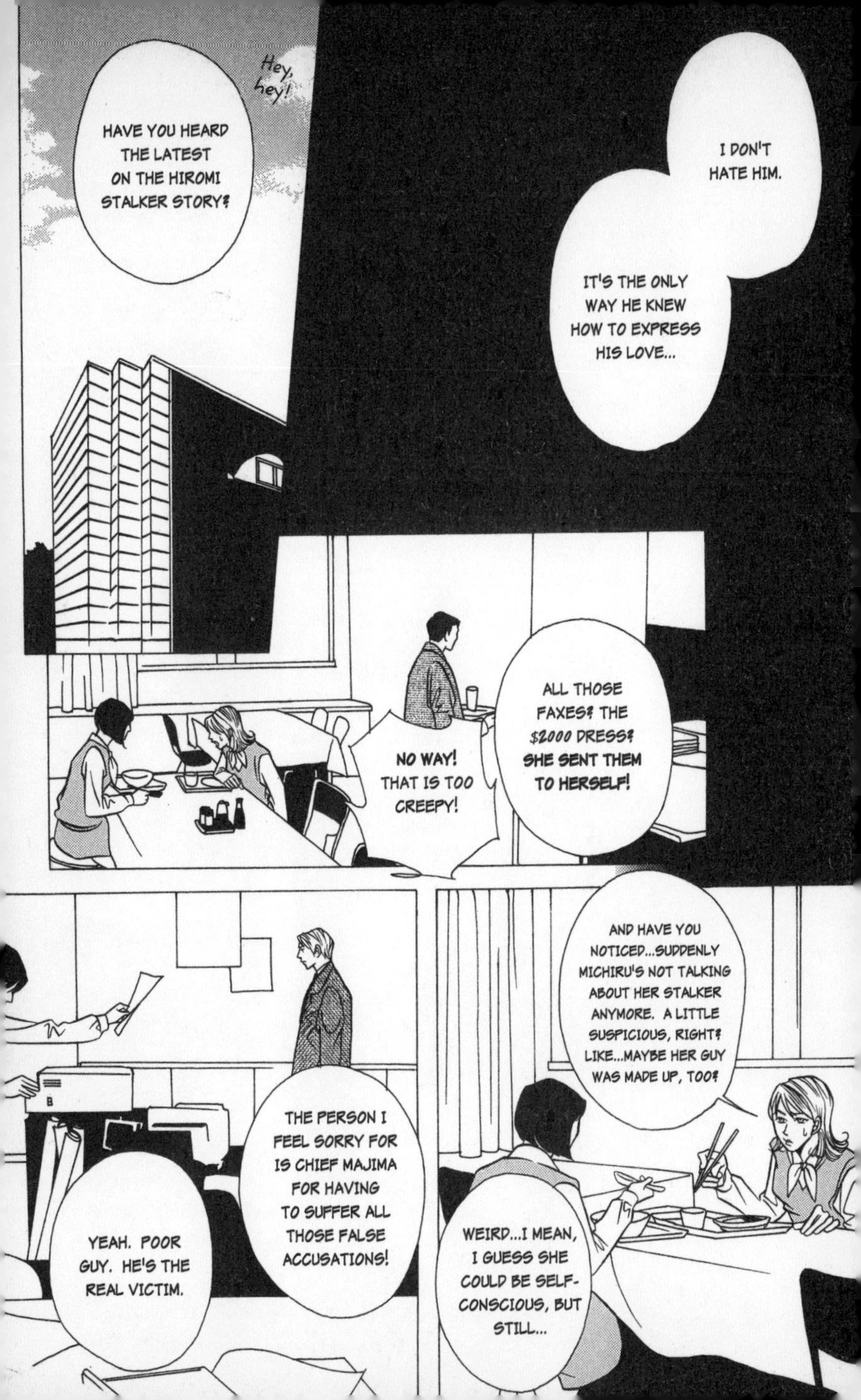
I DON'T HATE HIM.
IT'S THE ONLY WAY HE KNEW HOW TO EXPRESS HIS LOVE...
Hey, hey!
HAVE YOU HEARD THE LATEST ON THE HIROMI STALKER STORY?
ALL THOSE FAXES? THE $2000 DRESS? SHE SENT THEM TO HERSELF!
NO WAY! THAT IS TOO CREEPY!
AND HAVE YOU NOTICED...SUDDENLY MICHIRU'S NOT TALKING ABOUT HER STALKER ANYMORE. A LITTLE SUSPICIOUS, RIGHT? LIKE...MAYBE HER GUY WAS MADE UP, TOO?
WEIRD...I MEAN, I GUESS SHE COULD BE SELF-CONSCIOUS, BUT STILL...
THE PERSON I FEEL SORRY FOR IS CHIEF MAJIMA FOR HAVING TO SUFFER ALL THOSE FALSE ACCUSATIONS!
YEAH. POOR GUY. HE'S THE REAL VICTIM.

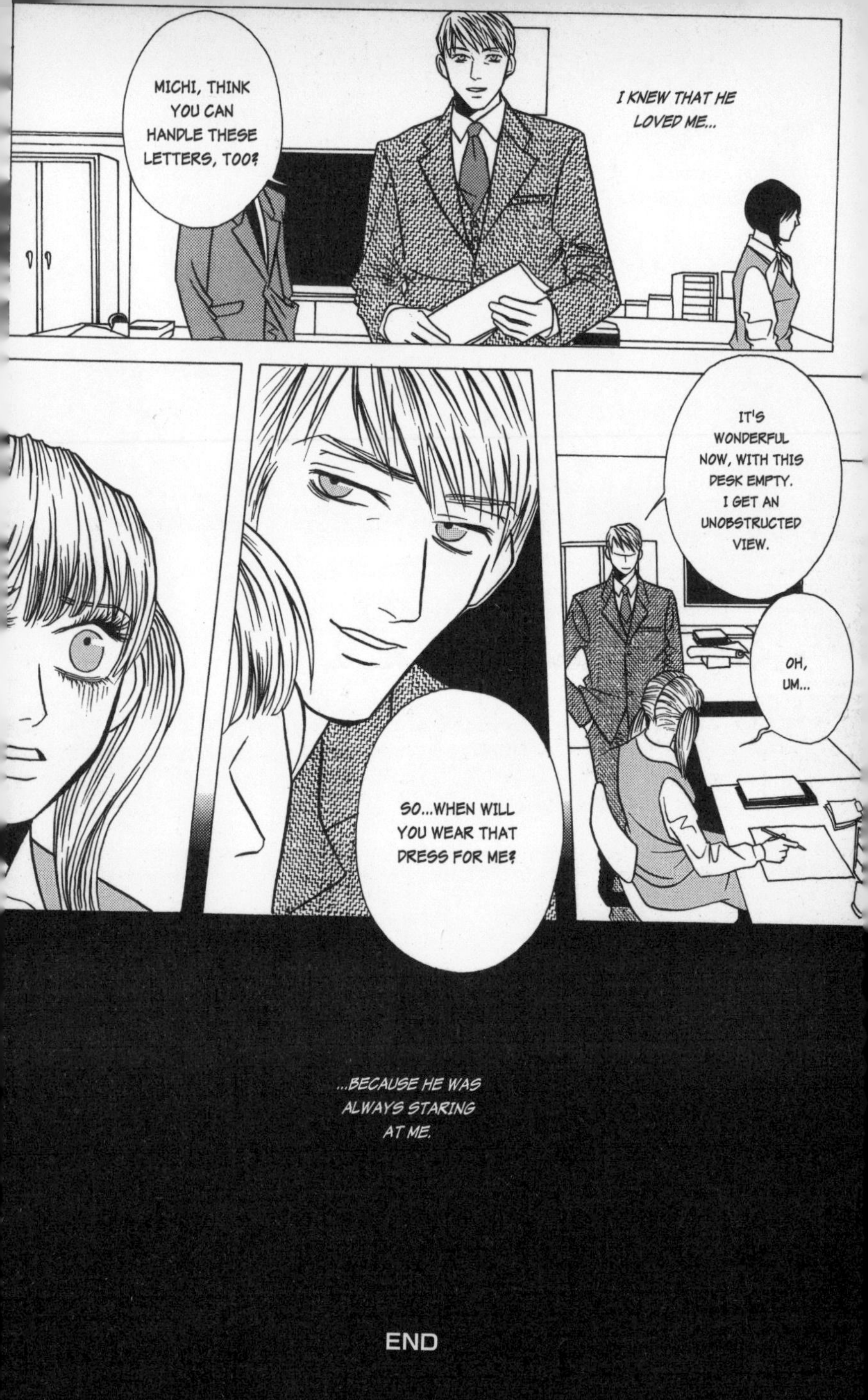
I KNEW THAT HE LOVED ME...
MICHI, THINK YOU CAN HANDLE THESE LETTERS, TOO?
IT'S WONDERFUL NOW, WITH THIS DESK EMPTY. I GET AN UNOBSTRUCTED VIEW.
OH, UM...
SO...WHEN WILL YOU WEAR THAT DRESS FOR ME?
...BECAUSE HE WAS ALWAYS STARING AT ME.
END

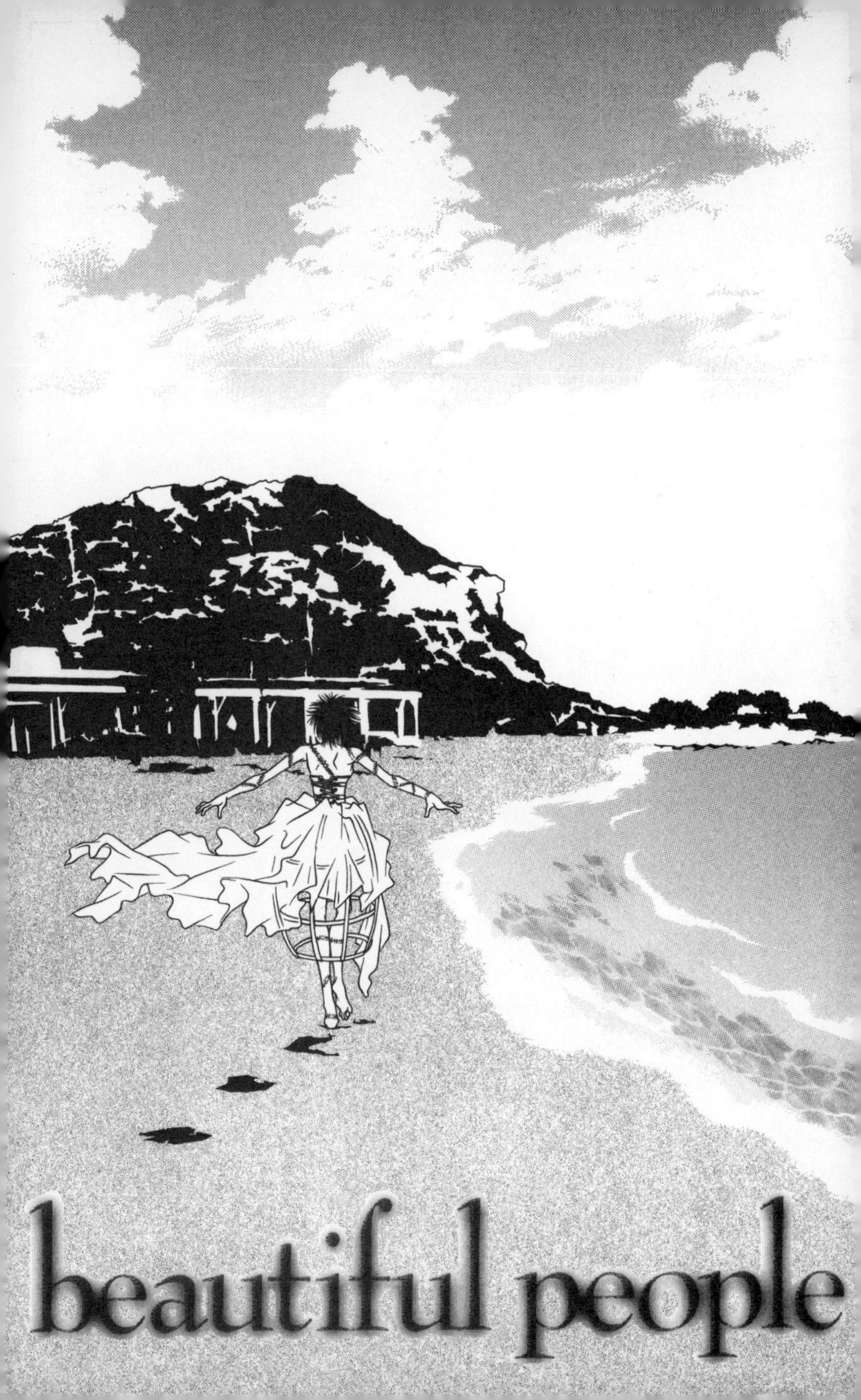
beautiful people

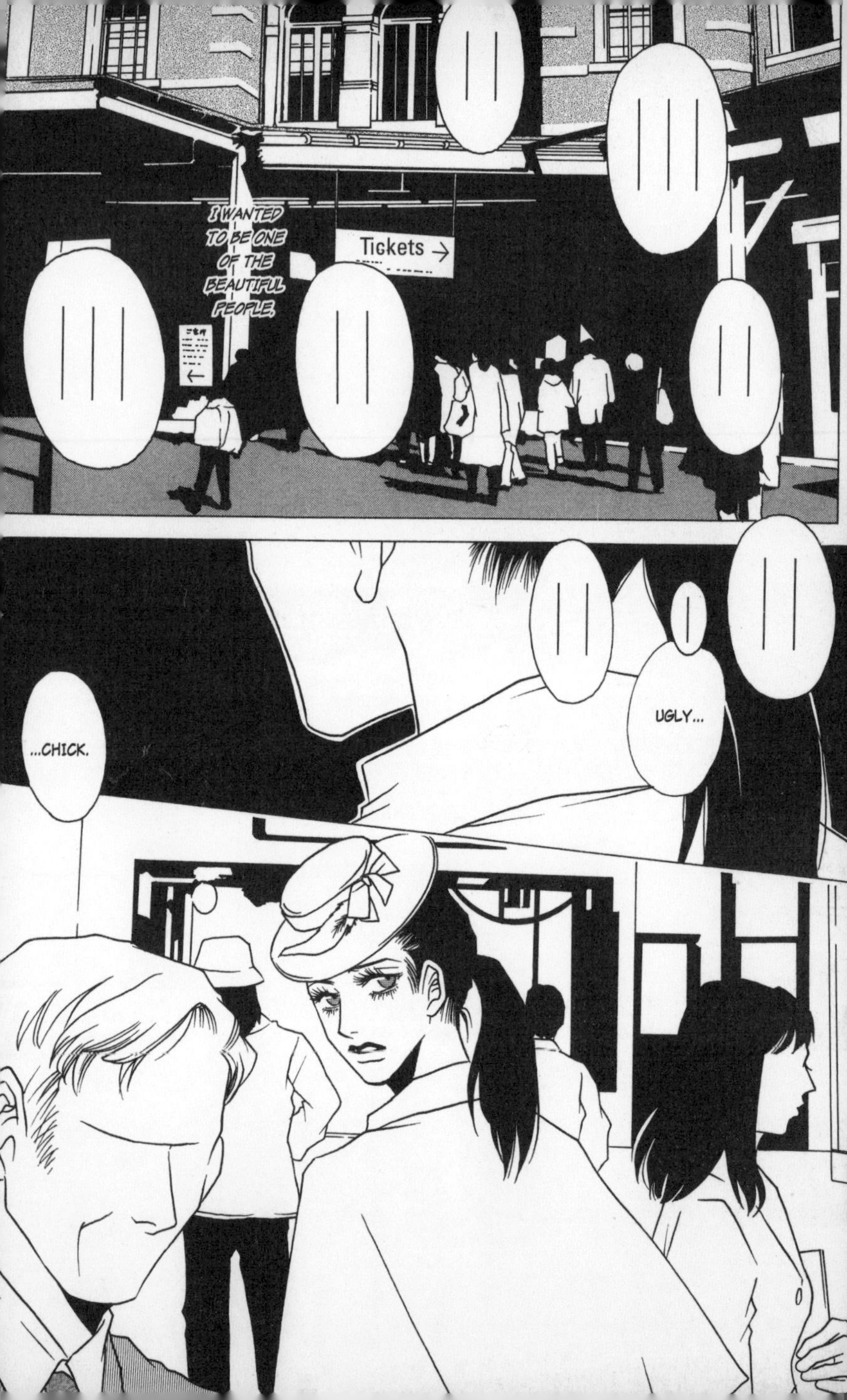
I WANTED TO BE ONE OF THE BEAUTIFUL PEOPLE.
Tickets →
UGLY...
...CHICK.

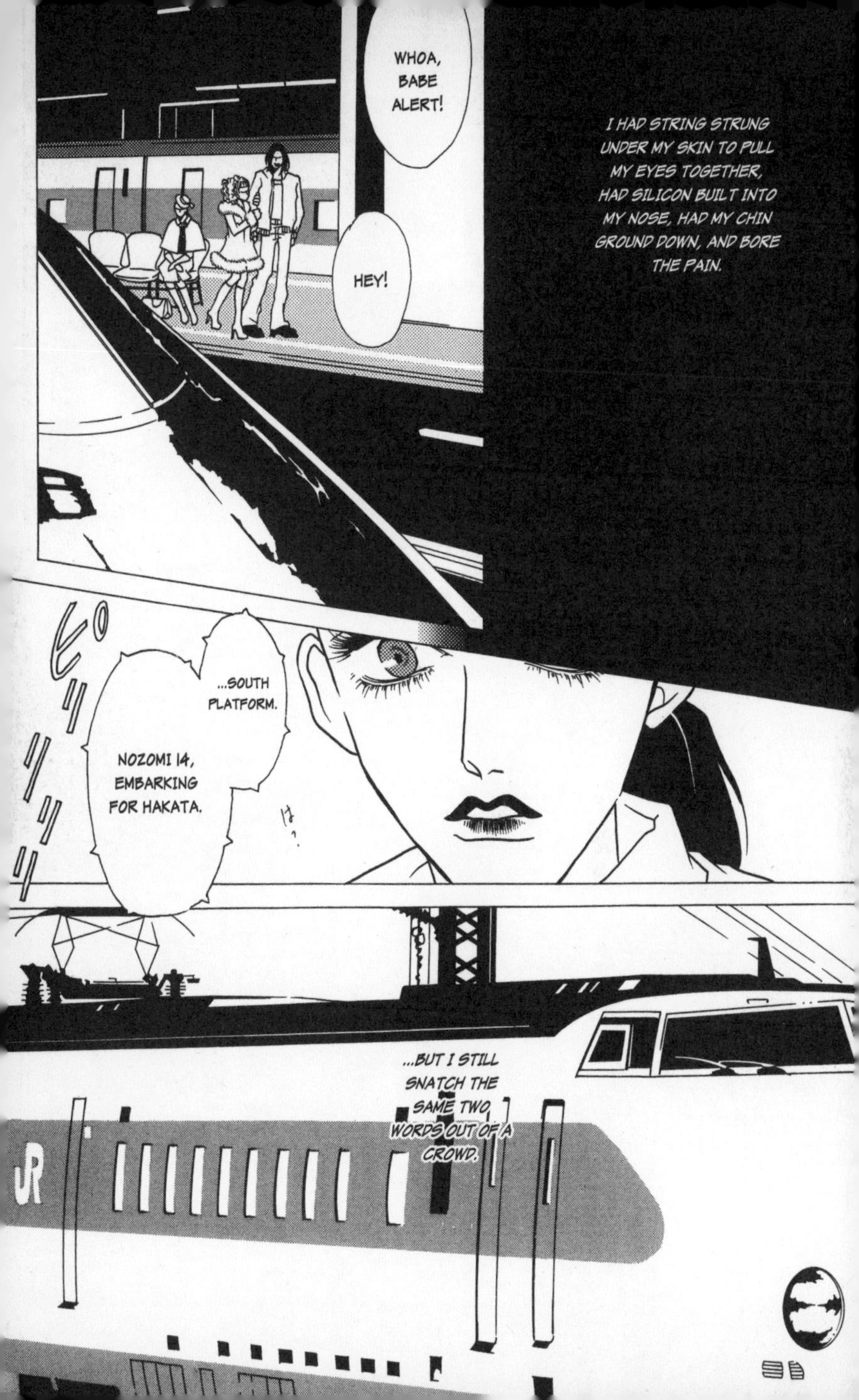
I HAD STRING STRUNG UNDER MY SKIN TO PULL MY EYES TOGETHER, HAD SILICON BUILT INTO MY NOSE, HAD MY CHIN GROUND DOWN, AND BORE THE PAIN.
WHOA, BABE ALERT!
HEY!
...SOUTH PLATFORM.
NOZOMI 14, EMBARKING FOR HAKATA.
は?
...BUT I STILL SNATCH THE SAME TWO WORDS OUT OF A CROWD.

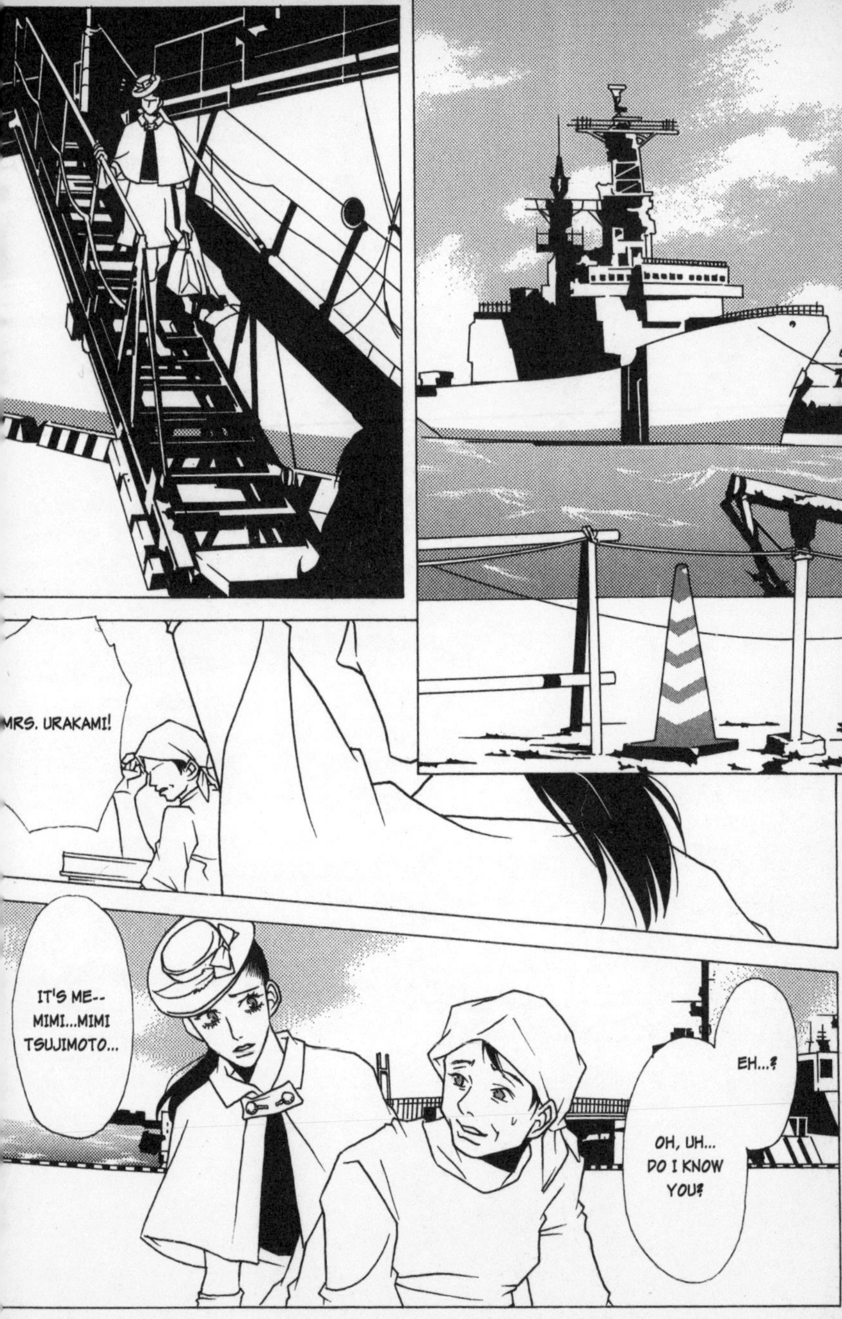
MRS. URAKAMI!
IT'S ME-- MIMI...MIMI TSUJIMOTO...
EH...?
OH, UH... DO I KNOW YOU?

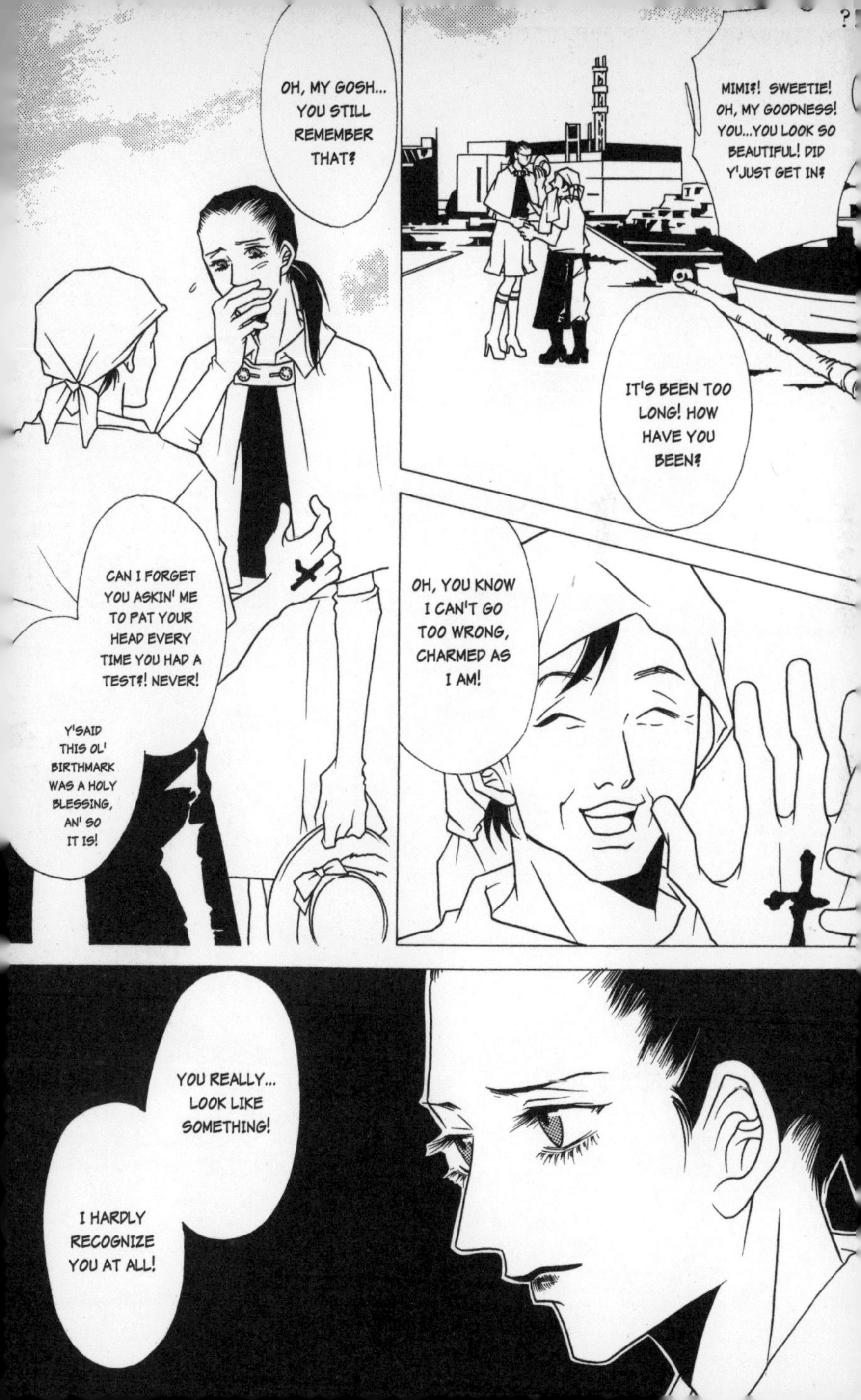
MIMI?! SWEETIE! OH, MY GOODNESS! YOU...YOU LOOK SO BEAUTIFUL! DID Y'JUST GET IN?
IT'S BEEN TOO LONG! HOW HAVE YOU BEEN?
OH, YOU KNOW I CAN'T GO TOO WRONG, CHARMED AS I AM!
OH, MY GOSH... YOU STILL REMEMBER THAT?
CAN I FORGET YOU ASKIN' ME TO PAT YOUR HEAD EVERY TIME YOU HAD A TEST?! NEVER!
Y'SAID THIS OL' BIRTHMARK WAS A HOLY BLESSING, AN' SO IT IS!
YOU REALLY... LOOK LIKE SOMETHING!
I HARDLY RECOGNIZE YOU AT ALL!

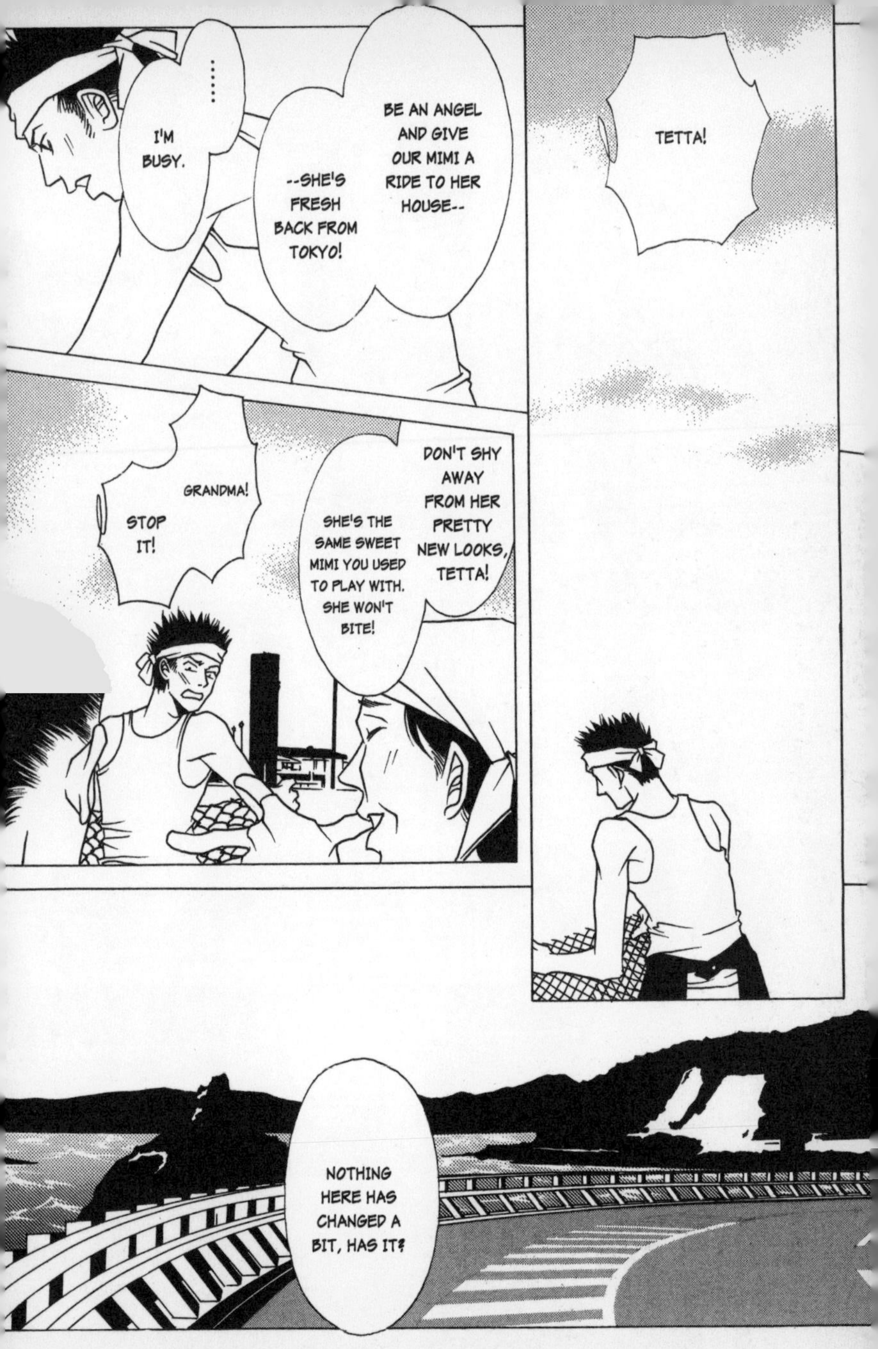
TETTA!
BE AN ANGEL AND GIVE OUR MIMI A RIDE TO HER HOUSE--
--SHE'S FRESH BACK FROM TOKYO!
......
I'M BUSY.
DON'T SHY AWAY FROM HER PRETTY NEW LOOKS, TETTA!
SHE'S THE SAME SWEET MIMI YOU USED TO PLAY WITH. SHE WON'T BITE!
GRANDMA!
STOP IT!
NOTHING HERE HAS CHANGED A BIT, HAS IT?

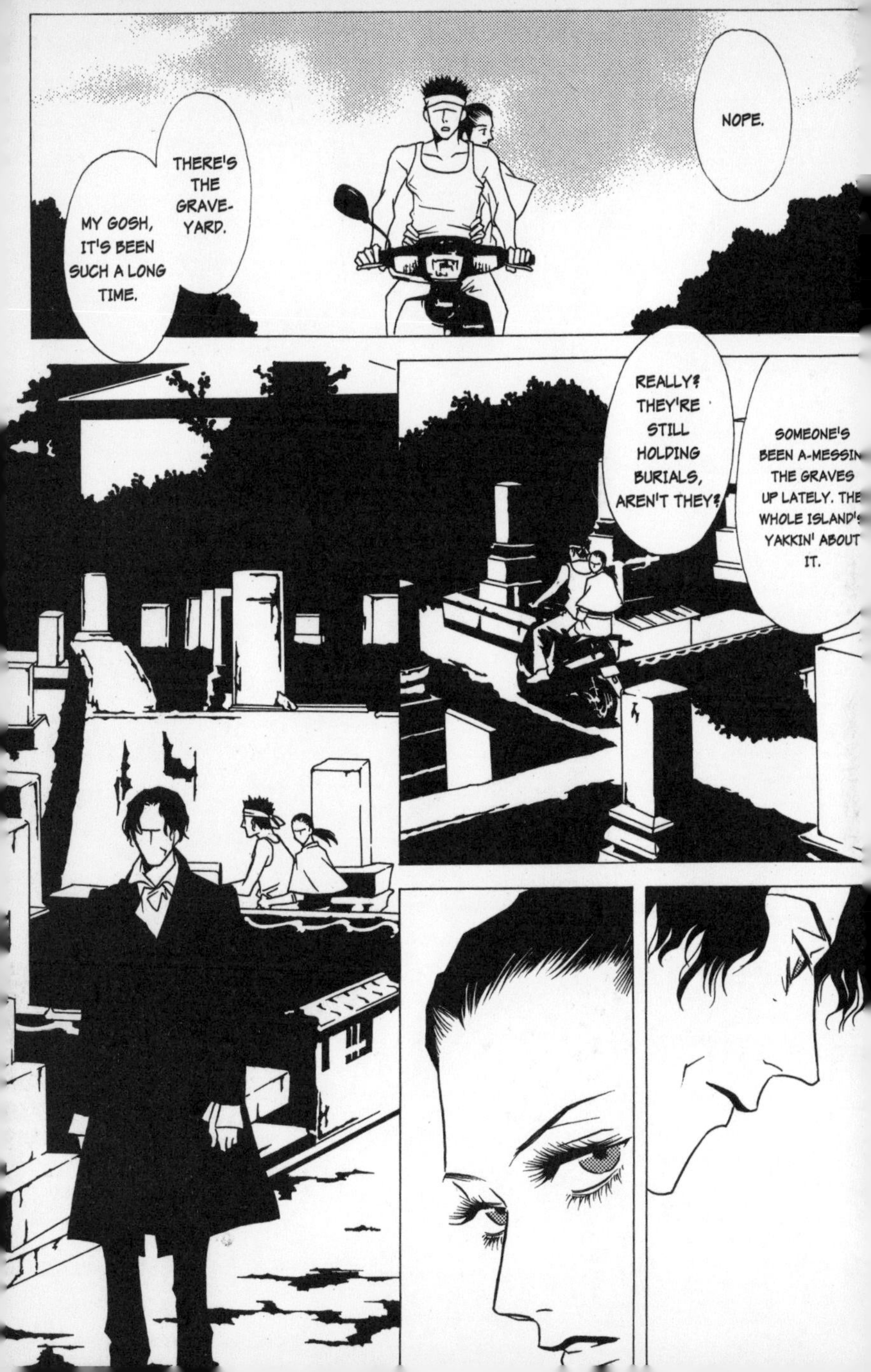
NOPE.
THERE'S THE GRAVE-YARD.
MY GOSH, IT'S BEEN SUCH A LONG TIME.
SOMEONE'S BEEN A-MESSIN THE GRAVES UP LATELY. THE WHOLE ISLAND'S YAKKIN' ABOUT IT.
REALLY? THEY'RE STILL HOLDING BURIALS, AREN'T THEY?

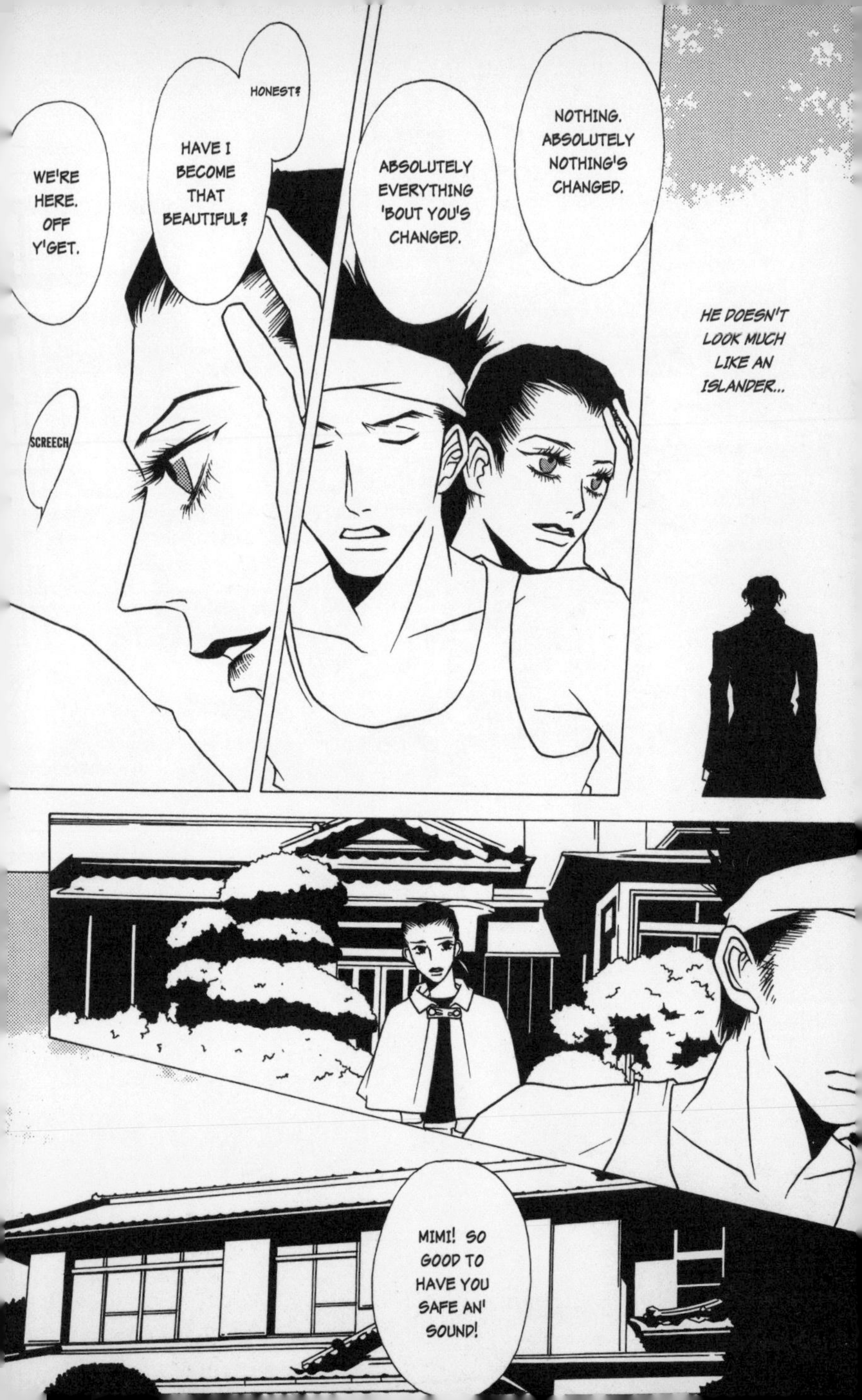
HE DOESN'T LOOK MUCH LIKE AN ISLANDER...
NOTHING. ABSOLUTELY NOTHING'S CHANGED.
ABSOLUTELY EVERYTHING 'BOUT YOU'S CHANGED.
HONEST?
HAVE I BECOME THAT BEAUTIFUL?
WE'RE HERE. OFF Y'GET.
SCREECH
MIMI! SO GOOD TO HAVE YOU SAFE AN' SOUND!

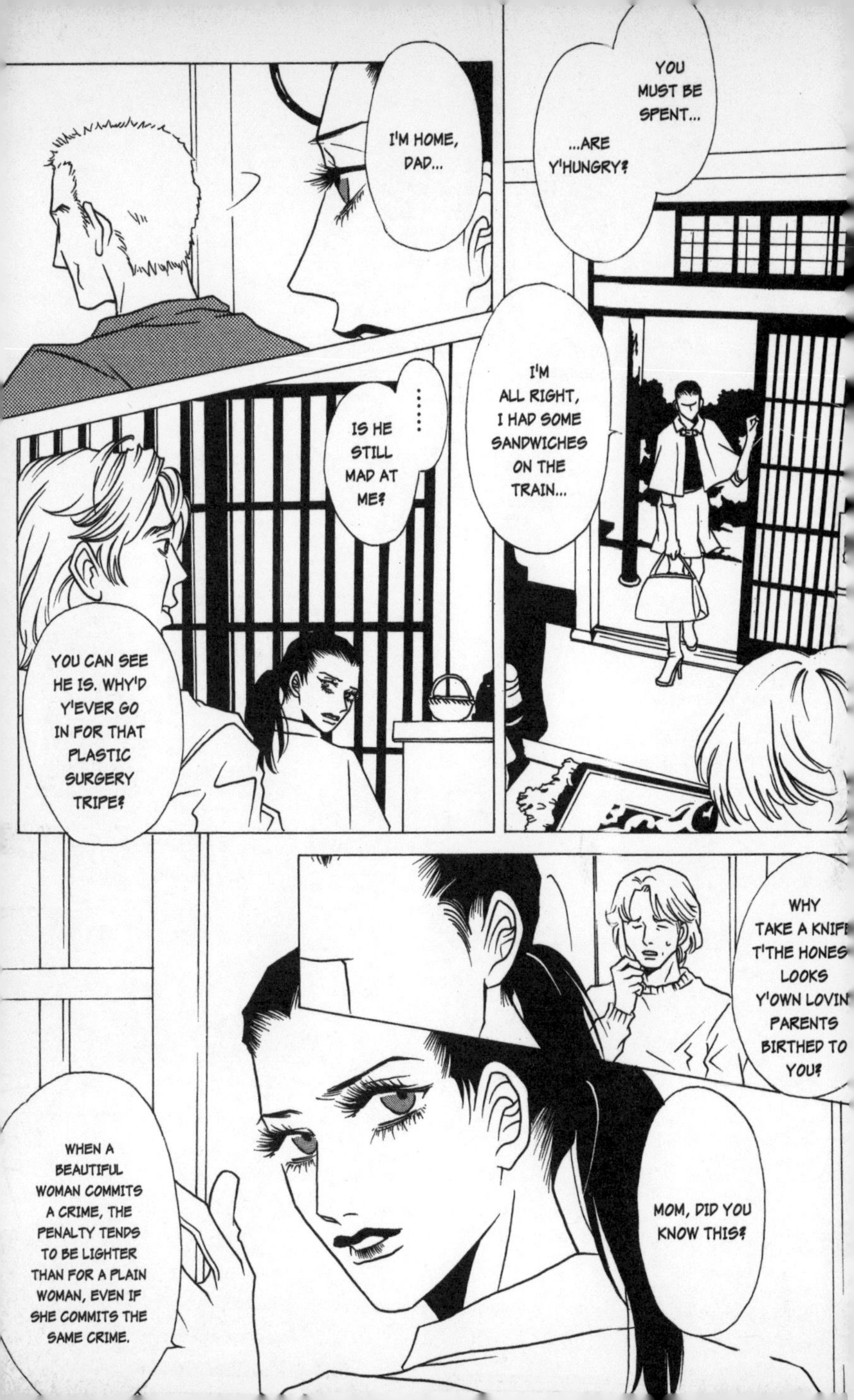

YOU MUST BE SPENT...
...ARE Y'HUNGRY?
I'M ALL RIGHT, I HAD SOME SANDWICHES ON THE TRAIN...
I'M HOME, DAD...
......
IS HE STILL MAD AT ME?
YOU CAN SEE HE IS. WHY'D Y'EVER GO IN FOR THAT PLASTIC SURGERY TRIPE?
WHY TAKE A KNIF T'THE HONES LOOKS Y'OWN LOVIN PARENTS BIRTHED TO YOU?
MOM, DID YOU KNOW THIS?
WHEN A BEAUTIFUL WOMAN COMMITS A CRIME, THE PENALTY TENDS TO BE LIGHTER THAN FOR A PLAIN WOMAN, EVEN IF SHE COMMITS THE SAME CRIME.

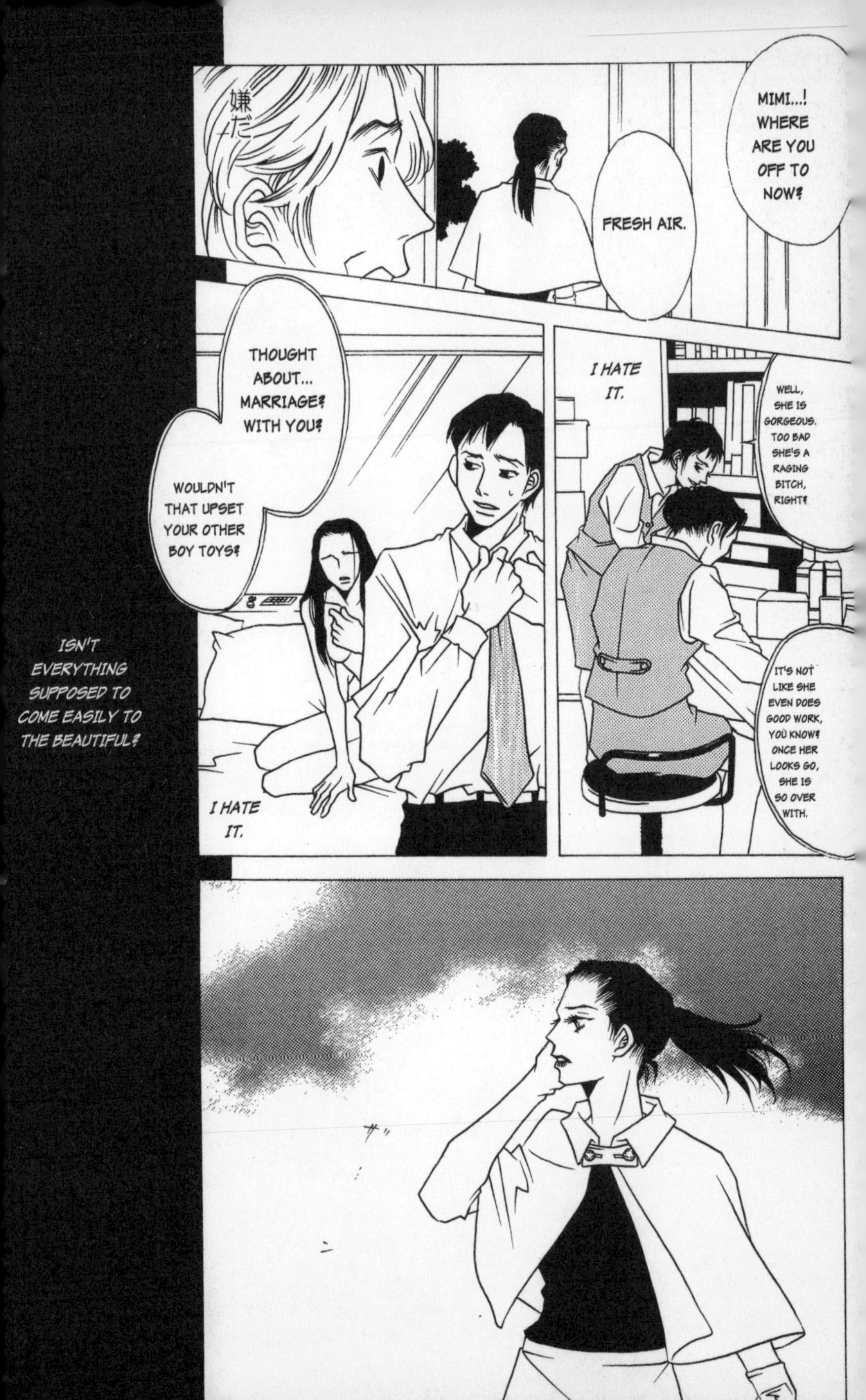
MIMI...! WHERE ARE YOU OFF TO NOW?
FRESH AIR.
嫌だ
WELL, SHE IS GORGEOUS. TOO BAD SHE'S A RAGING BITCH, RIGHT?
I HATE IT.
IT'S NOT LIKE SHE EVEN DOES GOOD WORK, YOU KNOW? ONCE HER LOOKS GO, SHE IS SO OVER WITH.
THOUGHT ABOUT... MARRIAGE? WITH YOU?
WOULDN'T THAT UPSET YOUR OTHER BOY TOYS?
I HATE IT.
ISN'T EVERYTHING SUPPOSED TO COME EASILY TO THE BEAUTIFUL?
ザ

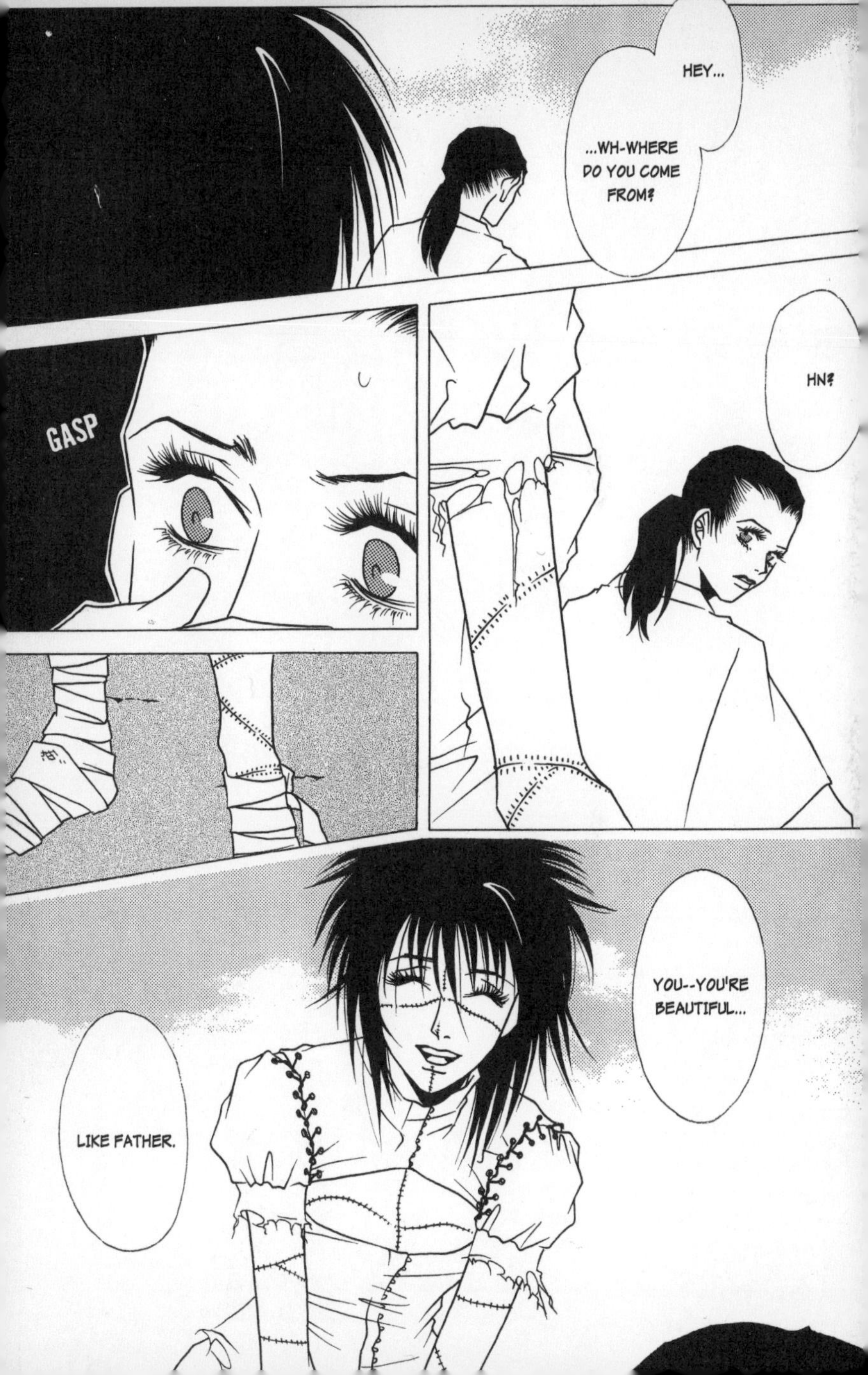
HEY...
...WH-WHERE DO YOU COME FROM?
HN?
GASP
YOU--YOU'RE BEAUTIFUL...
LIKE FATHER.

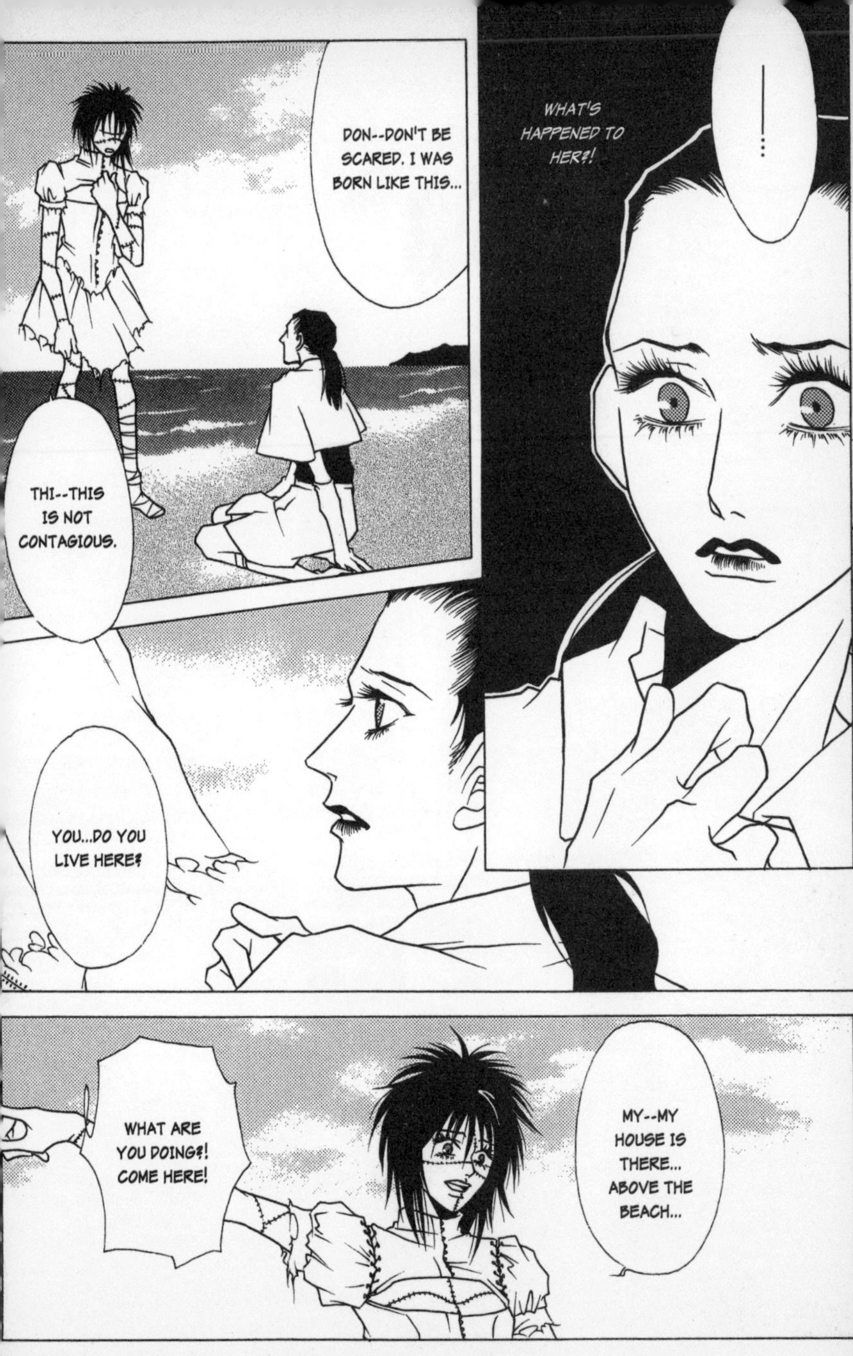
......
WHAT'S HAPPENED TO HER?!
DON--DON'T BE SCARED. I WAS BORN LIKE THIS...
THI--THIS IS NOT CONTAGIOUS.
YOU...DO YOU LIVE HERE?
MY--MY HOUSE IS THERE... ABOVE THE BEACH...
WHAT ARE YOU DOING?! COME HERE!

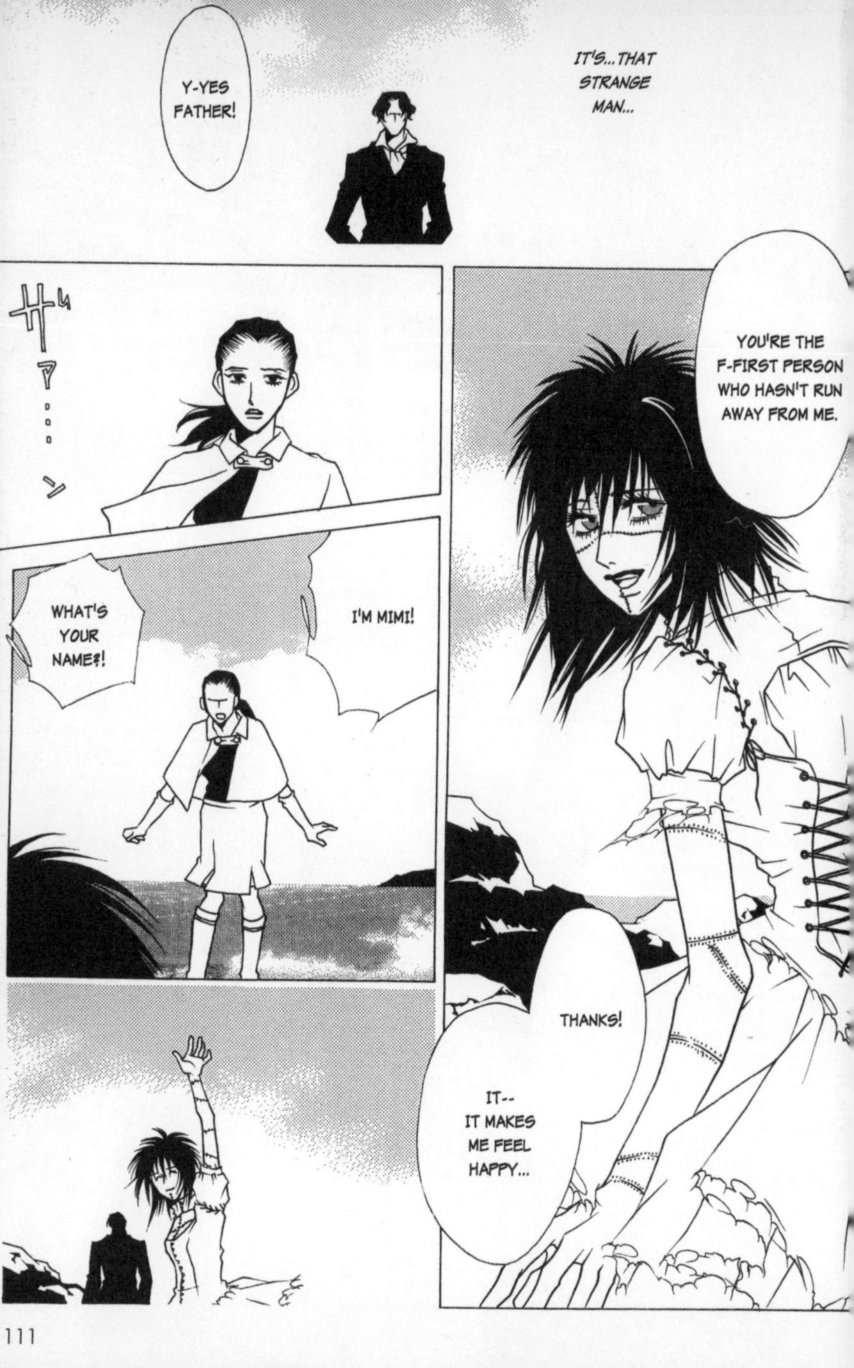
IT'S...THAT STRANGE MAN...
Y-YES FATHER!
YOU'RE THE F-FIRST PERSON WHO HASN'T RUN AWAY FROM ME.
THANKS!
IT-- IT MAKES ME FEEL HAPPY...
ザァ・・・ン
I'M MIMI!
WHAT'S YOUR NAME?!

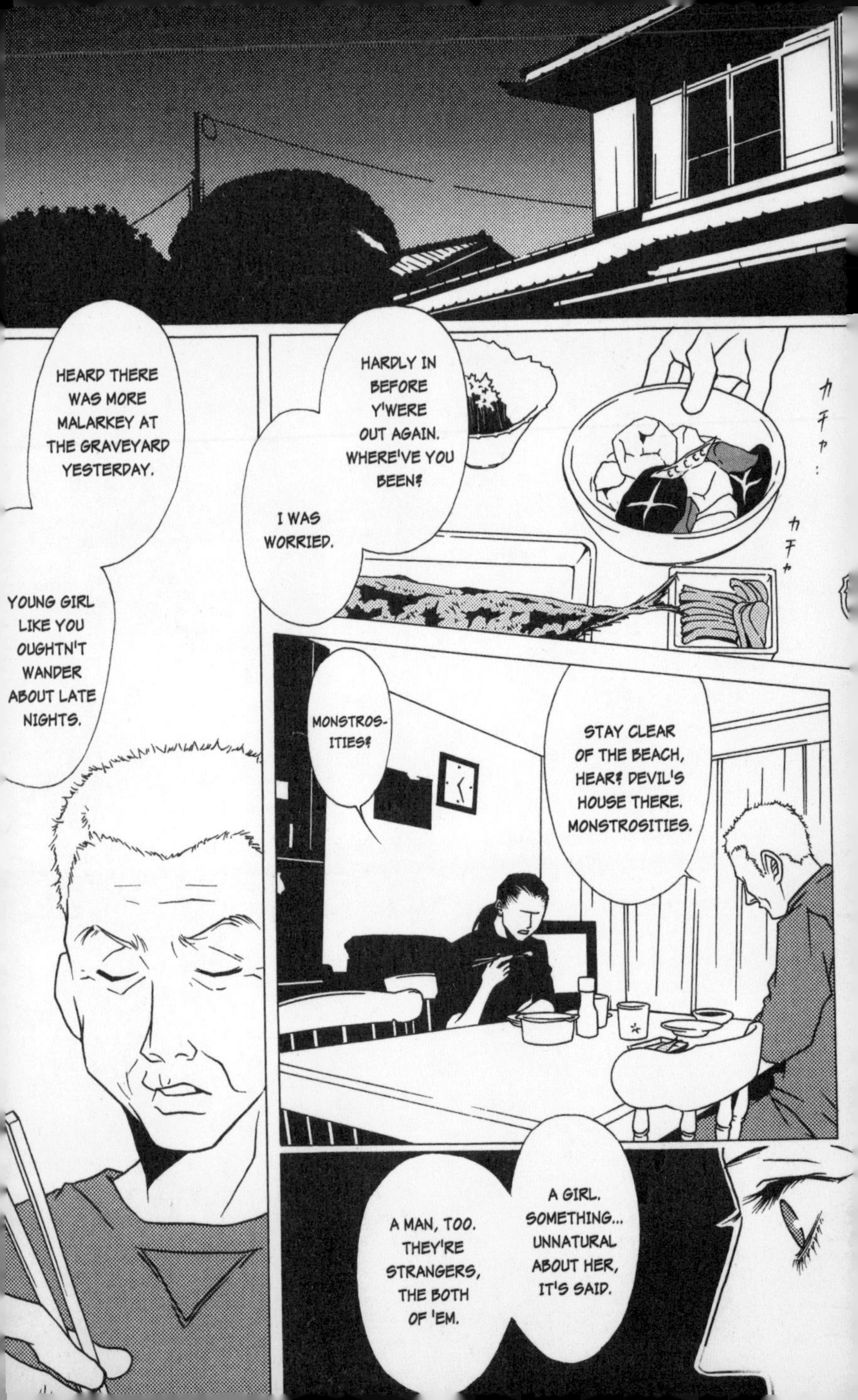
カチャ…
カチャ
HARDLY IN BEFORE Y'WERE OUT AGAIN. WHERE'VE YOU BEEN?
I WAS WORRIED.
HEARD THERE WAS MORE MALARKEY AT THE GRAVEYARD YESTERDAY.
YOUNG GIRL LIKE YOU OUGHTN'T WANDER ABOUT LATE NIGHTS.
STAY CLEAR OF THE BEACH, HEAR? DEVIL'S HOUSE THERE. MONSTROSITIES.
MONSTROS-ITIES?
A GIRL. SOMETHING... UNNATURAL ABOUT HER, IT'S SAID.
A MAN, TOO. THEY'RE STRANGERS, THE BOTH OF 'EM.

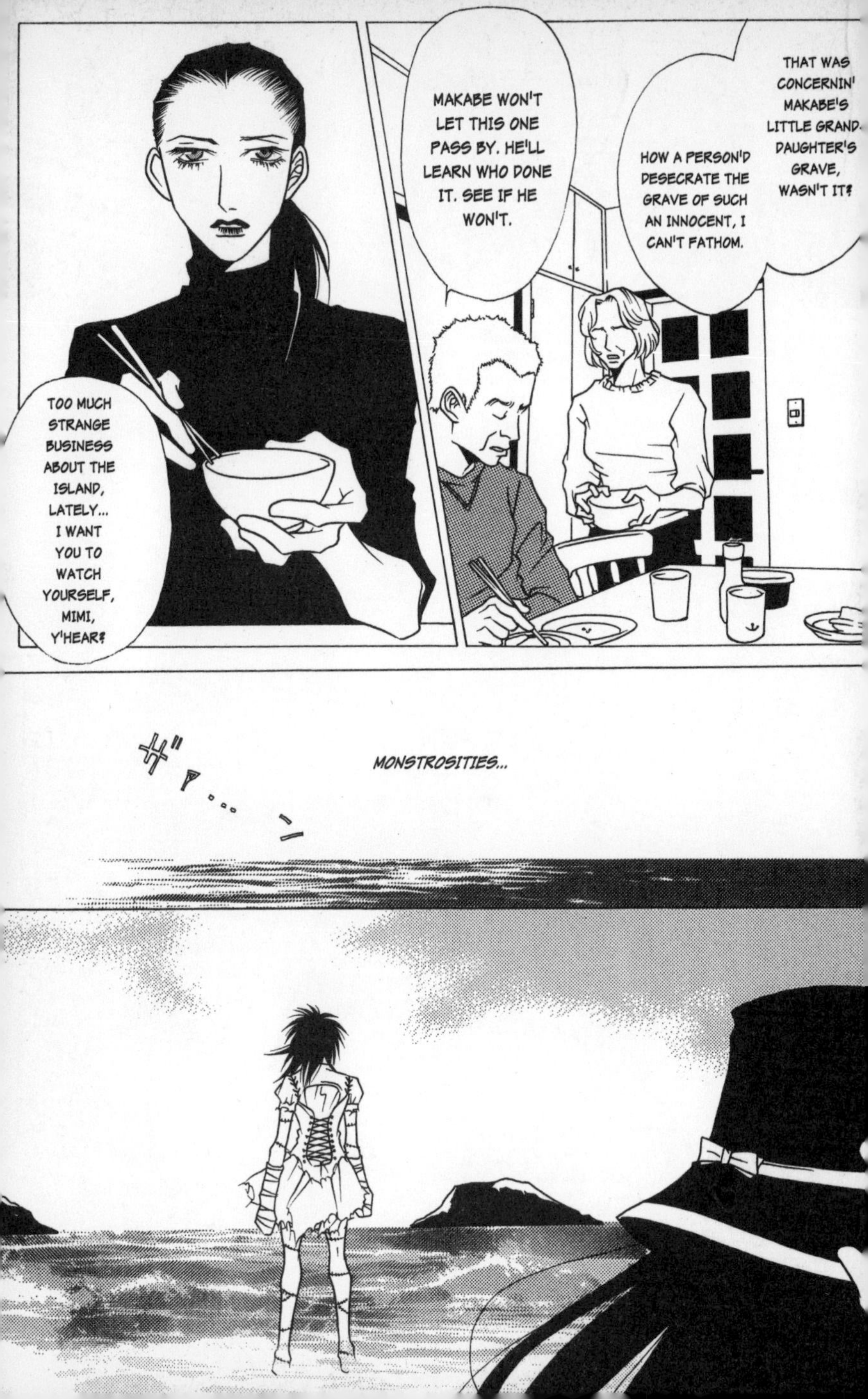
THAT WAS CONCERNIN' MAKABE'S LITTLE GRAND-DAUGHTER'S GRAVE, WASN'T IT?
HOW A PERSON'D DESECRATE THE GRAVE OF SUCH AN INNOCENT, I CAN'T FATHOM.
MAKABE WON'T LET THIS ONE PASS BY. HE'LL LEARN WHO DONE IT. SEE IF HE WON'T.
TOO MUCH STRANGE BUSINESS ABOUT THE ISLAND, LATELY... I WANT YOU TO WATCH YOURSELF, MIMI, Y'HEAR?
MONSTROSITIES...

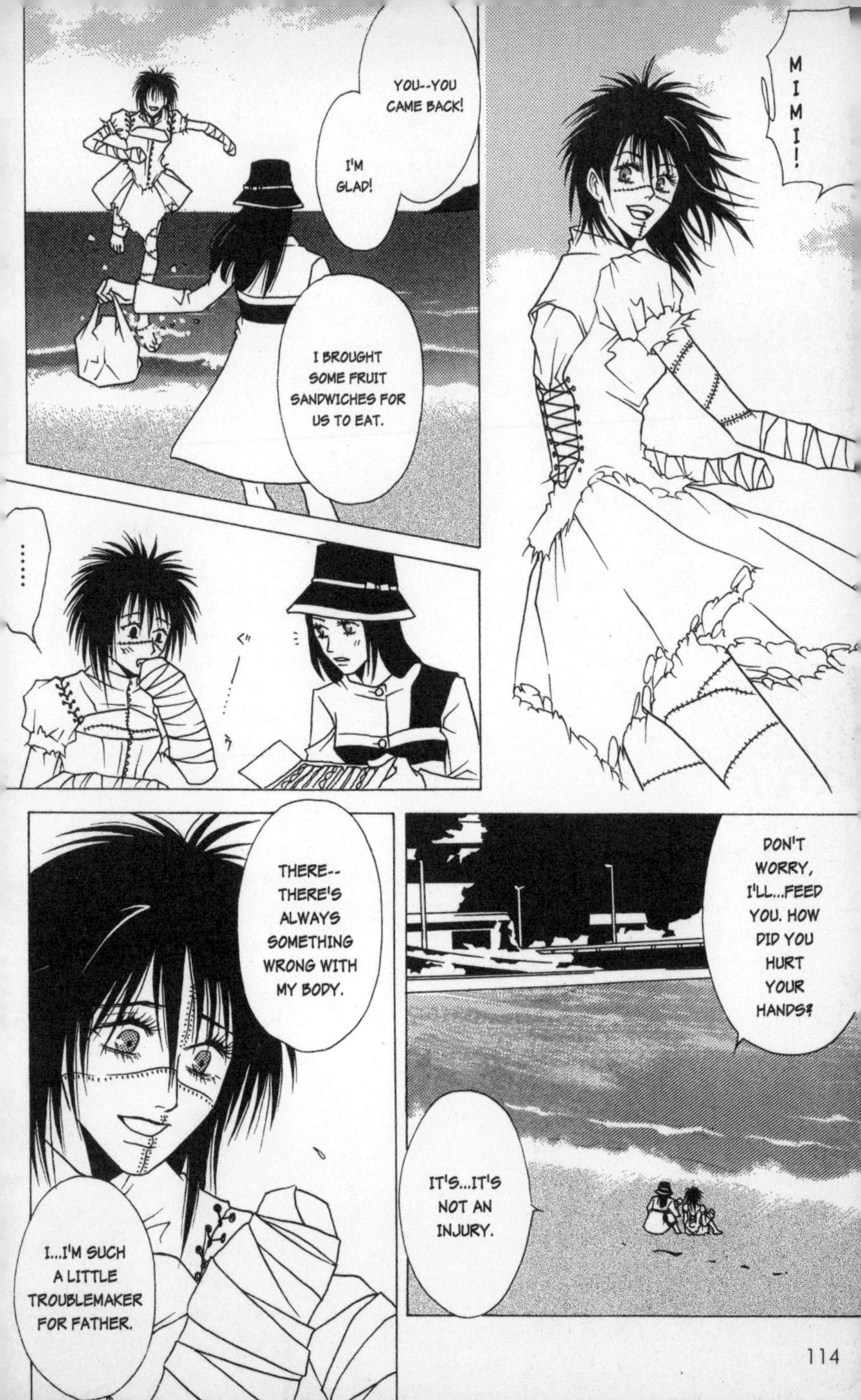
MIMI!
YOU--YOU CAME BACK!
I'M GLAD!
I BROUGHT SOME FRUIT SANDWICHES FOR US TO EAT.
......
DON'T WORRY, I'LL...FEED YOU. HOW DID YOU HURT YOUR HANDS?
IT'S...IT'S NOT AN INJURY.
THERE--THERE'S ALWAYS SOMETHING WRONG WITH MY BODY.
I...I'M SUCH A LITTLE TROUBLEMAKER FOR FATHER.

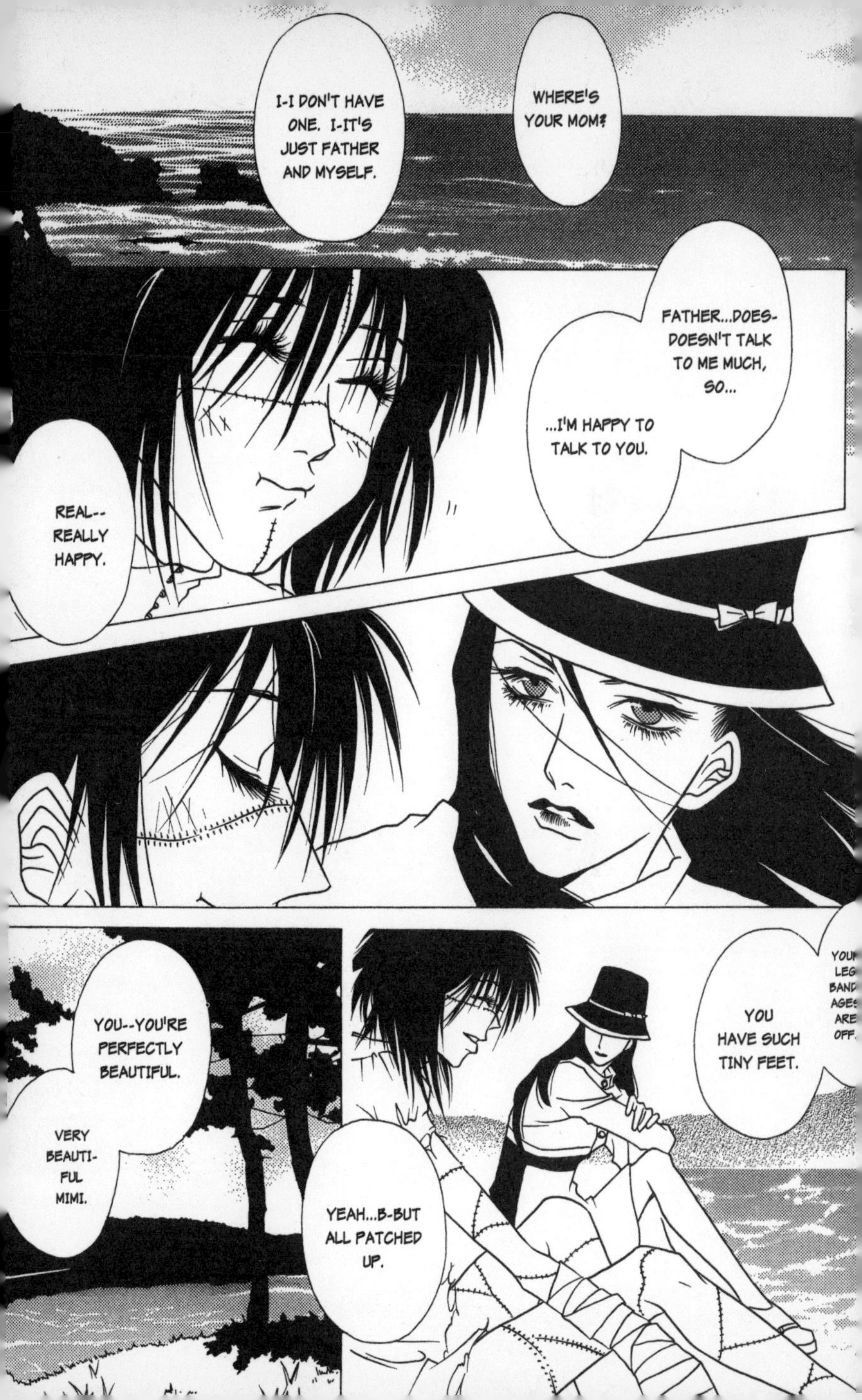
WHERE'S YOUR MOM?
I-I DON'T HAVE ONE. I-IT'S JUST FATHER AND MYSELF.
FATHER...DOES-DOESN'T TALK TO ME MUCH, SO...
...I'M HAPPY TO TALK TO YOU.
REAL--REALLY HAPPY.
YOU HAVE SUCH TINY FEET.
YEAH...B-BUT ALL PATCHED UP.
YOU--YOU'RE PERFECTLY BEAUTIFUL.
VERY BEAUTI-FUL MIMI.

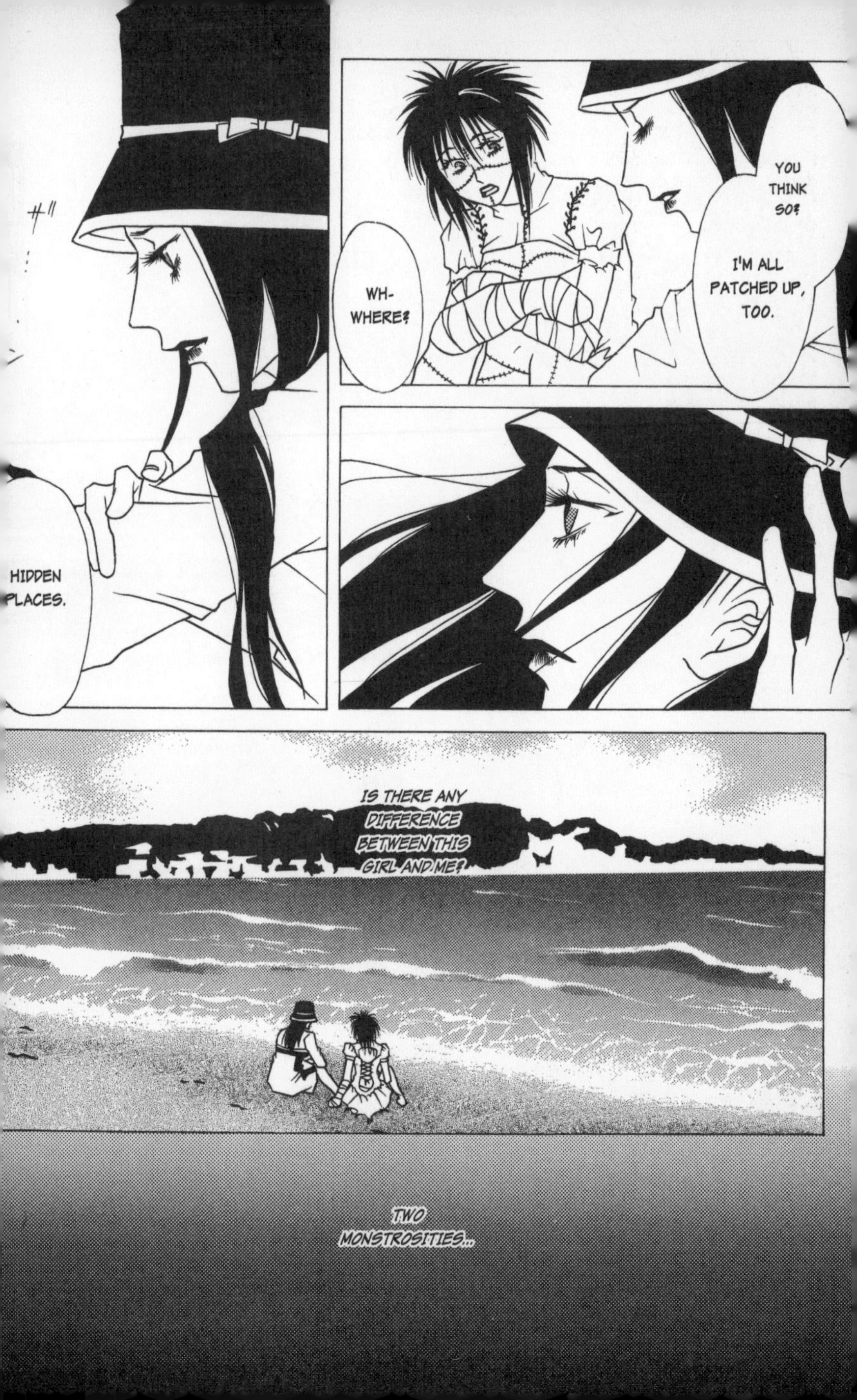
YOU THINK SO?
I'M ALL PATCHED UP, TOO.
WH- WHERE?
HIDDEN PLACES.
IS THERE ANY DIFFERENCE BETWEEN THIS GIRL AND ME?
TWO MONSTROSITIES...

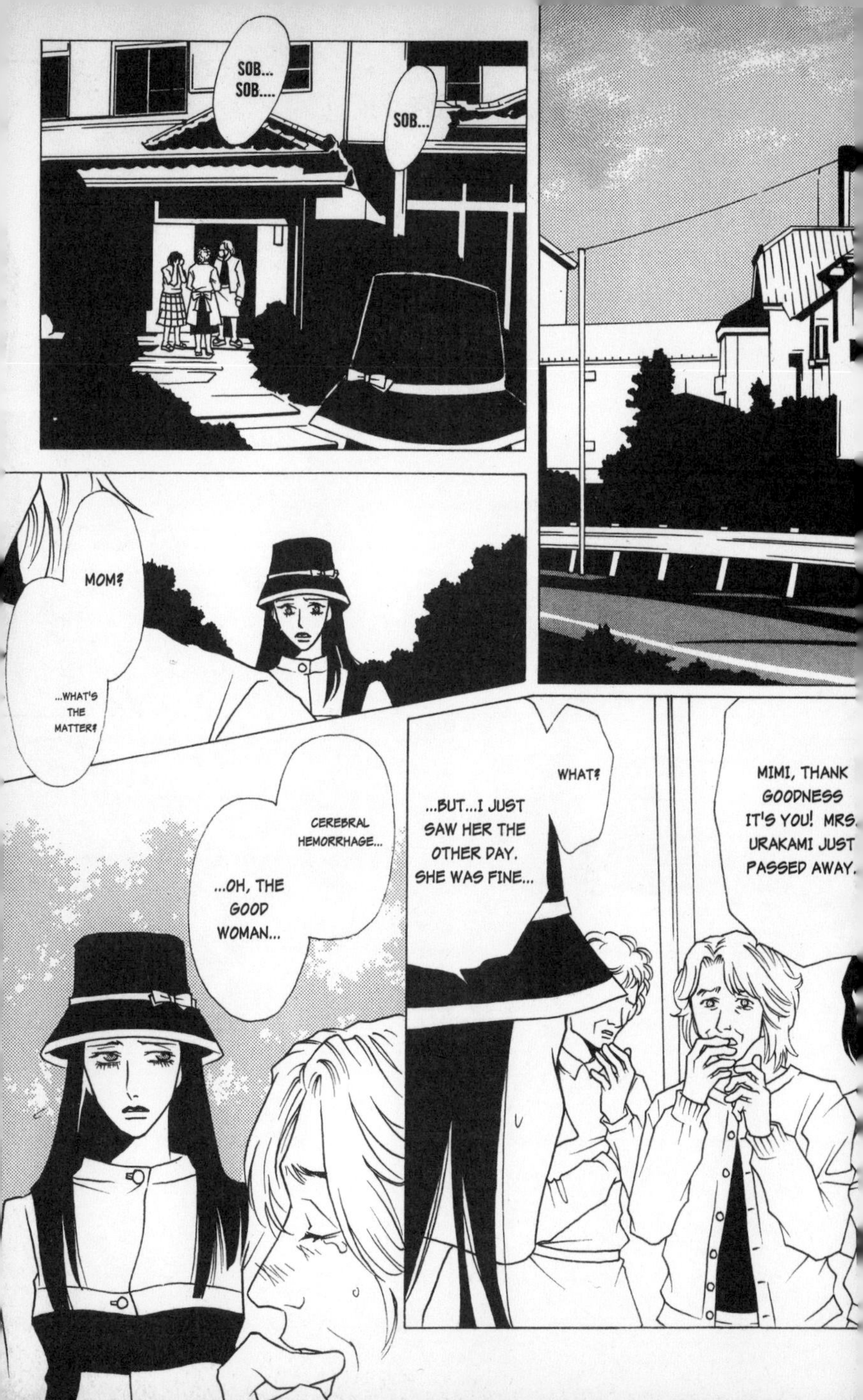
SOB...
SOB... SOB....
MOM?
...WHAT'S THE MATTER?
MIMI, THANK GOODNESS IT'S YOU! MRS. URAKAMI JUST PASSED AWAY.
WHAT?
...BUT...I JUST SAW HER THE OTHER DAY. SHE WAS FINE...
CEREBRAL HEMORRHAGE...
...OH, THE GOOD WOMAN...

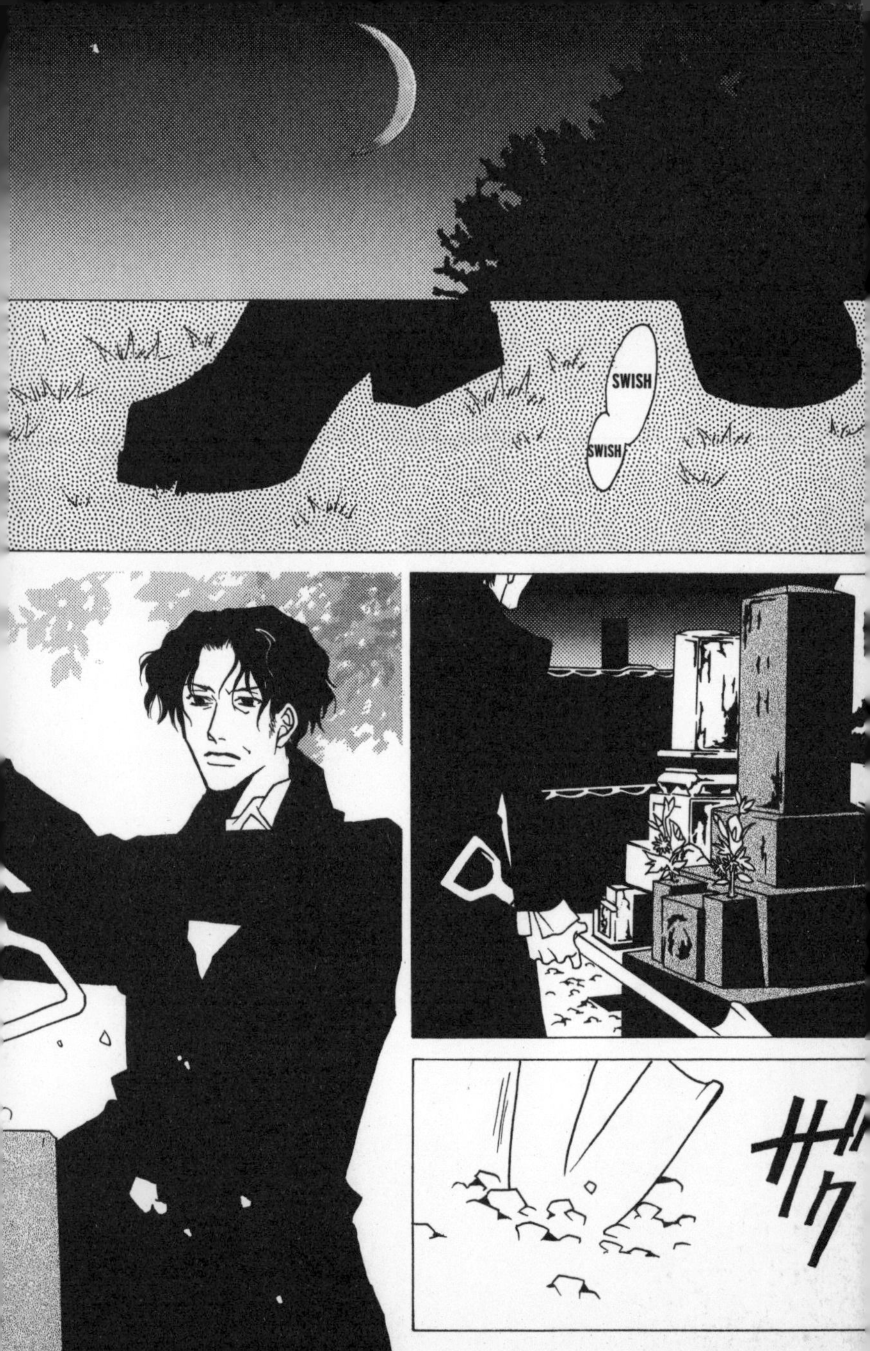
SWISH
SWISH
ザク

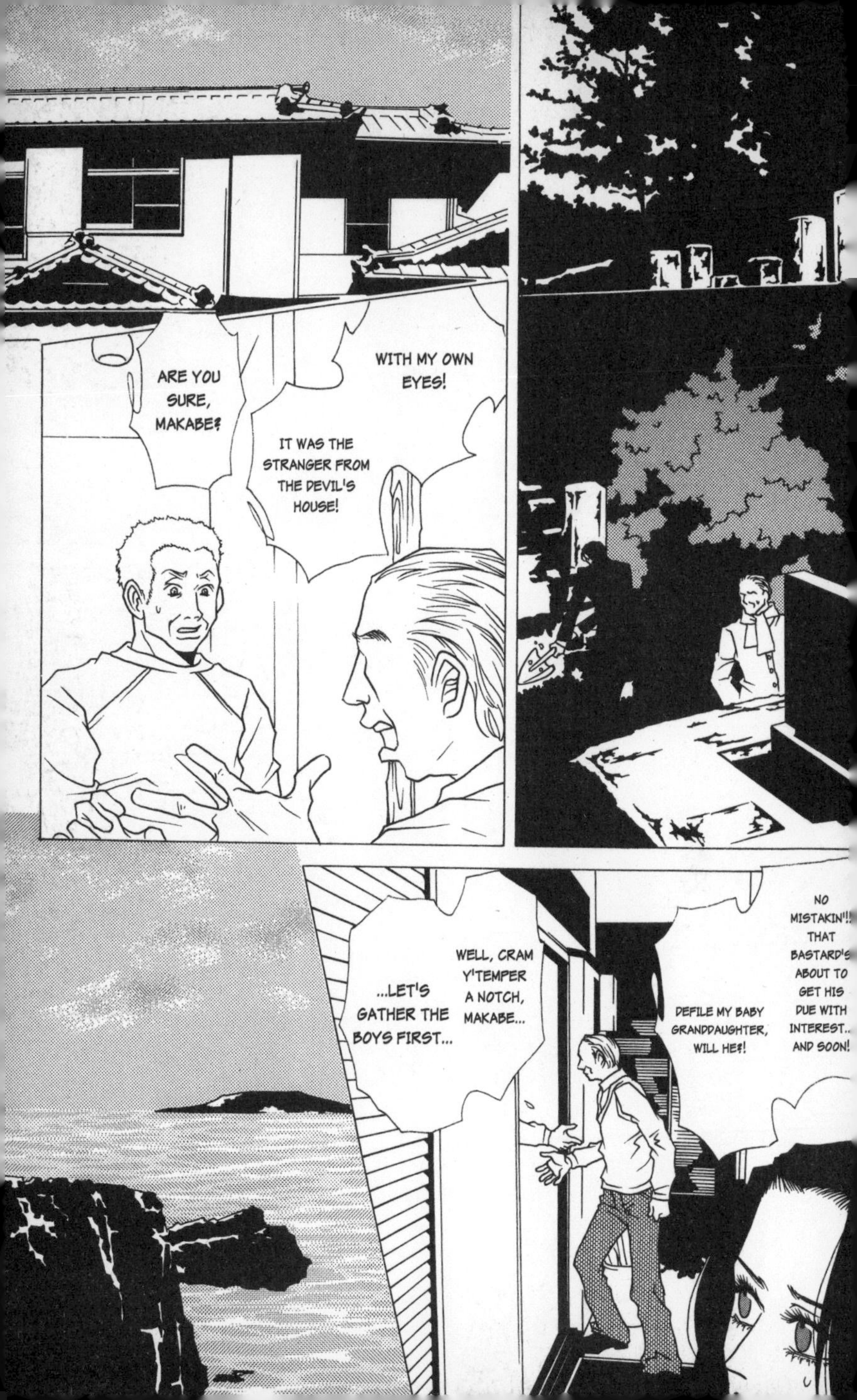
WITH MY OWN EYES!
IT WAS THE STRANGER FROM THE DEVIL'S HOUSE!
ARE YOU SURE, MAKABE?
NO MISTAKIN'!! THAT BASTARD'S ABOUT TO GET HIS DUE WITH INTEREST.. AND SOON!
DEFILE MY BABY GRANDDAUGHTER, WILL HE?!
WELL, CRAM Y'TEMPER A NOTCH, MAKABE...
...LET'S GATHER THE BOYS FIRST...

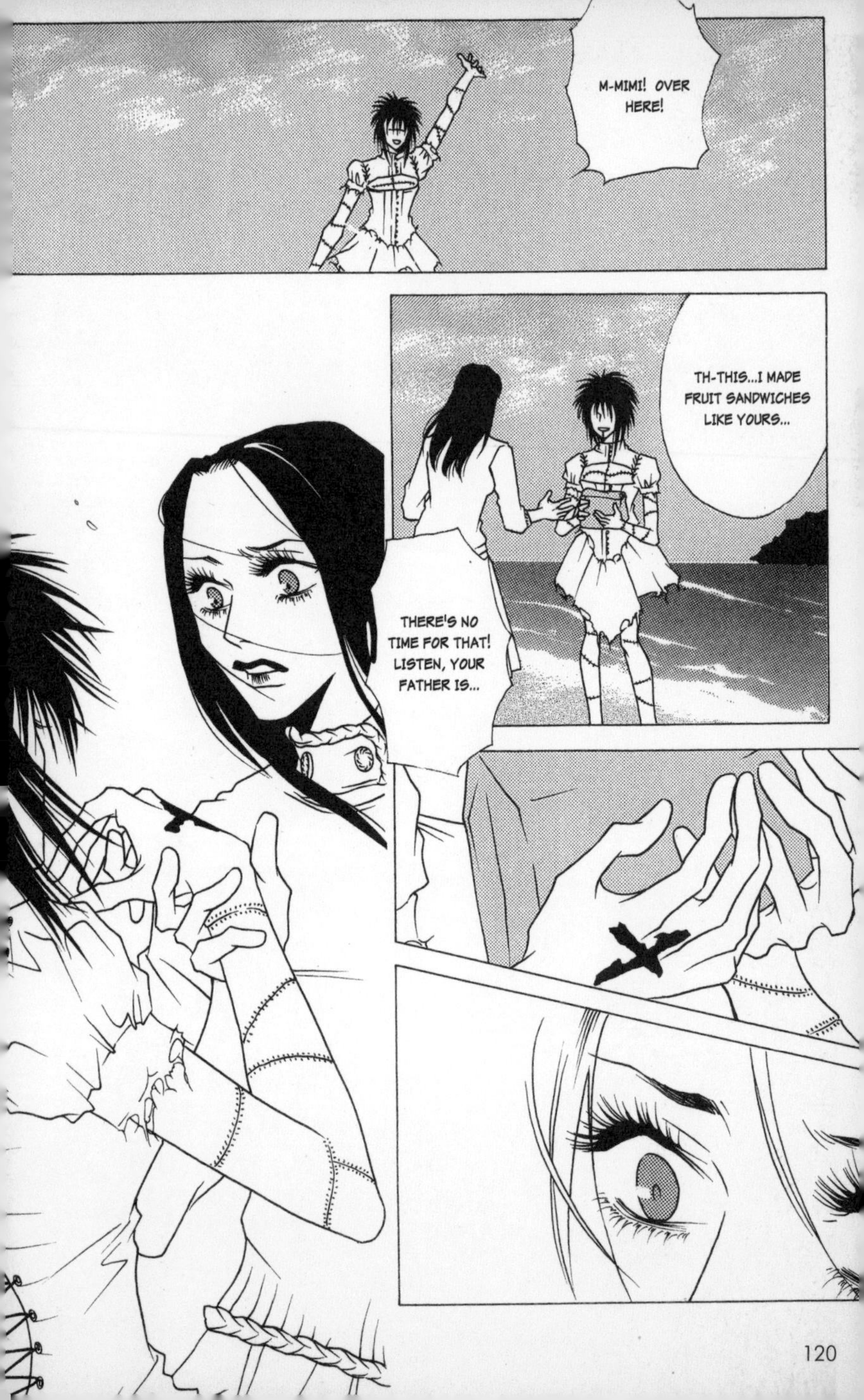
M-MIMI! OVER HERE!
TH-THIS...I MADE FRUIT SANDWICHES LIKE YOURS...
THERE'S NO TIME FOR THAT! LISTEN, YOUR FATHER IS...

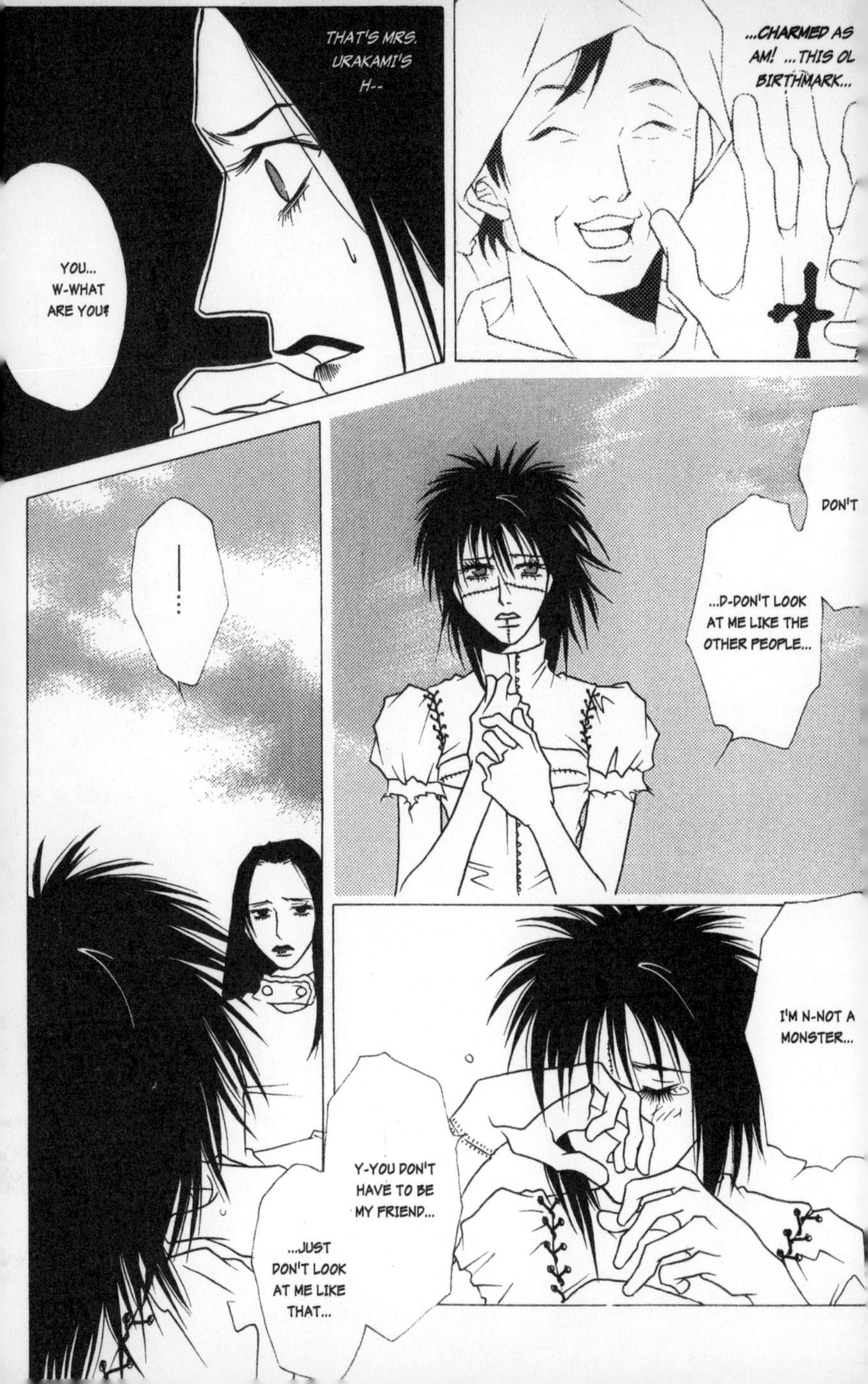
...CHARMED AS AM! ...THIS OL BIRTHMARK...
THAT'S MRS. URAKAMI'S H--
YOU... W-WHAT ARE YOU?
DON'T
...D-DON'T LOOK AT ME LIKE THE OTHER PEOPLE...
—...
I'M N-NOT A MONSTER...
Y-YOU DON'T HAVE TO BE MY FRIEND...
...JUST DON'T LOOK AT ME LIKE THAT...

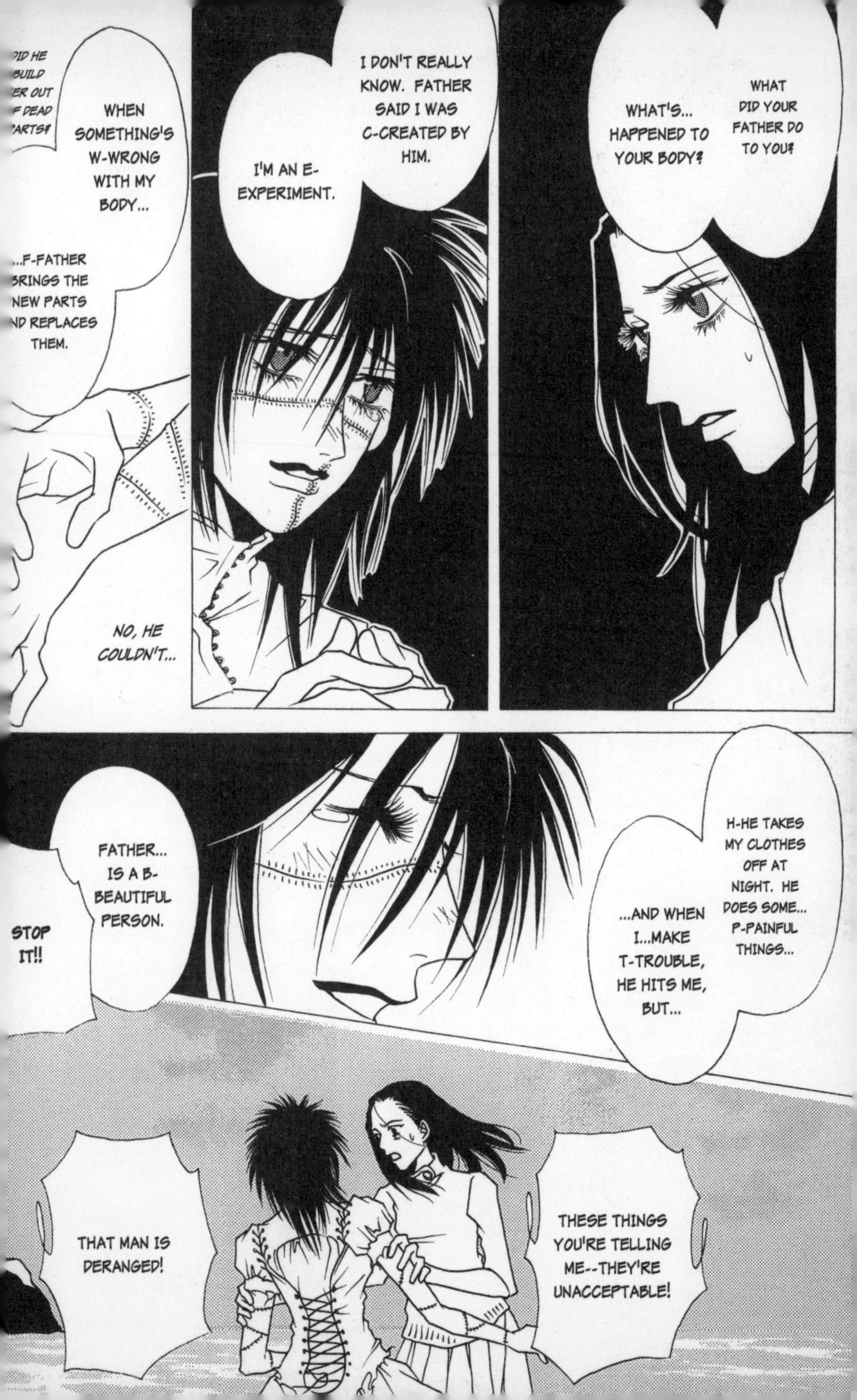
WHAT DID YOUR FATHER DO TO YOU?
WHAT'S... HAPPENED TO YOUR BODY?
I DON'T REALLY KNOW. FATHER SAID I WAS C-CREATED BY HIM.
I'M AN E-EXPERIMENT.
WHEN SOMETHING'S W-WRONG WITH MY BODY...
ID HE BUILD ER OUT F DEAD ARTS?
...F-FATHER BRINGS THE NEW PARTS ND REPLACES THEM.
NO, HE COULDN'T...
H-HE TAKES MY CLOTHES OFF AT NIGHT. HE DOES SOME... P-PAINFUL THINGS...
...AND WHEN I...MAKE T-TROUBLE, HE HITS ME, BUT...
FATHER... IS A B-BEAUTIFUL PERSON.
STOP IT!!
THESE THINGS YOU'RE TELLING ME--THEY'RE UNACCEPTABLE!
THAT MAN IS DERANGED!

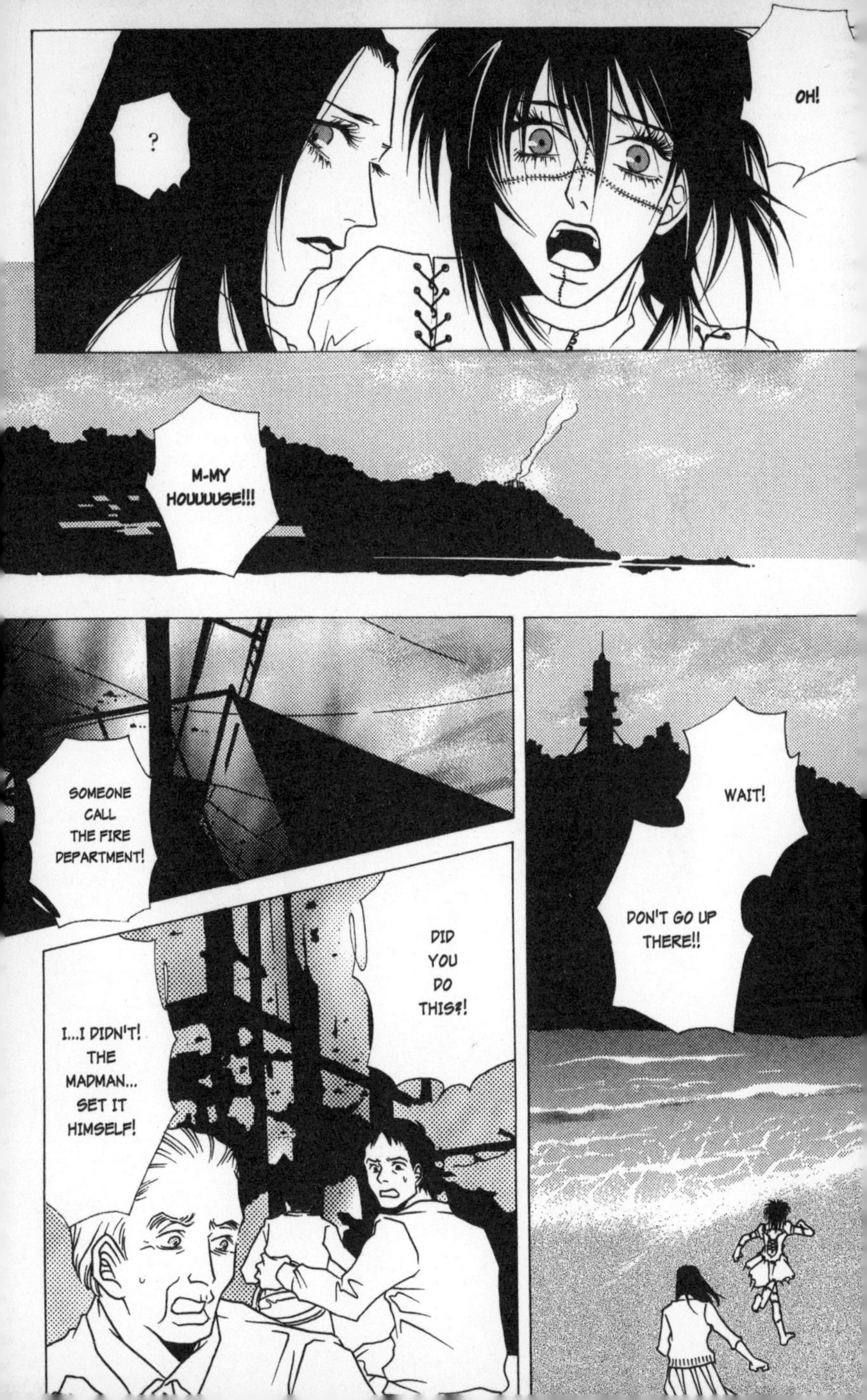
OH!
?
M-MY HOUUUUSE!!!
WAIT!
DON'T GO UP THERE!!
SOMEONE CALL THE FIRE DEPARTMENT!
DID YOU DO THIS?!
I...I DIDN'T! THE MADMAN... SET IT HIMSELF!

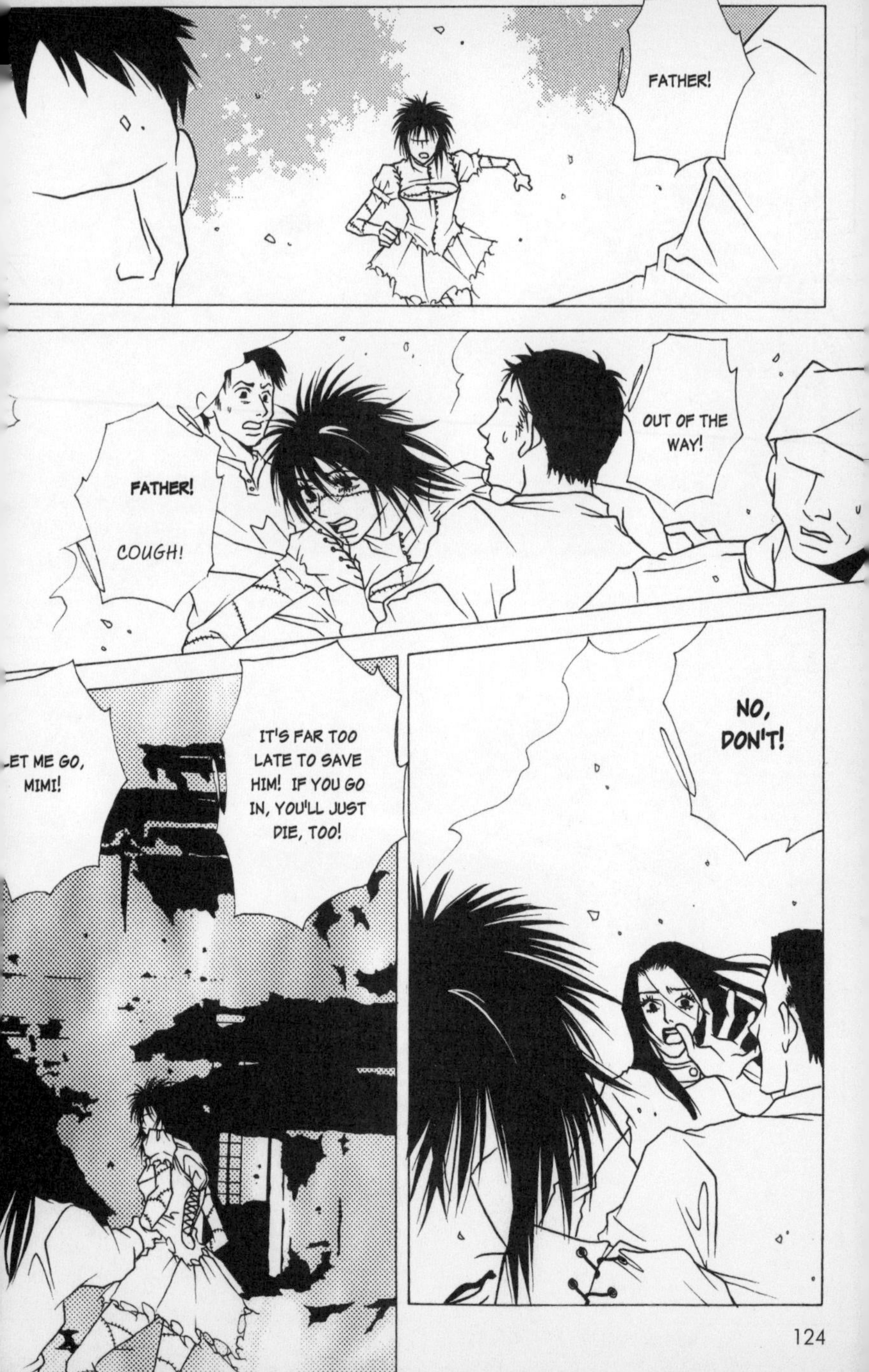
FATHER!
OUT OF THE WAY!
FATHER!
COUGH!
NO, DON'T!
IT'S FAR TOO LATE TO SAVE HIM! IF YOU GO IN, YOU'LL JUST DIE, TOO!
ET ME GO, MIMI!

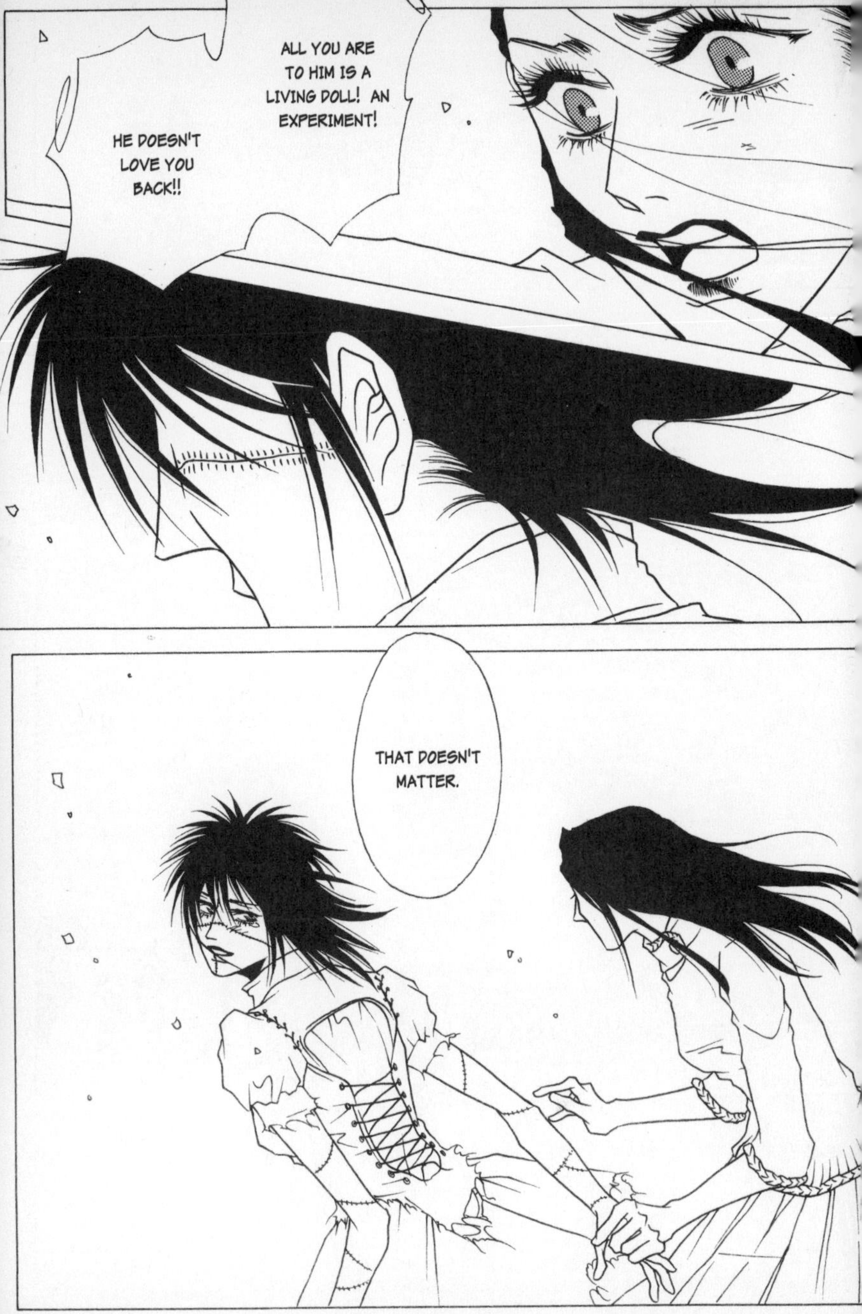
ALL YOU ARE TO HIM IS A LIVING DOLL! AN EXPERIMENT!
HE DOESN'T LOVE YOU BACK!!
THAT DOESN'T MATTER.

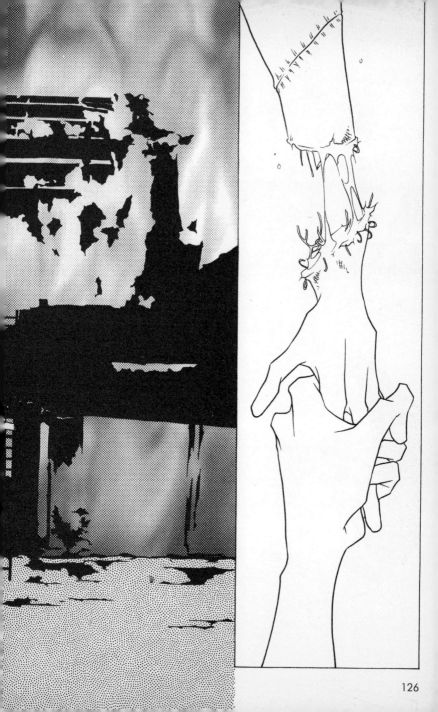

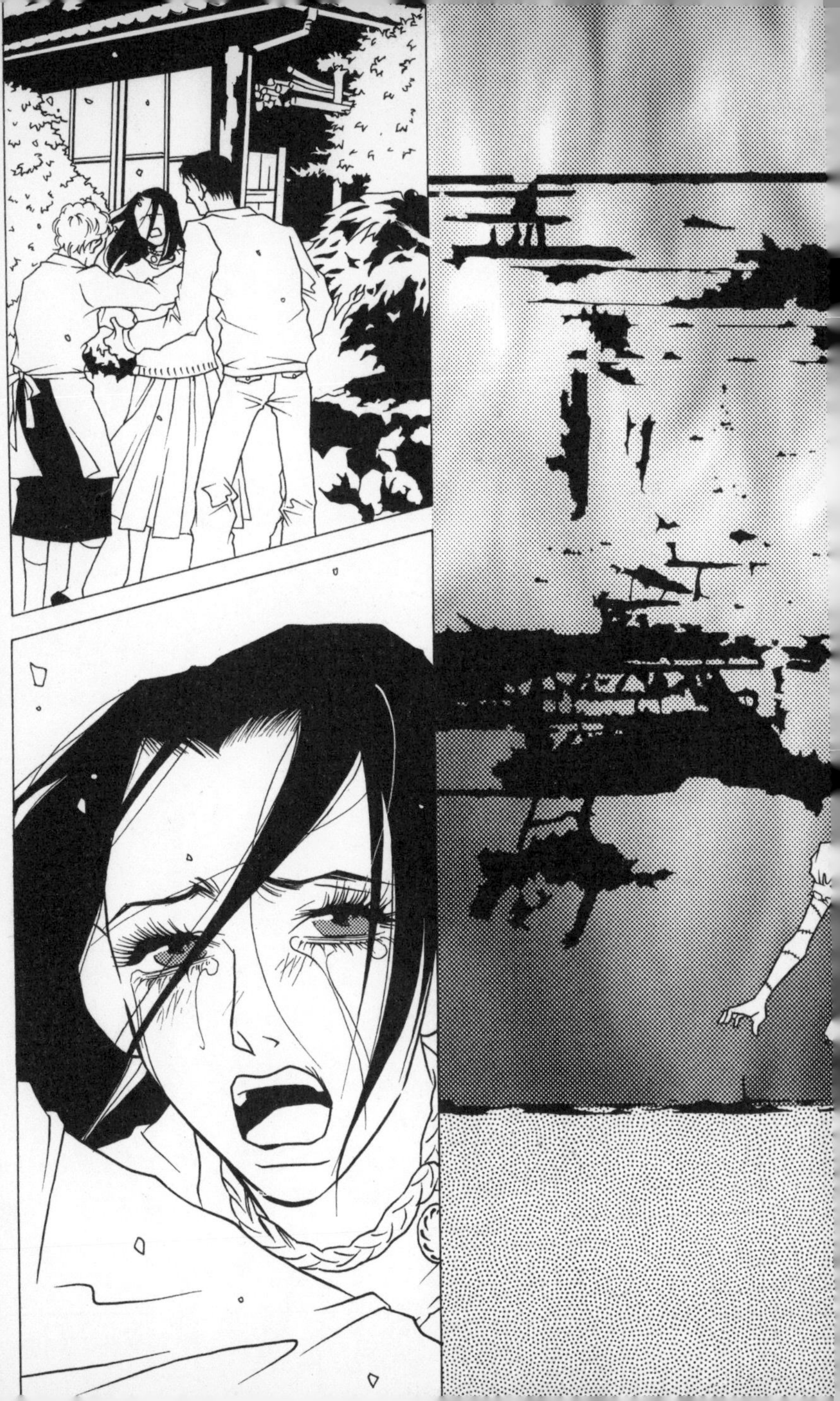

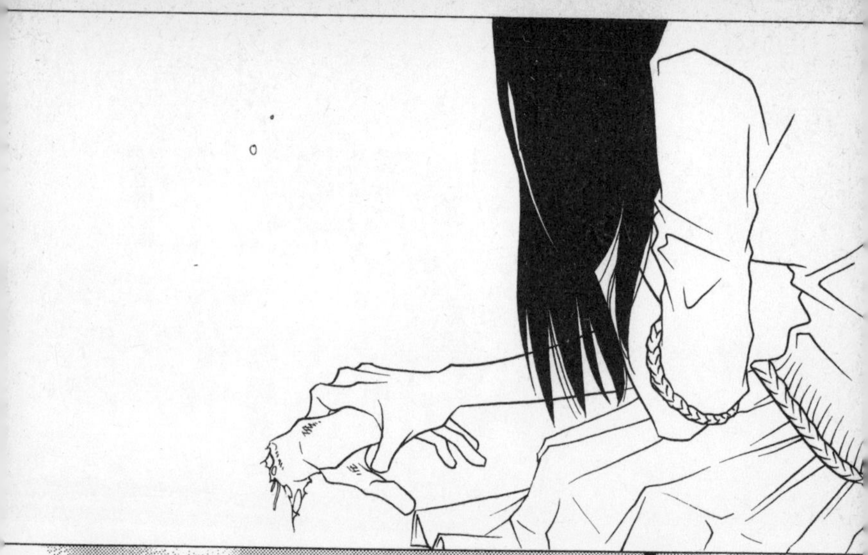
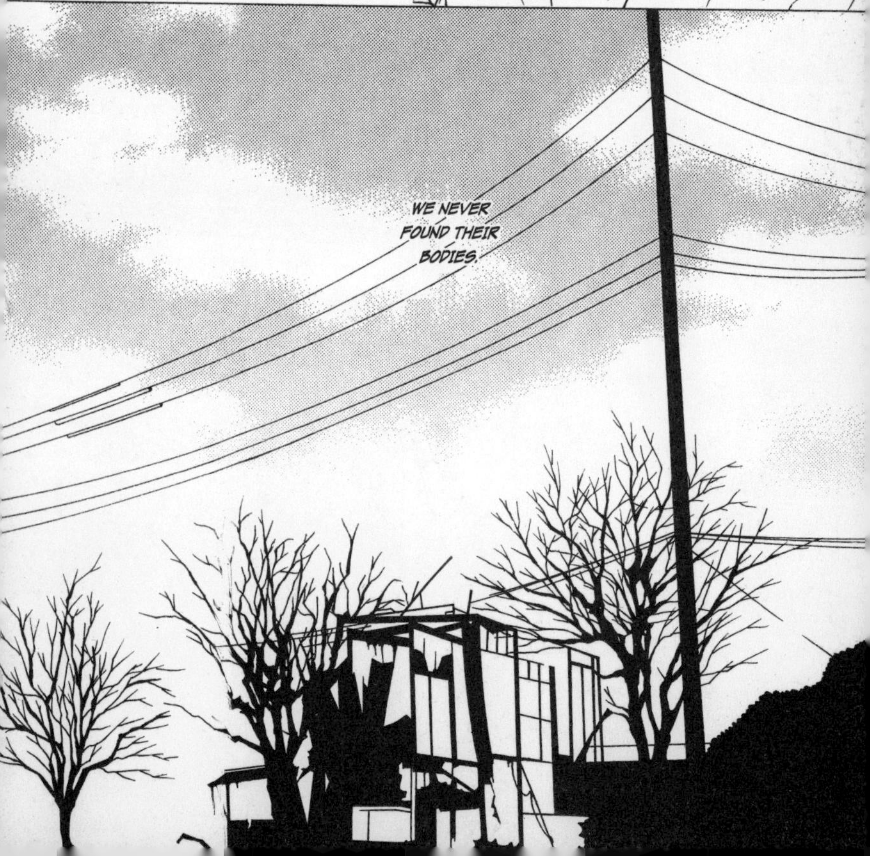
WE NEVER
FOUND THEIR
BODIES.

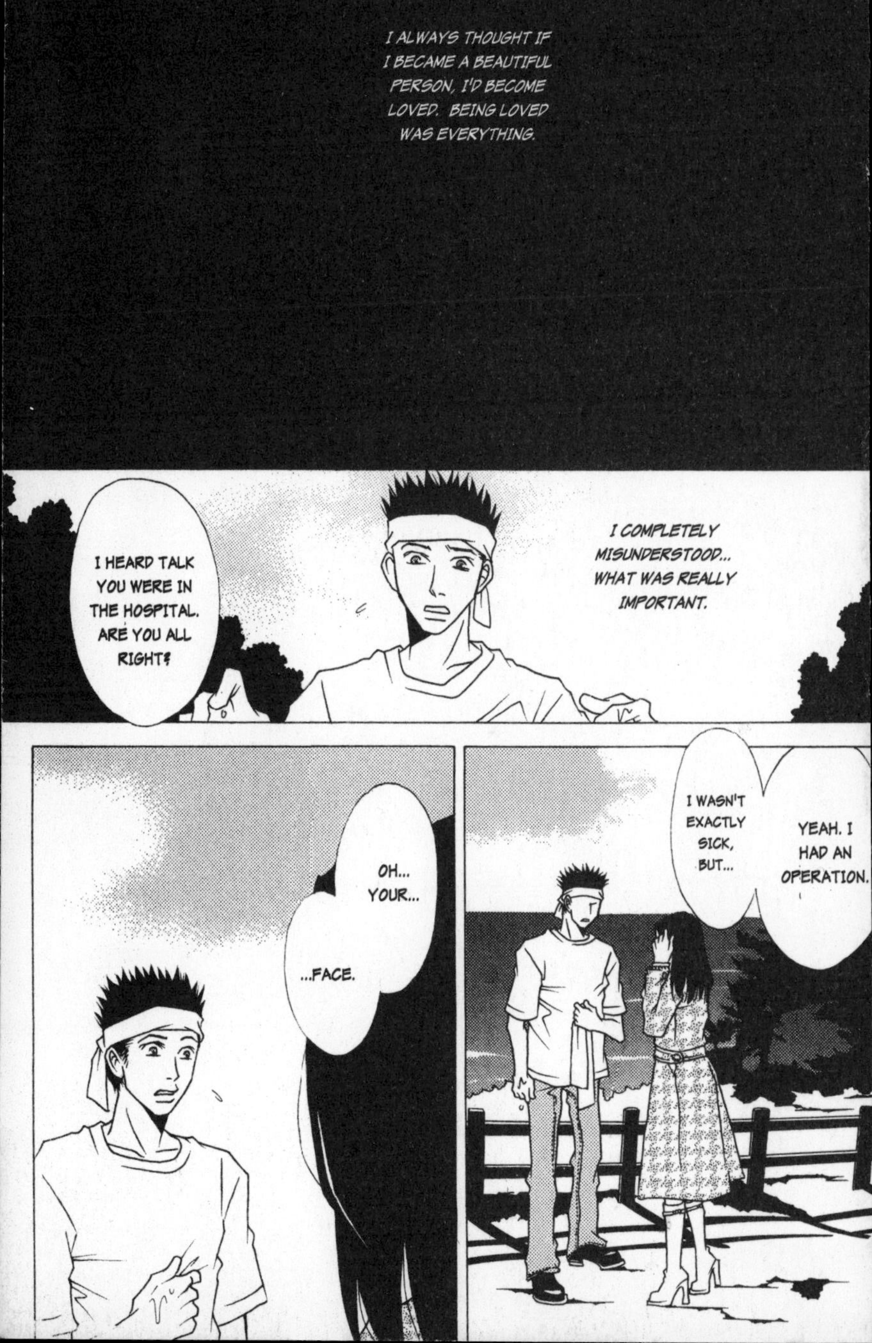
I ALWAYS THOUGHT IF I BECAME A BEAUTIFUL PERSON, I'D BECOME LOVED. BEING LOVED WAS EVERYTHING.
I COMPLETELY MISUNDERSTOOD... WHAT WAS REALLY IMPORTANT.
I HEARD TALK YOU WERE IN THE HOSPITAL. ARE YOU ALL RIGHT?
YEAH. I HAD AN OPERATION.
I WASN'T EXACTLY SICK, BUT...
OH... YOUR...
...FACE.

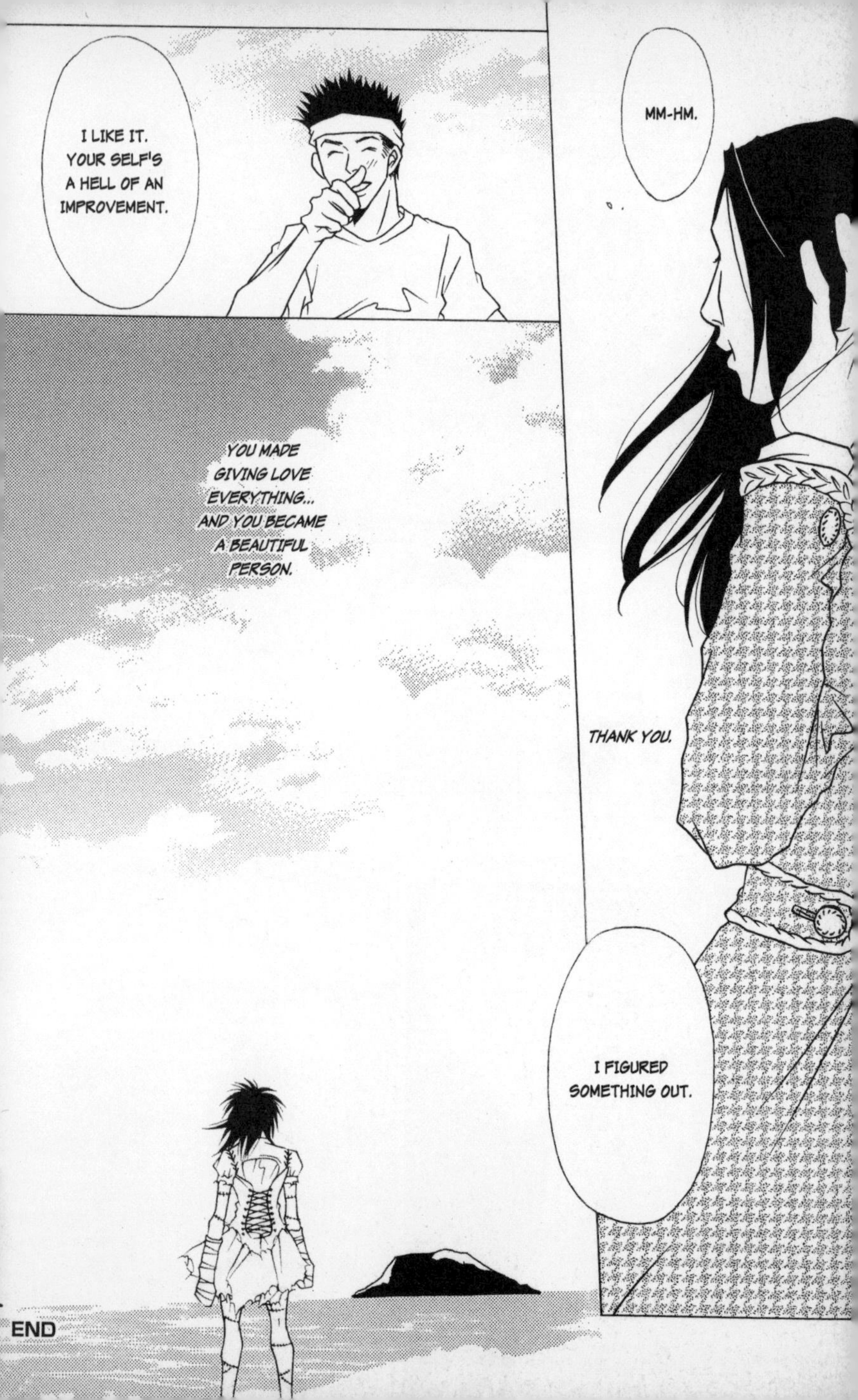
MM-HM.
THANK YOU.
I FIGURED SOMETHING OUT.
I LIKE IT. YOUR SELF'S A HELL OF AN IMPROVEMENT.
YOU MADE GIVING LOVE EVERYTHING... AND YOU BECAME A BEAUTIFUL PERSON.
END

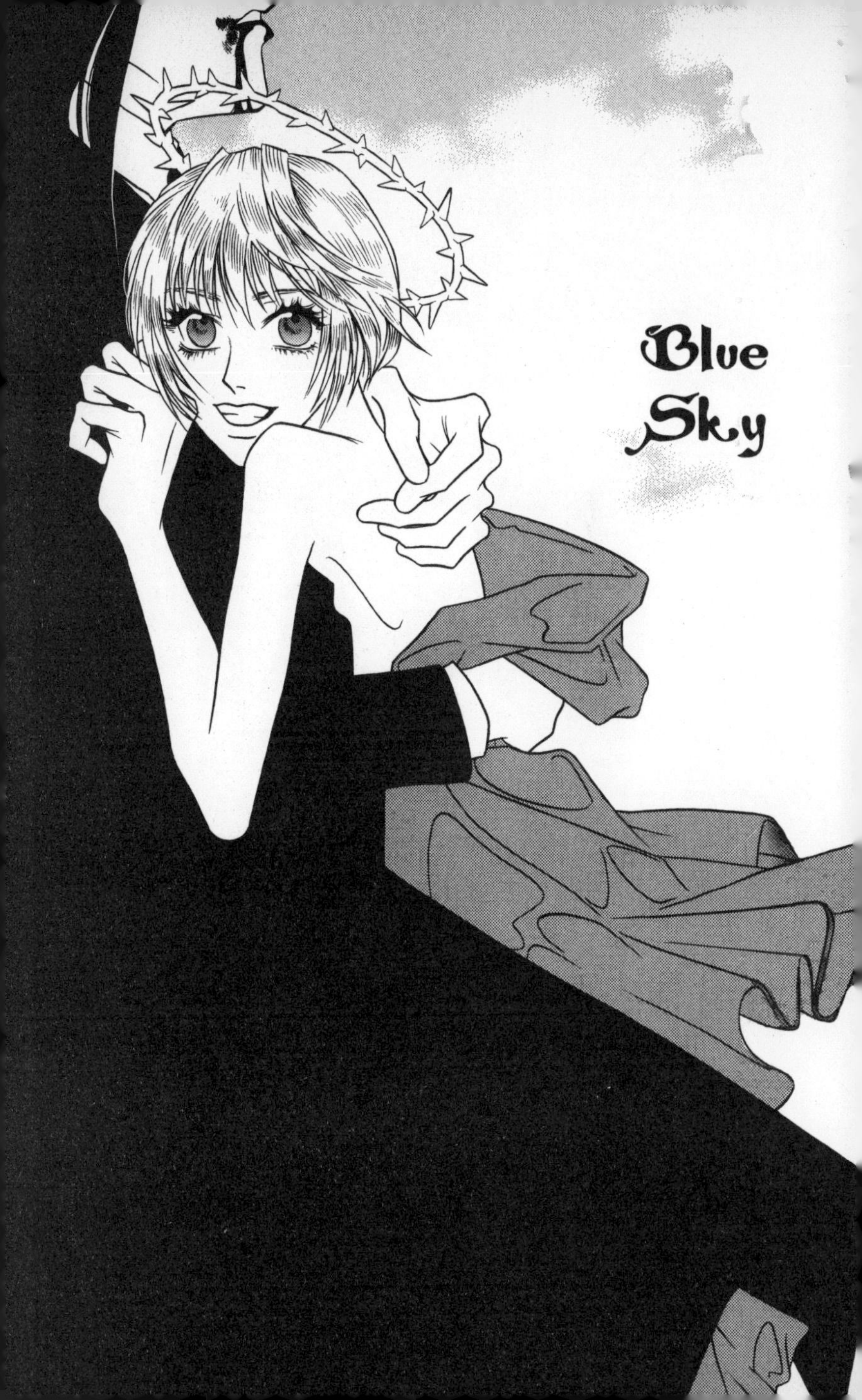
Blue
Sky

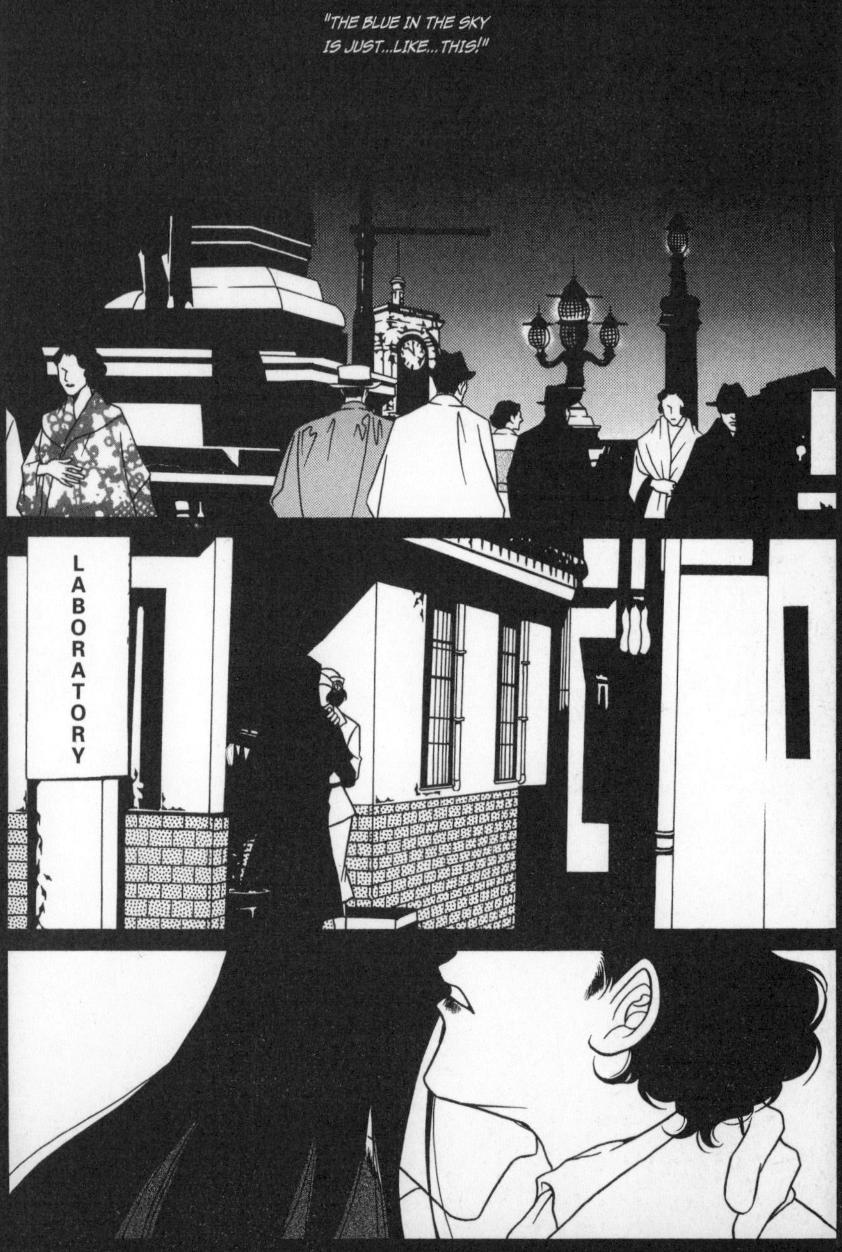
"THE BLUE IN THE SKY
IS JUST...LIKE...THIS!"
LABORATORY

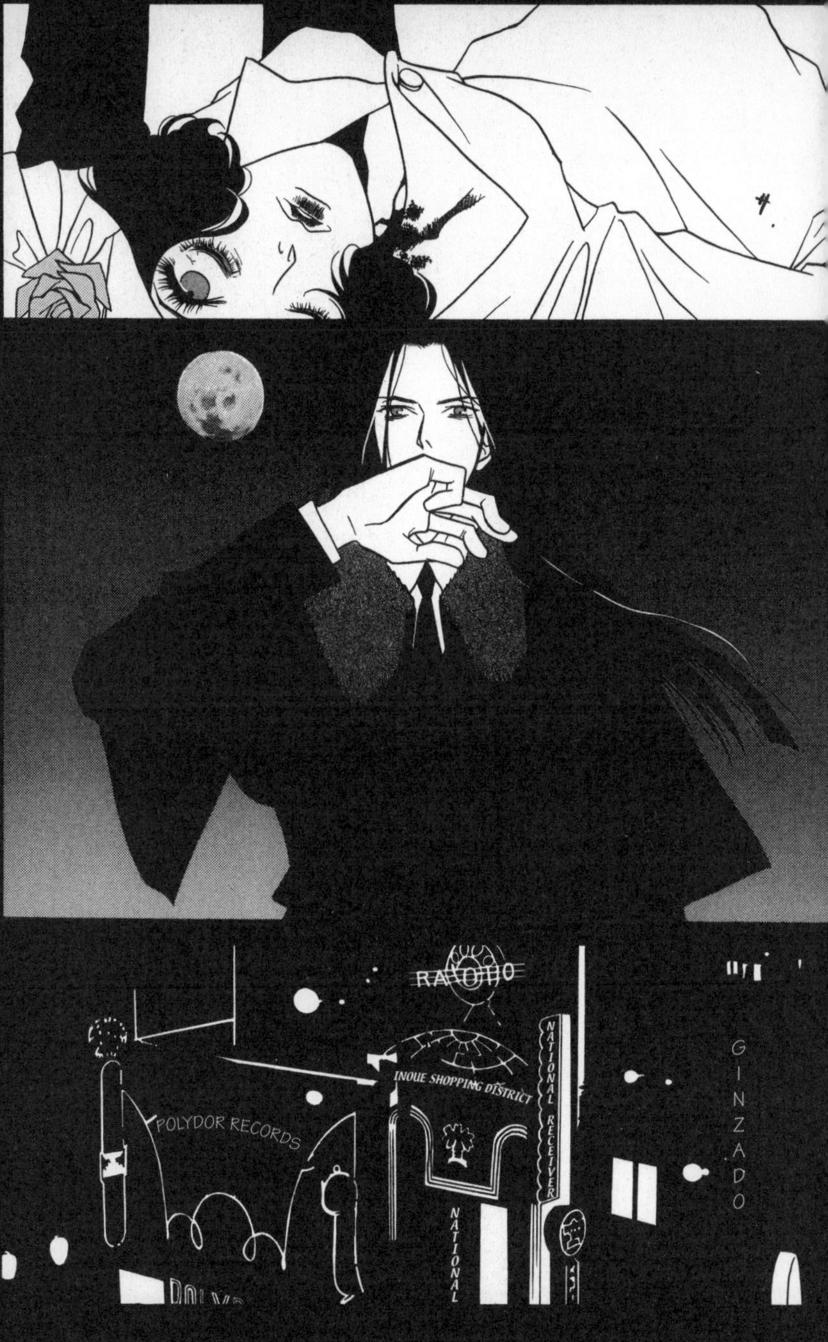
GINZADO
NATIONAL RECEIVER
INOUE SHOPPING DISTRICT
NATIONAL
POLYDOR RECORDS

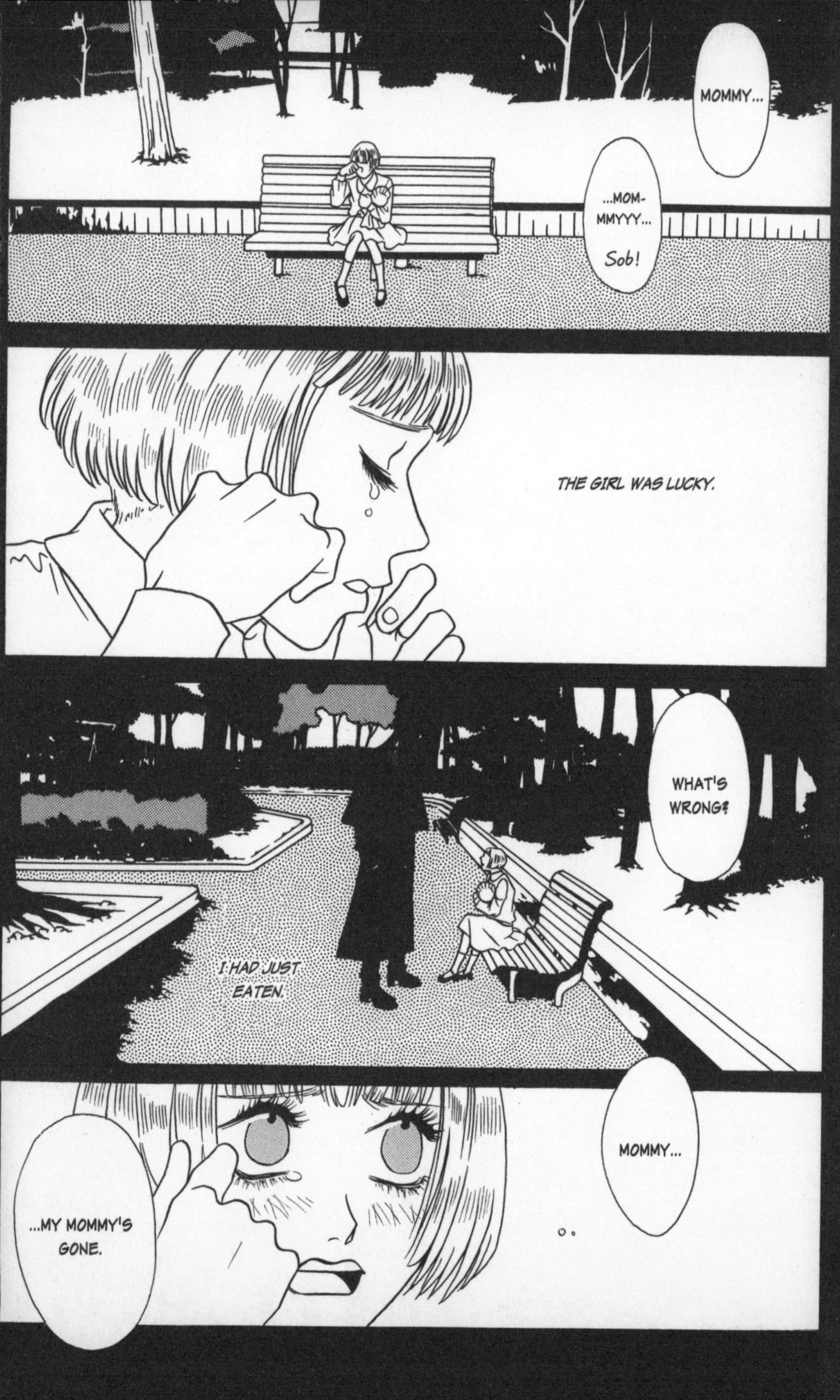
MOMMY...
...MOM-MMYYY...
Sob!
THE GIRL WAS LUCKY.
WHAT'S WRONG?
I HAD JUST EATEN.
MOMMY...
...MY MOMMY'S GONE.

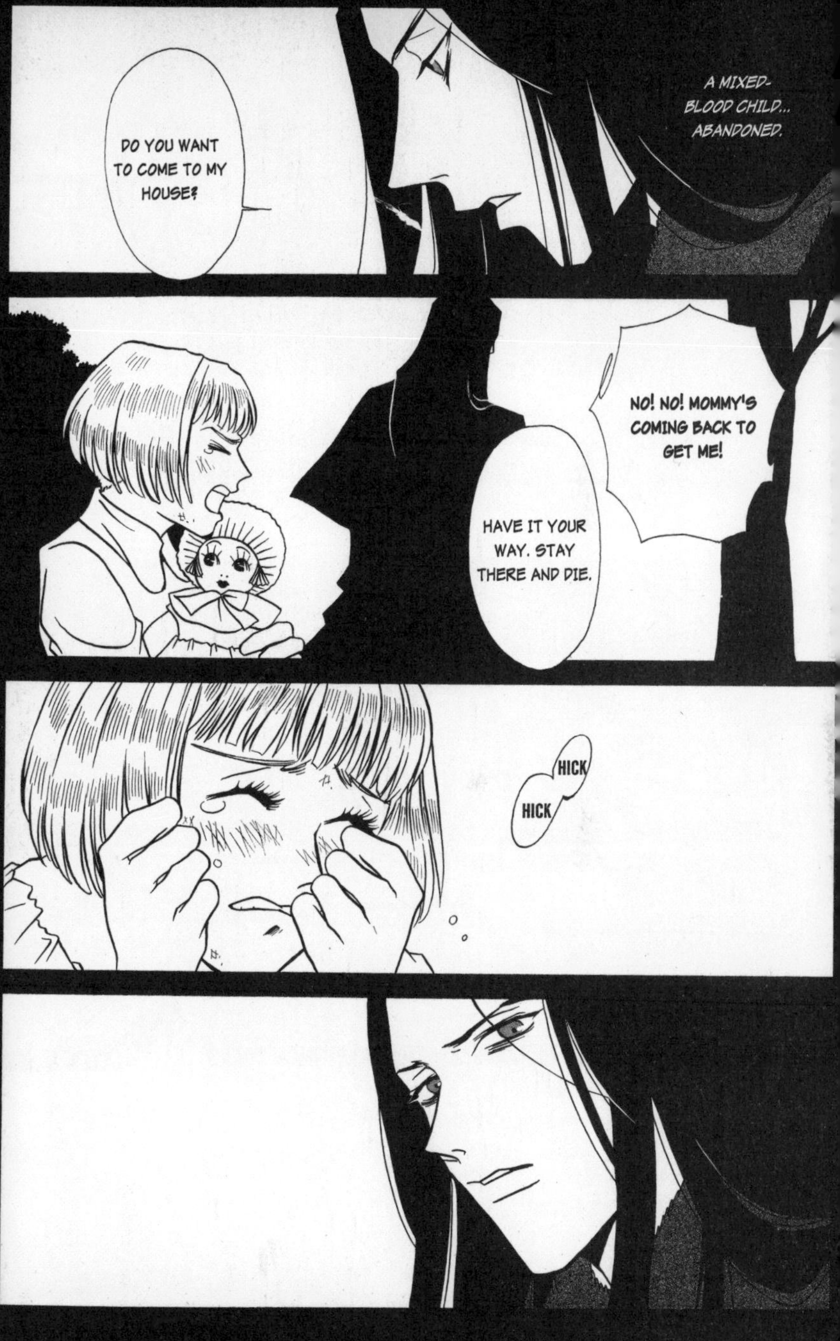
A MIXED-BLOOD CHILD... ABANDONED.
DO YOU WANT TO COME TO MY HOUSE?
NO! NO! MOMMY'S COMING BACK TO GET ME!
HAVE IT YOUR WAY. STAY THERE AND DIE.
HICK
HICK

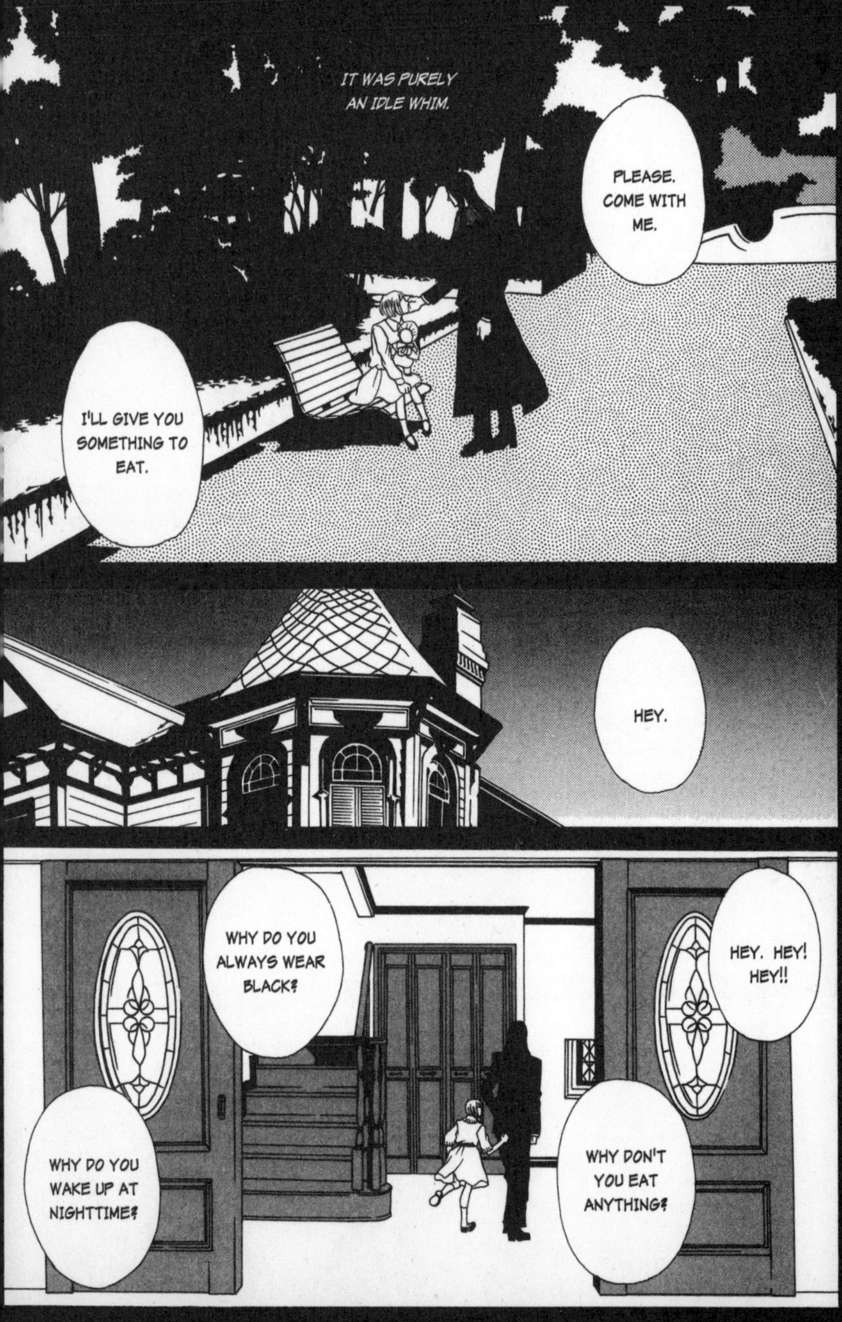
IT WAS PURELY AN IDLE WHIM.
PLEASE. COME WITH ME.
I'LL GIVE YOU SOMETHING TO EAT.
HEY.
HEY. HEY! HEY!!
WHY DO YOU ALWAYS WEAR BLACK?
WHY DON'T YOU EAT ANYTHING?
WHY DO YOU WAKE UP AT NIGHTTIME?

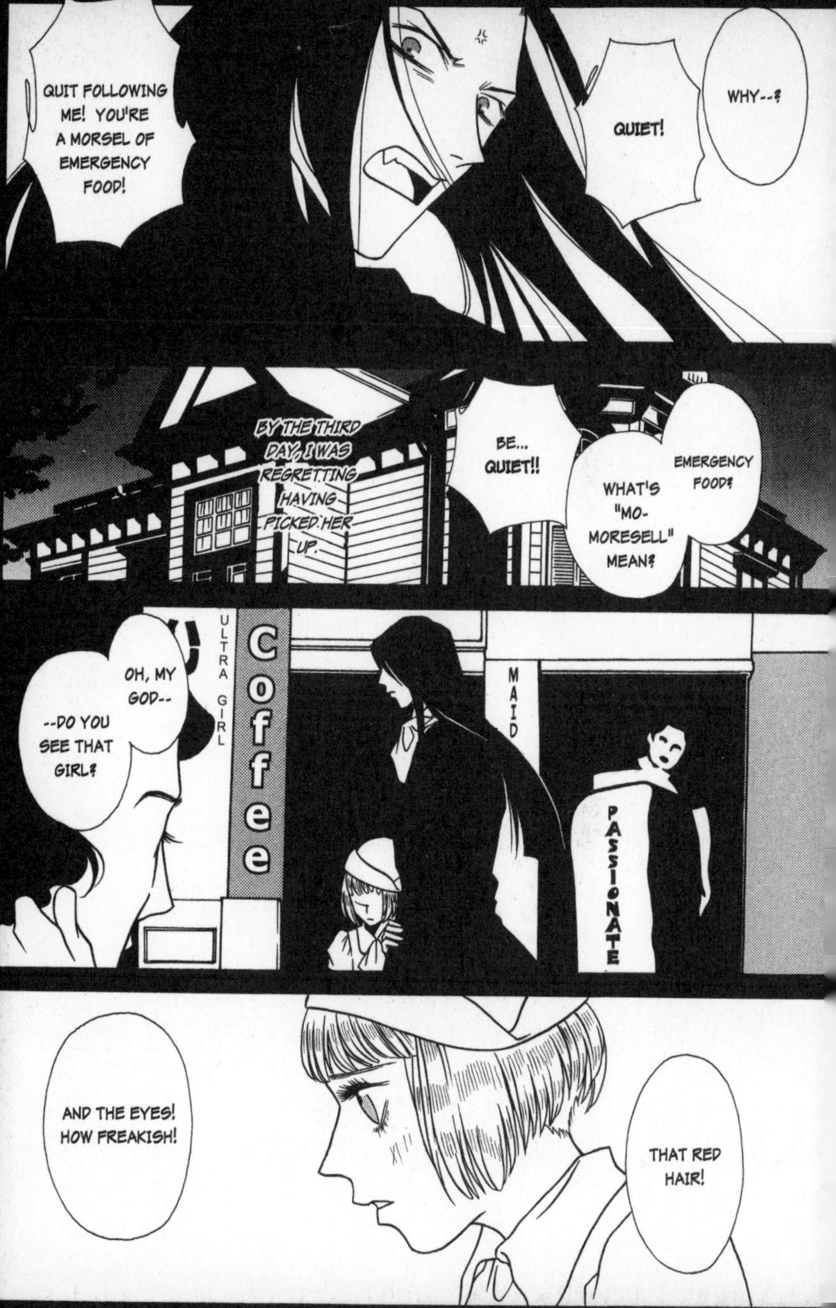
WHY--?
QUIET!
QUIT FOLLOWING ME! YOU'RE A MORSEL OF EMERGENCY FOOD!
EMERGENCY FOOD?
WHAT'S "MO-MORESELL" MEAN?
BE... QUIET!!
BY THE THIRD DAY, I WAS REGRETTING HAVING PICKED HER UP.
PASSIONATE
MAID
Coffee
ULTRA GIRL
OH, MY GOD--
--DO YOU SEE THAT GIRL?
THAT RED HAIR!
AND THE EYES! HOW FREAKISH!

IGNORE THEM. THEY ARE CHAFF.
PERHAPS I DIDN'T DISPOSE OF HER BECAUSE SHE WAS AN ABERRATION, LIKE MYSELF.
BLUE SKY...
BLUE WATER...
BLUE.
HMM...I DON'T KNOW HOW TO DRAW IT RIGHT. THE REAL SKY IS MORE...
YOU NEVER SAW THE SKY BE BLUE? REALLY?!

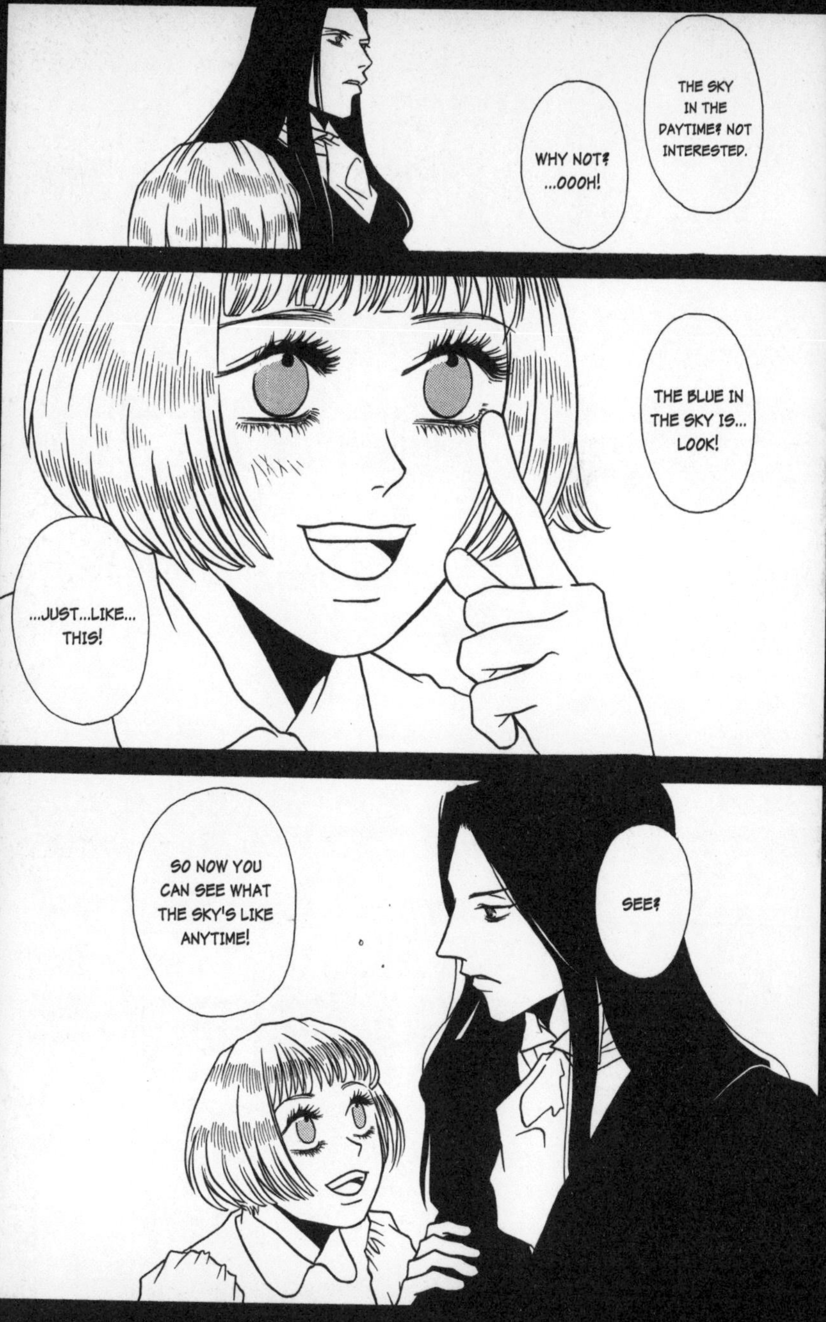
THE SKY IN THE DAYTIME? NOT INTERESTED.
WHY NOT? ...OOOH!
THE BLUE IN THE SKY IS... LOOK!
...JUST...LIKE... THIS!
SEE?
SO NOW YOU CAN SEE WHAT THE SKY'S LIKE ANYTIME!

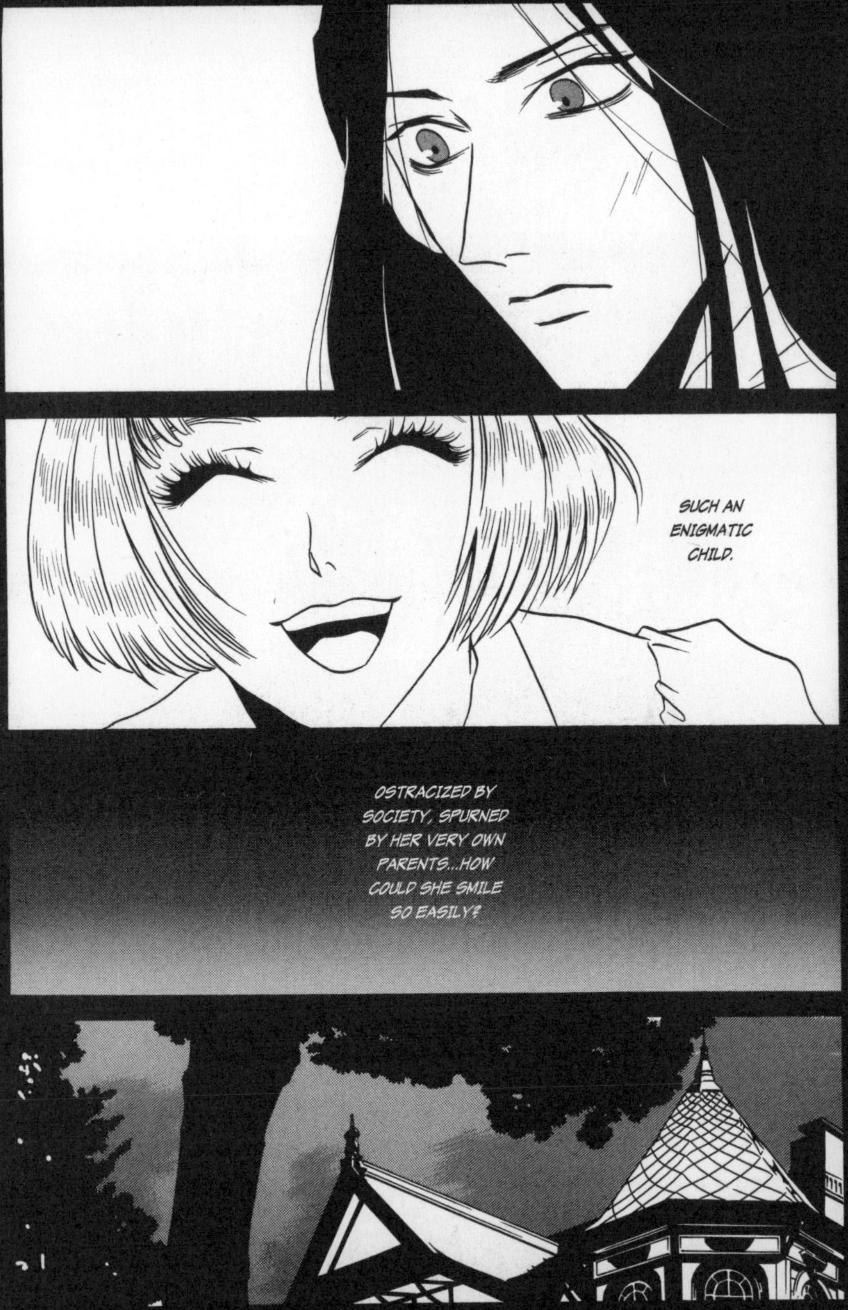
SUCH AN ENIGMATIC CHILD.
OSTRACIZED BY SOCIETY, SPURNED BY HER VERY OWN PARENTS...HOW COULD SHE SMILE SO EASILY?

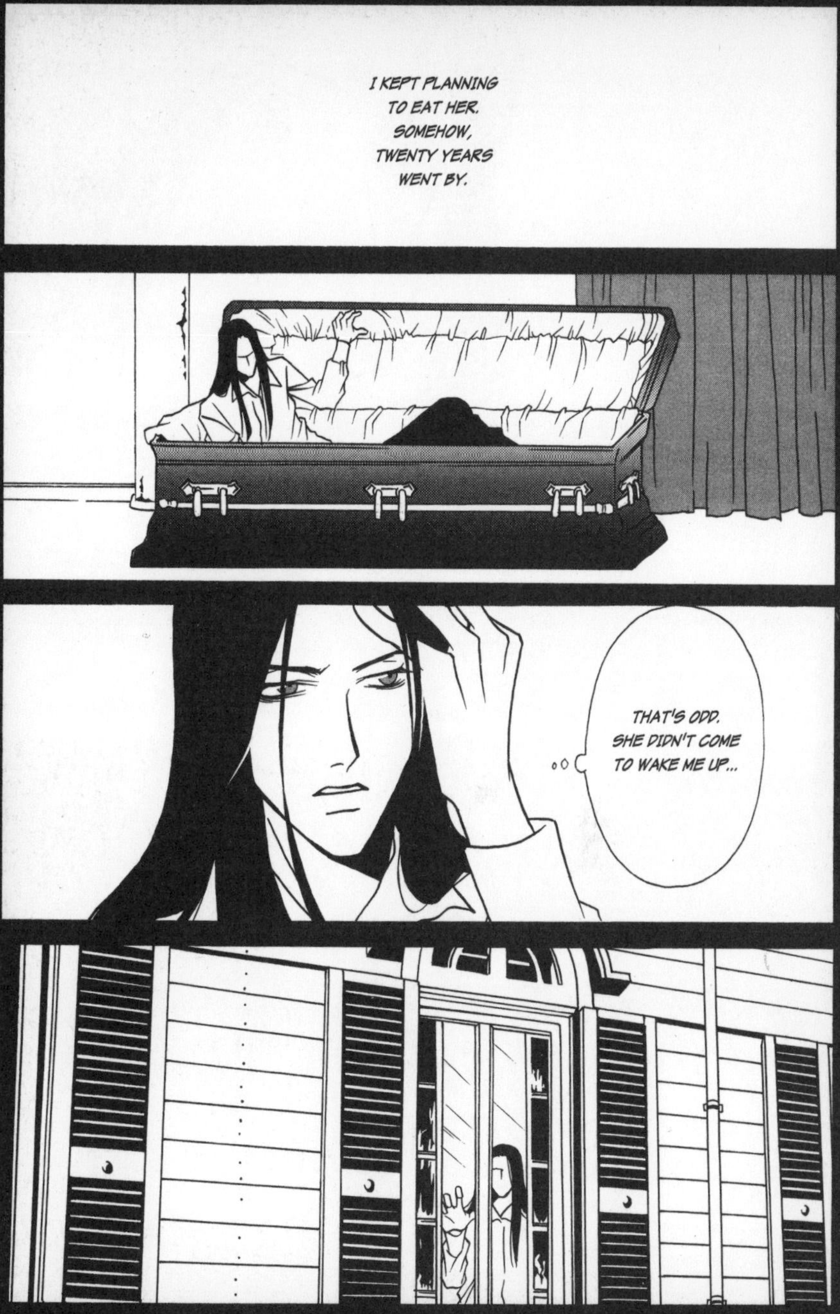
I KEPT PLANNING TO EAT HER. SOMEHOW, TWENTY YEARS WENT BY.
THAT'S ODD. SHE DIDN'T COME TO WAKE ME UP...

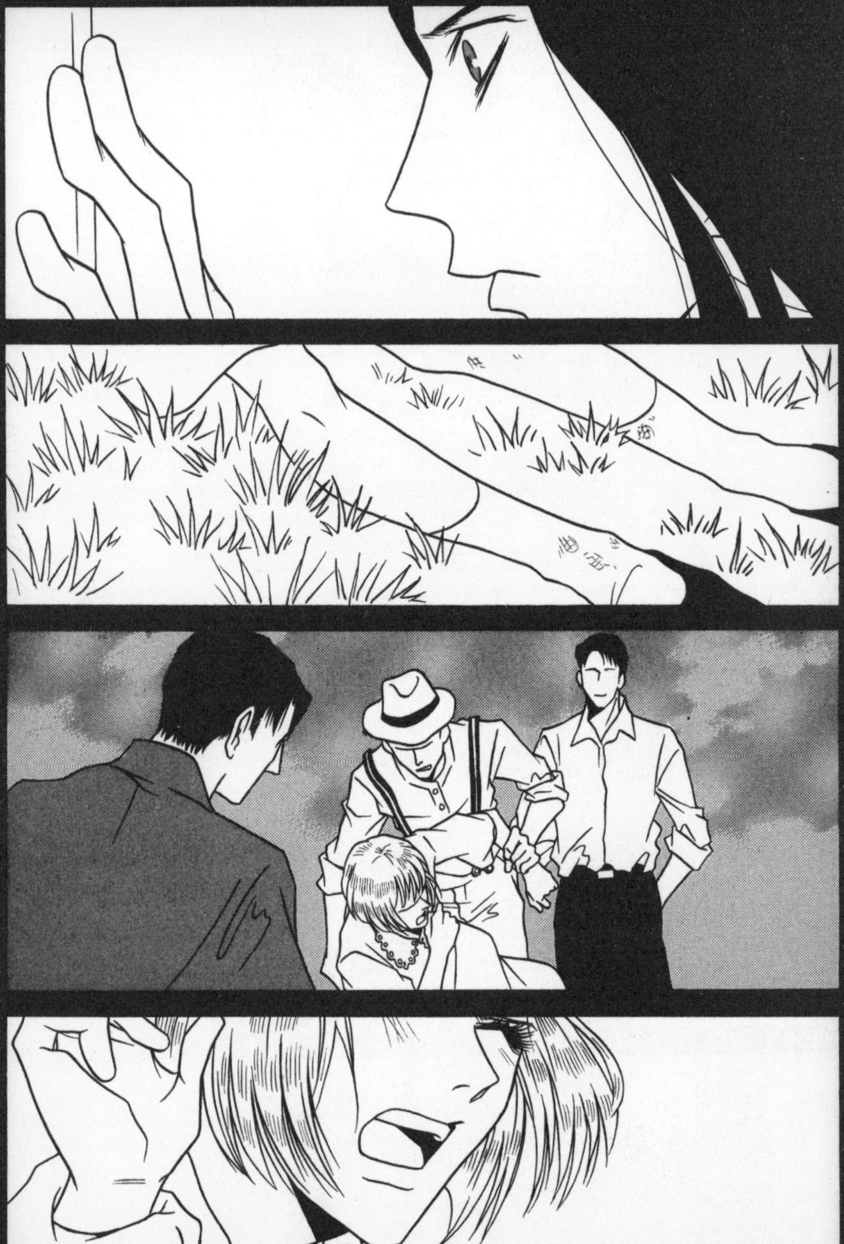

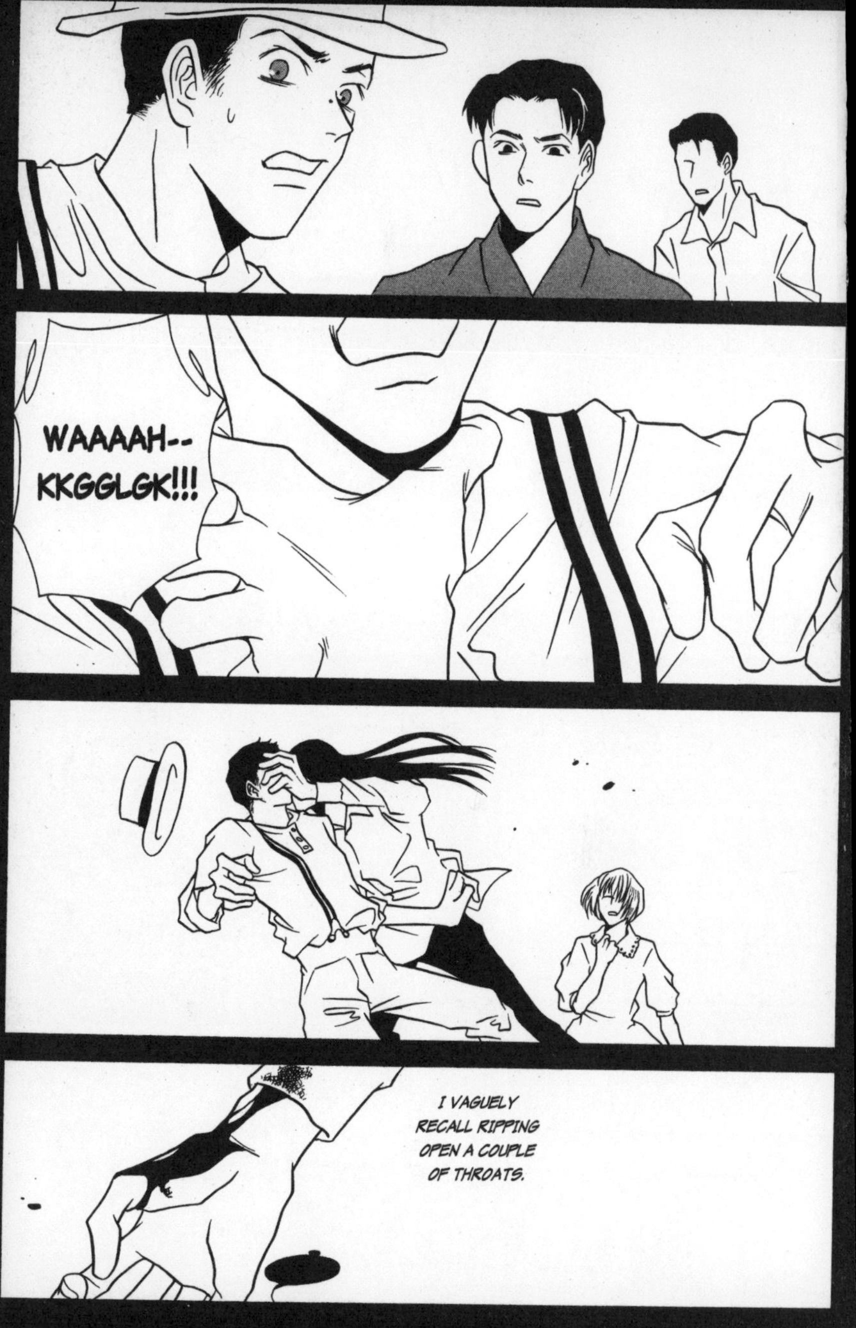
WAAAAH--
KKGGLGK!!!
I VAGUELY RECALL RIPPING OPEN A COUPLE OF THROATS.

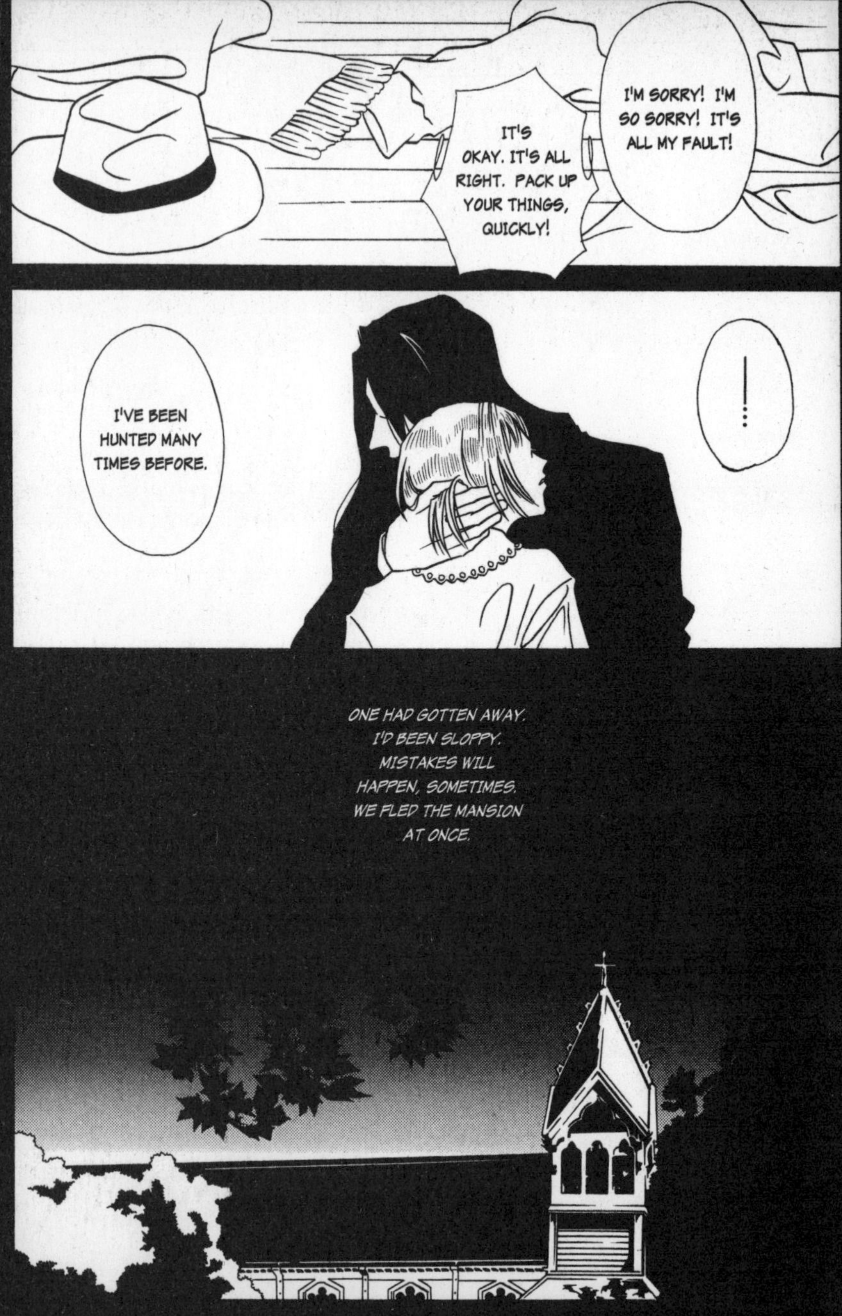
I'M SORRY! I'M SO SORRY! IT'S ALL MY FAULT!
IT'S OKAY. IT'S ALL RIGHT. PACK UP YOUR THINGS, QUICKLY!
!......
I'VE BEEN HUNTED MANY TIMES BEFORE.
ONE HAD GOTTEN AWAY. I'D BEEN SLOPPY. MISTAKES WILL HAPPEN, SOMETIMES. WE FLED THE MANSION AT ONCE.

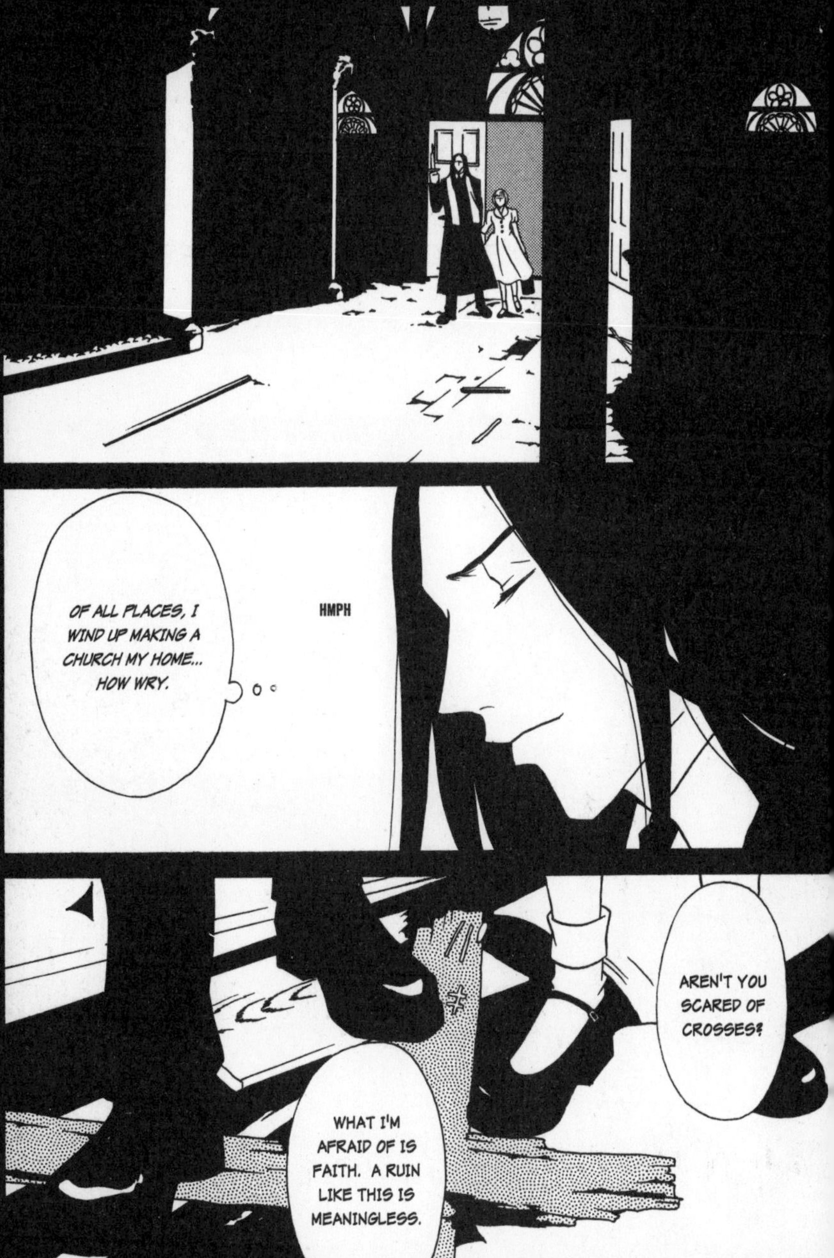
HMPH
OF ALL PLACES, I WIND UP MAKING A CHURCH MY HOME... HOW WRY.
AREN'T YOU SCARED OF CROSSES?
WHAT I'M AFRAID OF IS FAITH. A RUIN LIKE THIS IS MEANINGLESS.

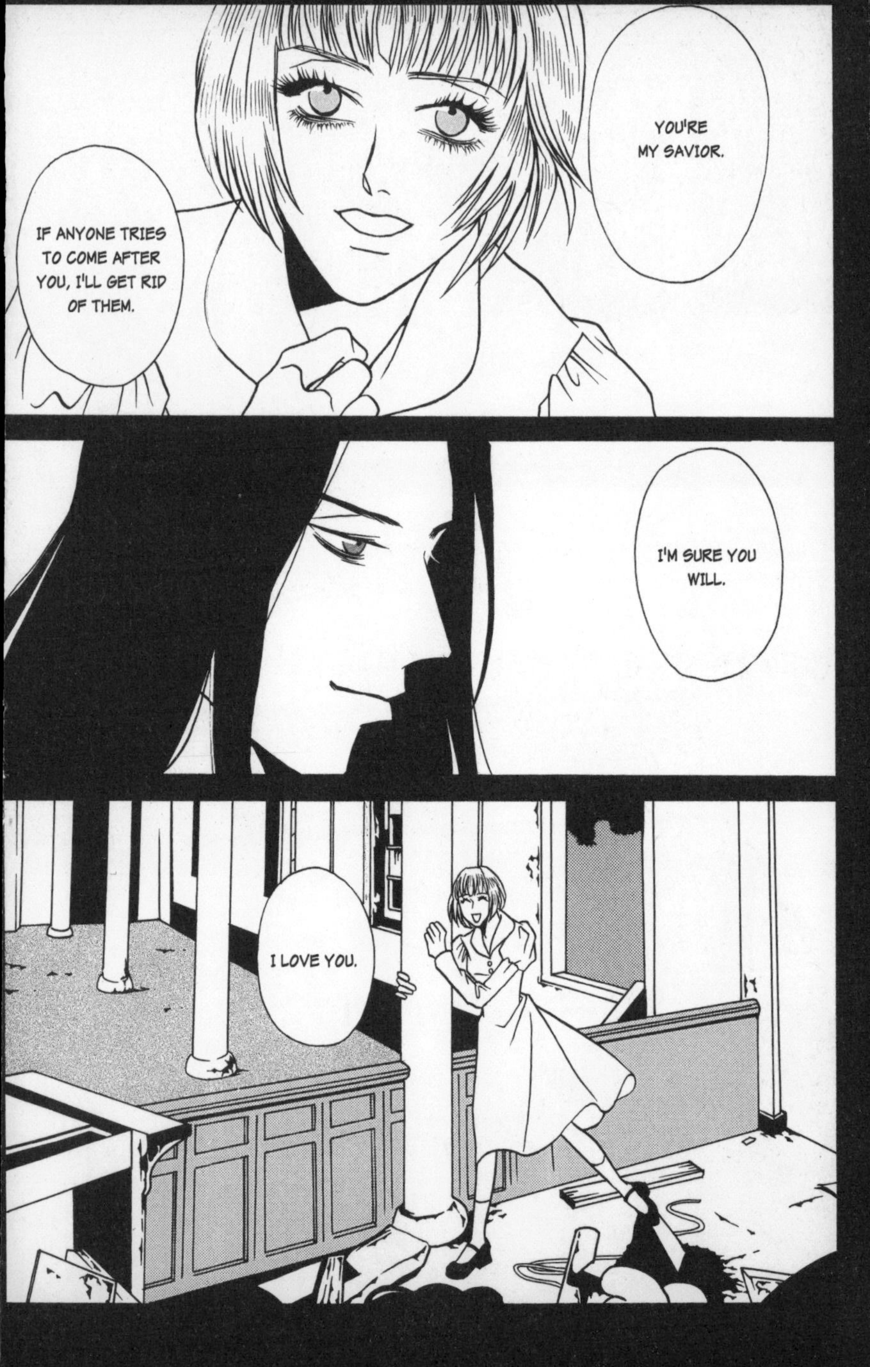
YOU'RE MY SAVIOR.
IF ANYONE TRIES TO COME AFTER YOU, I'LL GET RID OF THEM.
I'M SURE YOU WILL.
I LOVE YOU.

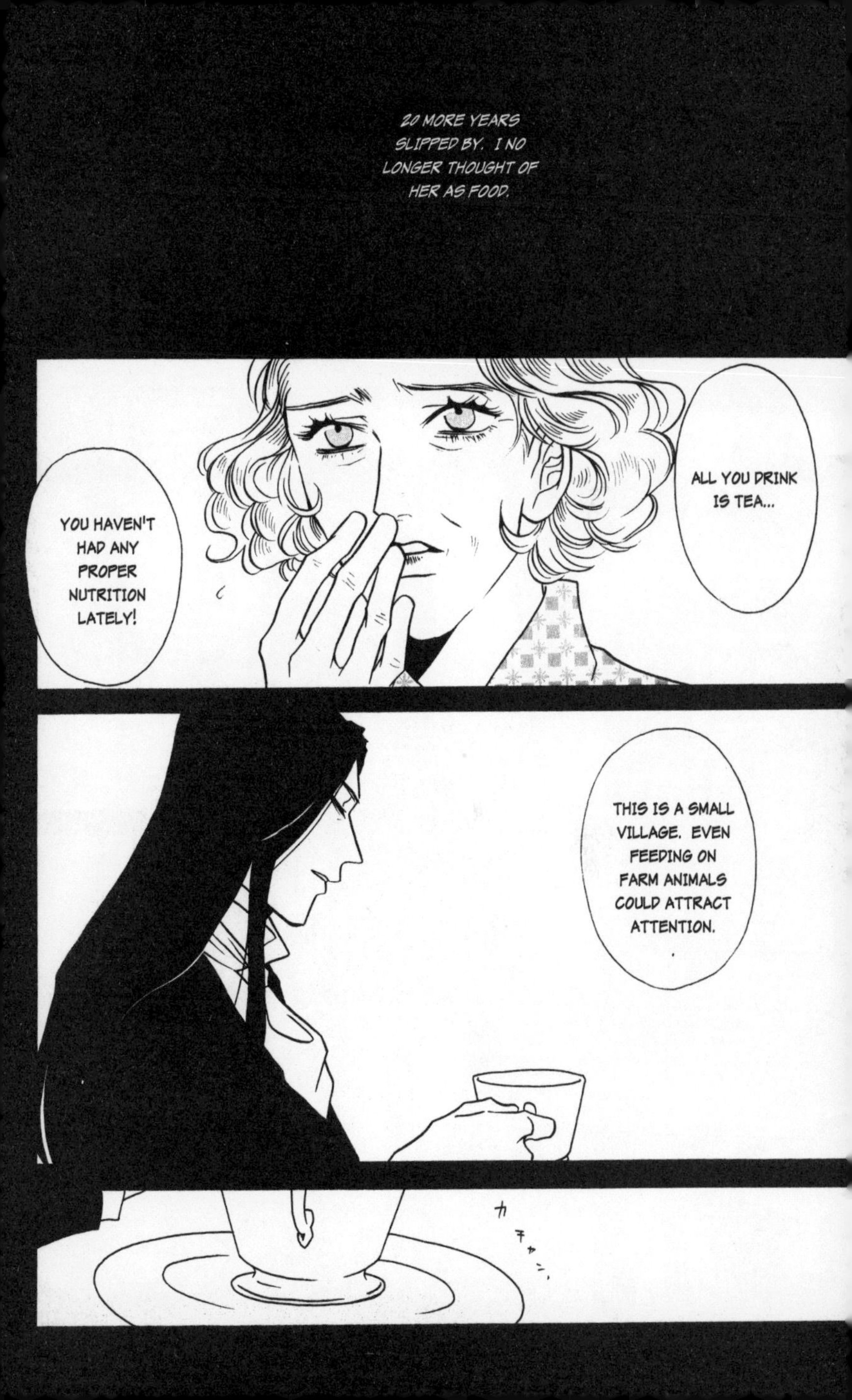
20 MORE YEARS SLIPPED BY. I NO LONGER THOUGHT OF HER AS FOOD.
ALL YOU DRINK IS TEA...
YOU HAVEN'T HAD ANY PROPER NUTRITION LATELY!
THIS IS A SMALL VILLAGE. EVEN FEEDING ON FARM ANIMALS COULD ATTRACT ATTENTION.
カチャン

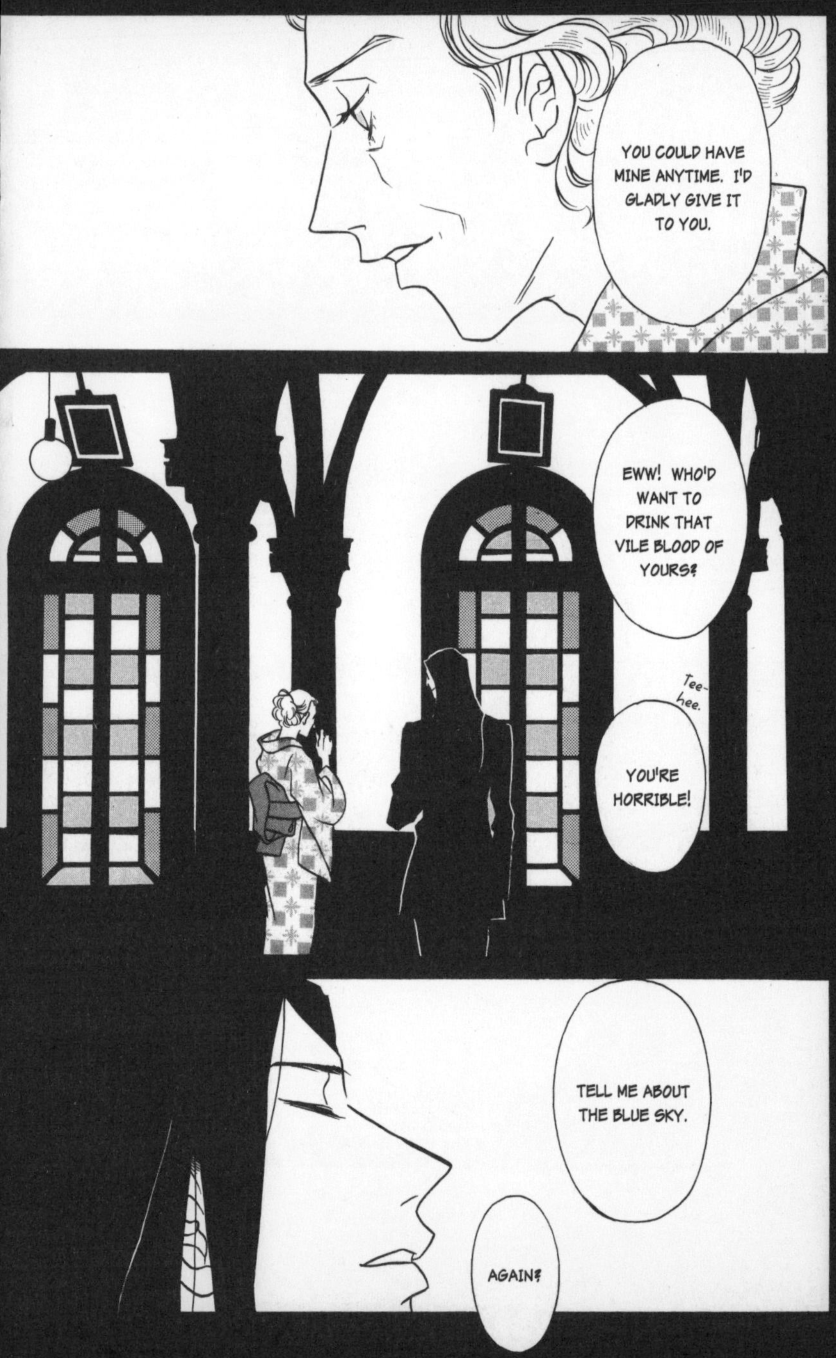
YOU COULD HAVE MINE ANYTIME. I'D GLADLY GIVE IT TO YOU.
EWW! WHO'D WANT TO DRINK THAT VILE BLOOD OF YOURS?
Tee-hee.
YOU'RE HORRIBLE!
TELL ME ABOUT THE BLUE SKY.
AGAIN?

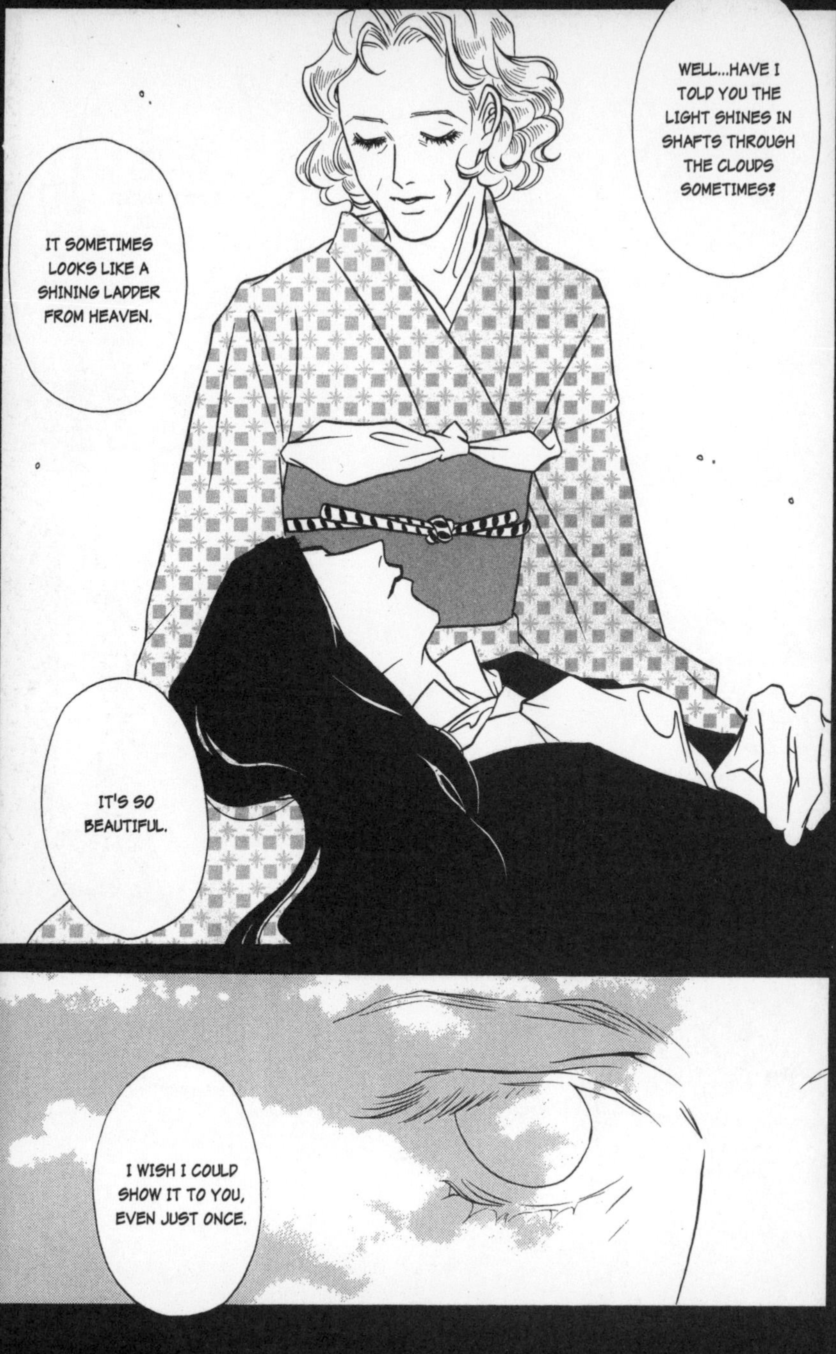
WELL...HAVE I TOLD YOU THE LIGHT SHINES IN SHAFTS THROUGH THE CLOUDS SOMETIMES?
IT SOMETIMES LOOKS LIKE A SHINING LADDER FROM HEAVEN.
IT'S SO BEAUTIFUL.
I WISH I COULD SHOW IT TO YOU, EVEN JUST ONCE.

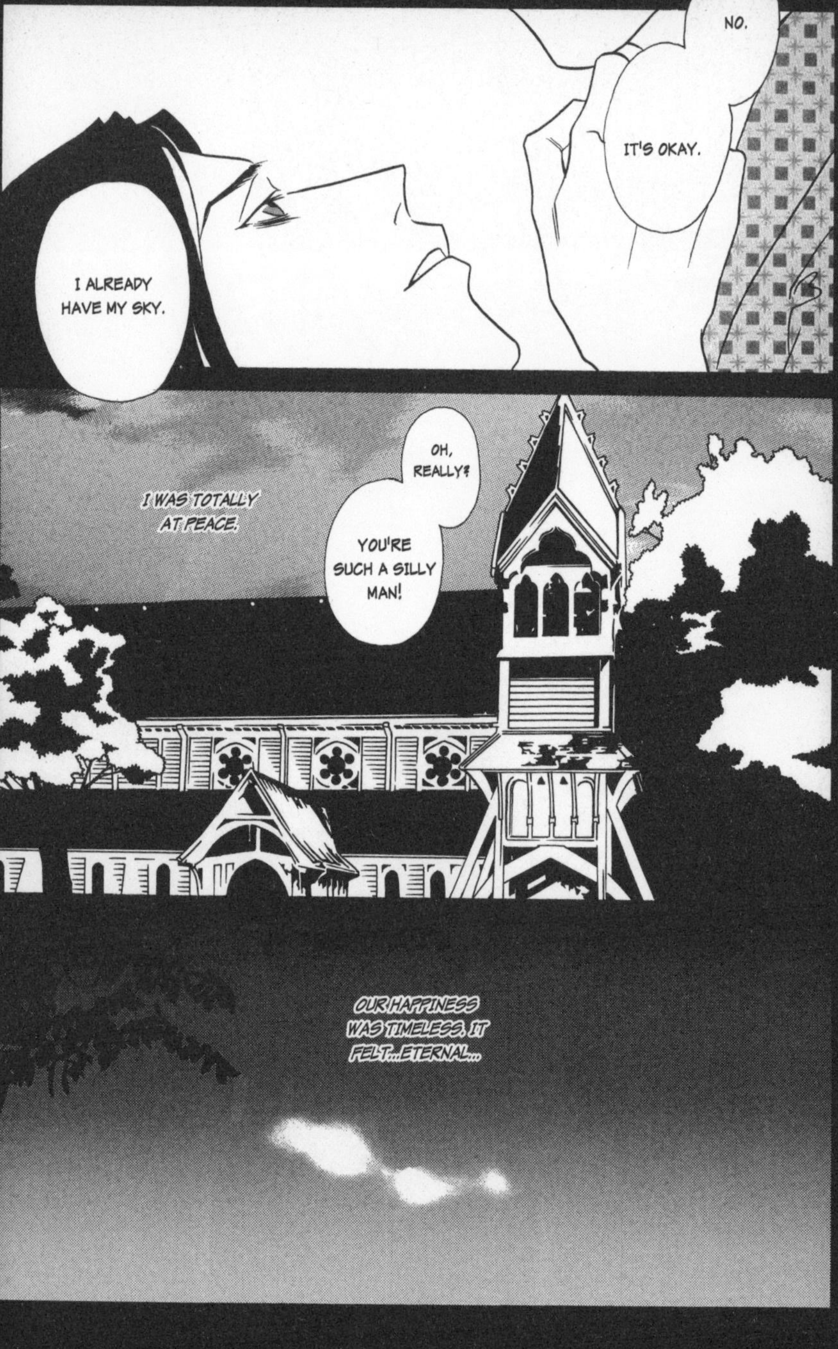
NO.
IT'S OKAY.
I ALREADY HAVE MY SKY.
OH, REALLY?
YOU'RE SUCH A SILLY MAN!
I WAS TOTALLY AT PEACE.
OUR HAPPINESS WAS TIMELESS. IT FELT...ETERNAL...

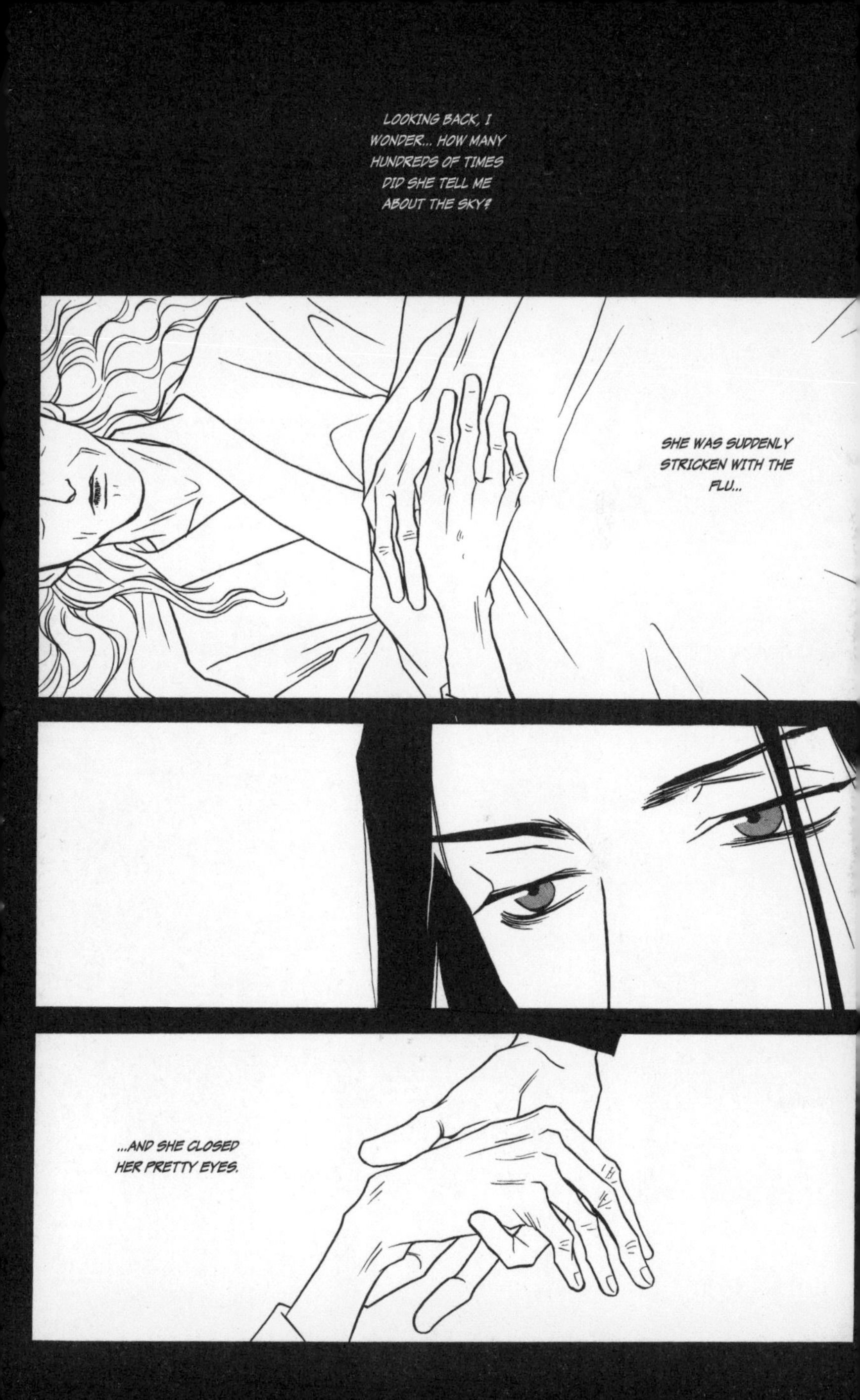
LOOKING BACK, I WONDER... HOW MANY HUNDREDS OF TIMES DID SHE TELL ME ABOUT THE SKY?
SHE WAS SUDDENLY STRICKEN WITH THE FLU...
...AND SHE CLOSED HER PRETTY EYES.

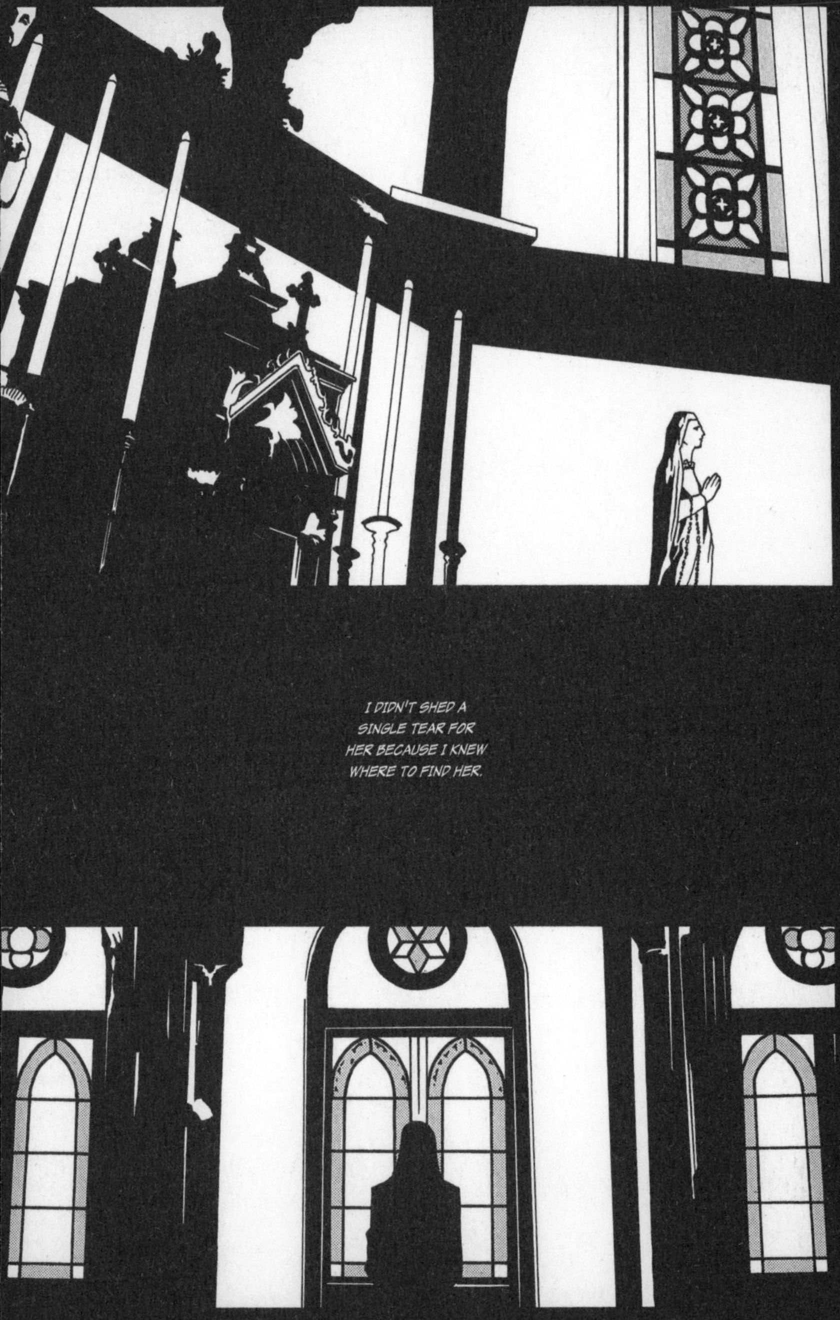
I DIDN'T SHED A SINGLE TEAR FOR HER BECAUSE I KNEW WHERE TO FIND HER.

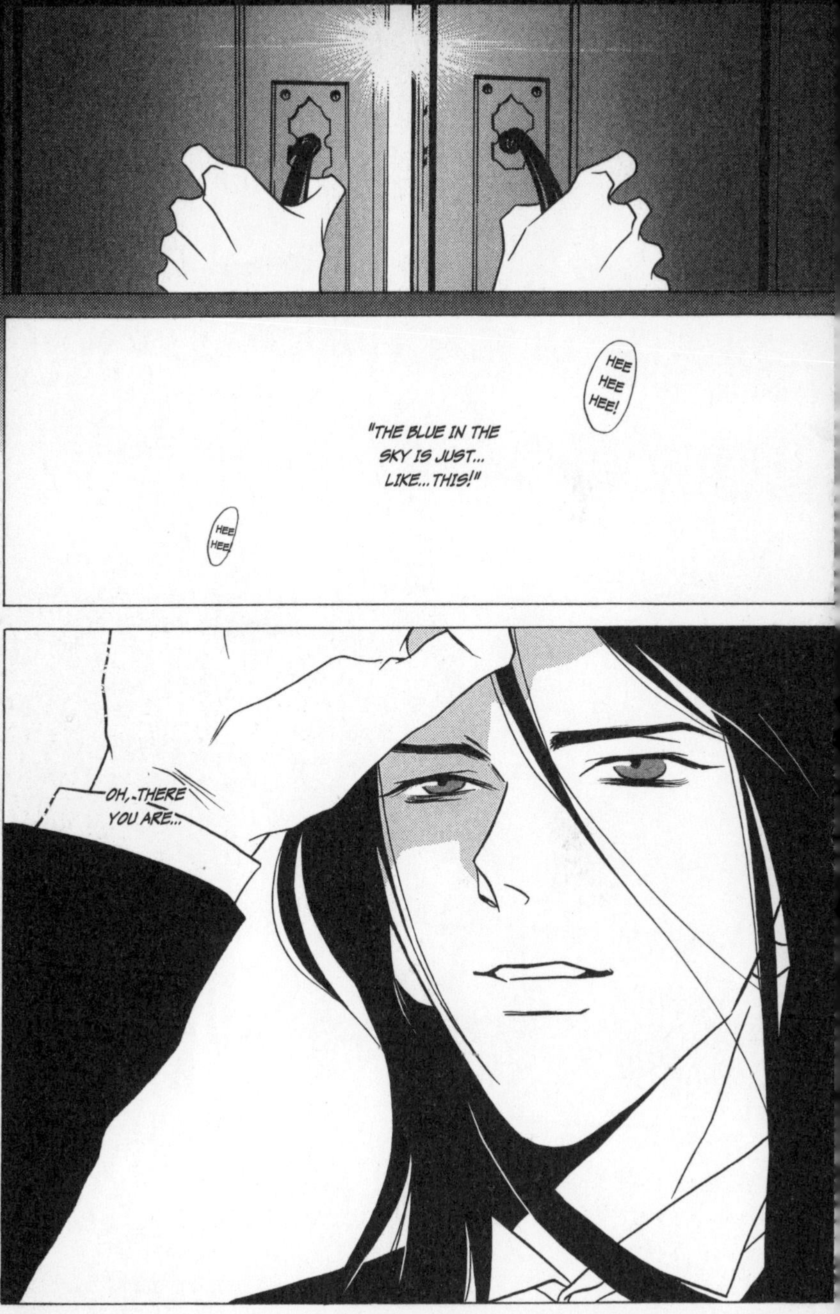
HEE HEE HEE!
"THE BLUE IN THE SKY IS JUST... LIKE...THIS!"
HEE HEE
OH, THERE YOU ARE...

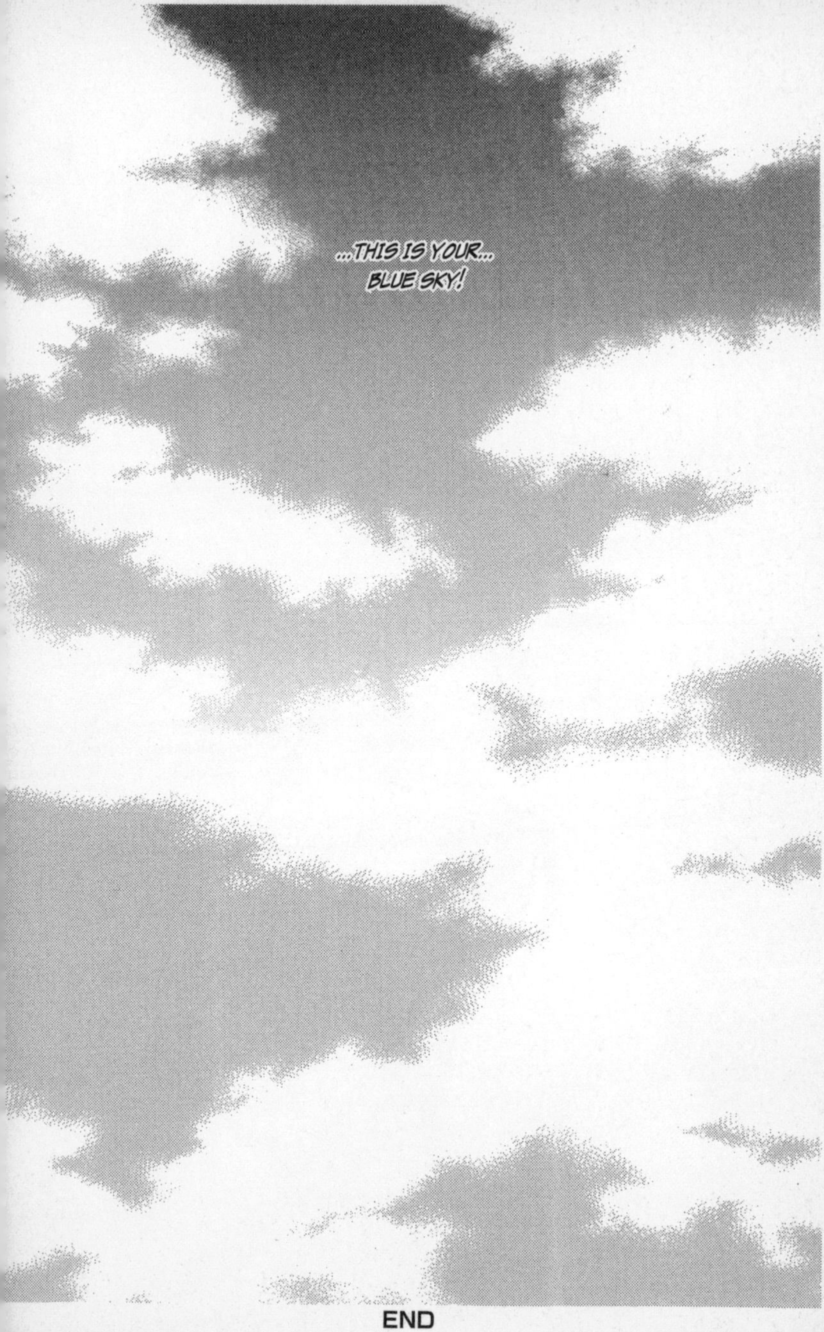
...THIS IS YOUR... BLUE SKY!
END

Some people are haunted by spirits of the dead who are intent on tormenting the living. "Sabbath" Obiga is haunted by his family, who are among the living, but intent on tormenting him!

A self-contained comedy that's like John Hughes meets the Addams Family, Mitsukazu Mihara's *Haunted House* is proof that there's nothing scarier than growing up...unless, of course, it's growing up in house full of goth pranksters.

Coming in 2006!

Ayumu struggles with her studies, and the all-important high school entrance exams are approaching. Fortunately, she has help from her best bud Shii-chan, who is at the top of the class. But when the test results come back, the friends are surprised: Ayumu surpasses Shii-chan's scores and gets into the school of her choice—without Shii-chan! Losing her friend is so painful for Ayumu that she starts cutting herself to ease her sorrow. Finally, Ayumu seeks comfort in a new friend, Manami. But will Manami prove to be the friend that Ayumu truly needs? Or will Ayumu continue down a dark path?

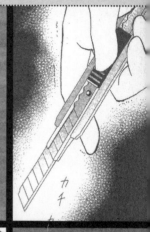

LIFE
Volume 1
Keiko Suenobu

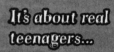

It's about real teenagers...

It's about real high school...

It's about real life.

LIFE
BY KEIKO SUENOBU

**Ordinary high school teenagers...
Except that they're not.**

READ THE ENTIRE FIRST CHAPTER ONLINE FOR FREE:

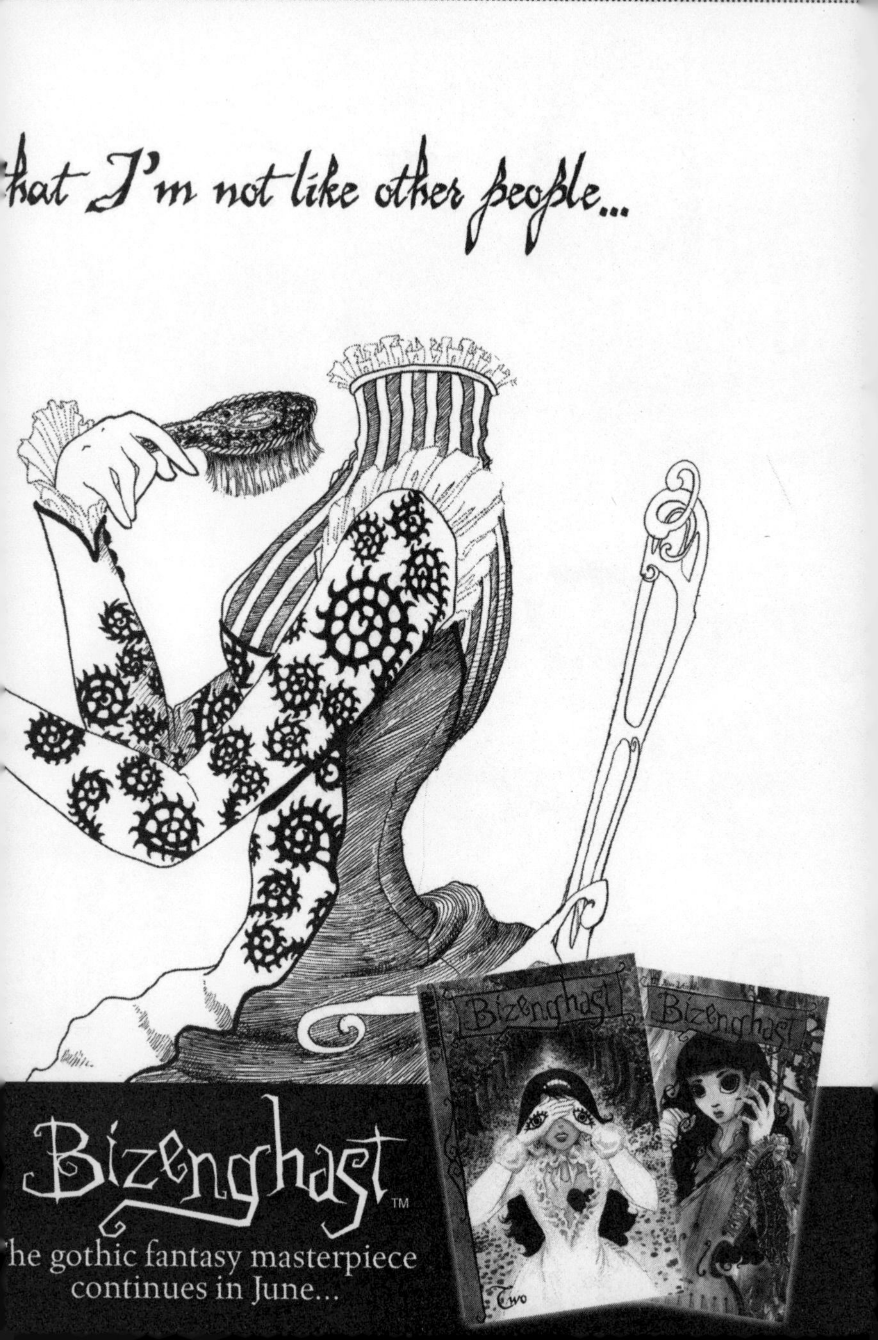
hat I'm not like other people...
Bizenghast™
he gothic fantasy masterpiece
continues in June...
Bizenghast
Two
Bizenghast

BIZENGHAST

Dear Diary,
I'm starting to feel

STOP!

This is the back of the book.
You wouldn't want to spoil a great ending!

This book is printed "manga-style," in the authentic Japanese right-to-left format. Since none of the artwork has been flipped or altered, readers get to experience the story just as the creator intended. You've been asking for it, so TOKYOPOP® delivered: authentic, hot-off-the-press, and far more fun!

DIRECTIONS

If this is your first time reading manga-style, here's a quick guide to help you understand how it works.

It's easy... just start in the top right panel and follow the numbers. Have fun, and look for more 100% authentic manga from TOKYOPOP®!